Gangland
MELBOURNE

James Morton
Susanna Lobez

VICTORY BOOKS
An imprint of Melbourne University Publishing Limited
187 Grattan Street, Carlton, Victoria 3053, Australia
mup-info@unimelb.edu.au
www.mup.com.au

First published 2011
Text © James Morton and Susanna Lobez, 2011
Design and typography © Melbourne University Publishing Ltd 2011

Text designed by Alice Graphics
Cover designed by Nada Backovic
Typeset in 9/14 pt Lino Letter Roman by Pauline Haas
Printed in Australia by Griffin Press, South Australia

Front cover photos, left to right: Kath Pettingill, © Newspix/Jay Town; Carl Williams, © Newspix/John Hart; Macchour Chaouk, © Newspix/Fiona Hamilton; Dennis Allen, © Newspix/News Ltd; Jason Moran, © Newspix/Jay Town; Alphonse Gangitano, © Newspix/Ben Swinnerton; Judy Moran, © Newspix/Trevor Pinder; Chopper Read, © Newspix/News Ltd. Background images © iStockphoto.com.

National Library of Australia Cataloguing-in-Publication entry:
Morton, James, 1938–
Gangland Melbourne / James Morton and Susanna Lobez.

9780522858693 (pbk.)

9780522860382 (ebook)

Includes bibliographical references and index.

Organized crime—Victoria—Melbourne—History.
Gangs—Victoria—Melbourne—History.
Mafia—Victoria—Melbourne—History.

Lobez, Susanna.

364.106099451

For Patricia Rose and Alec Masel
and Dock Bateson with love.

Contents

Preface   vii

1   Not So Marvelous Melbourne   1
2   Squizzy Taylor and Friends   12
3   Sex in the City   39
4   Unhappy Families   55
5   World War II   71
6   The Combine   84
7   Melbourne Market Matters   108
8   Some Painters and Dockers   124
9   Shooting Stars   141
10   Chopper Read and Mr Death   156
11   Victoria's Finest   167
12   Into the New Century   183

Notes   221
Selected Bibliography   233
Index   239

Preface

On the face of it people might not think that Melbourne numbers among the great crime cities of the world. There's Chicago and Al Capone; New York and the Five Families; certainly Detroit and its Purple Gang, Marseilles and its history of white slaving and dope dealing. London and the Kray Twins, yes. Berlin and Macau, possibly. But Melbourne? Come on, get real.

But they would be wrong. Throughout the last century the city has spawned a series of quality criminals—some, of course, better known than others. There have been the Bourke Street Rats, followed closely by Australia's 'favourite larrikin' Joseph Leslie Theodore 'Squizzy' Taylor and, in the 1920s, his henchman Norman Bruhn, whose descendents still operate today. In 1939 Melbourne had a higher crime rate per capita than London and its record for violent robberies was then the worst in Australia. And after the war there were some great robbers such as Ray 'Chuck' Bennett of the Great Bookie Robbery and his lesser known but almost as talented predecessor Leslie Woon. There have been great wars—Taylor and another offsider Harry Stokes against John 'Snowy' Cutmore and his mate Henry Slater, which ended in the deaths of both Taylor and Cutmore; the long-running Painters and Dockers' Union war of the 1970s, which saw the assassination of secretary Pat Shannon and resulted in the deaths or disappearances of up to forty dockers, their friends and innocent bystanders; the war for control of the Queen Victoria Market; and finally the Melbourne Gang War between the Carlton Crew and the New Boys from the late 1990s to the present day, in which the body count tallies over thirty—not including the standover men, brothel madams, cocaine, heroin, amphetamines and crack dealers and, regrettably, some police officers who, over the years, have changed sides. All in all, Melbourne can proudly take its place in the pantheon of crime cities. This, then, is the story of some of the men and women who have placed it there.

Some surprise may be expressed at the absence of names that have been on the lips of the cognoscenti over the past two decades—people who, it seems, have simply disappeared from the streets into a legal gulag. The reason for this is the number of suppression orders handed out by the courts to protect multiple killers who may be wheeled out in the future to give evidence for the prosecution in high-profile trials. These orders may easily last for half a decade or more. In the event of any of them being lifted their stories will appear in future editions.

Our thanks are due first and foremost to Dock Bateson, without whose help, guidance and research the book would never have seen the light of day. Then in strictly alphabetical order our thanks go to Anne Brooke, Cinzia Cavallaro, the late Clive Coleman, Foong Ling Kong, Diane Leyman, Barbara Levy, Sybil Nolan, Kath Pettingill, Russell Robinson, Adrian Tame, and many others on both sides of the criminal and judicial fences who have asked not to be named. Our thanks also go to NSW Supreme Court Public Information Officers Sonya Zadel and Lisa McGregor, NSW DPP Media Liaison Anna Cooper and Victorian Supreme Court Information Officer Anne Stanford, the staff of the State Archives of New South Wales, the Public Record Office of Victoria, the National Library of Australia, and the State Libraries of New South Wales, South Australia, Queensland, Victoria and Western Australia, the British Library, the Newspaper Library, Colindale, England, the National Archives, Kew, England. The following websites have been invaluable: www.austlii.edu.au, www.trove.nla.gov.au/newspaper, www.paperspast.natlib.govt.nz and www.news.google.com/archivesearch.

Not So Marvelous Melbourne

1

In the early hours of 2 April 1852 a team of men—some dressed as women, and led by James Duncan, James Morgan and John James, who had come together robbing diggers—rowed across Hobson's Bay in two boats stolen from a local hotel to the *Nelson*, a barque being loaded with 8000 ounces of gold worth around £30000 before sailing for London. Passengers and crew were nailed up in the stateroom, where they remained until a steward found them the next morning. The success of the robbers was short-lived. With a reward of £750 on offer, the leaders were caught within three weeks. Justice was swift and in May the trio received fifteen years apiece on road gangs; the first three were to be spent in irons. Only around £2260 was recovered. The rest was thought to have been fenced through a St Kilda publican, John Dascome. It was this raid that convinced the authorities that they needed a proper detective force, and men from Scotland Yard were brought out.

During the afternoon of 16 October that same year, four mounted and armed men (thought to be survivors of the *Nelson* raid) bailed up every individual they encountered on St Kilda Road. At sunset they galloped off into the bush towards South Yarra. Three days later John Flanigan and Thomas Williams were caught and sentenced to thirty years. Williams was later hanged for his part in the murder at Williamstown on 26 March 1857 of John Price, the highly unpopular and sadistic inspector of prisons.

Flanigan, who gave evidence against his former offsider, was released in 1862.

As Melbourne grew, in came the magsmen, or confidence tricksters, and the three-card merchants. There were also coiners and rather more organised burglars. Thefts, which until the 1860s had been opportunistic—from the back of wagons, unlocked houses and yards—became more professional. The detective division of the police was also on the up. John Christie, a champion boxer and rower and probably the best of the Melbourne detectives of the time, joined the force in 1867 when at the age of twenty-one he walked in off the street with a character reference. Within a matter of months his arrest record far surpassed those of other officers.

One of the more professional jobs in the late 1860s was a series of silk robberies, which for a time went unsolved despite a £250 reward. Then, with information received, in March 1869 Christie arrested a Thomas Griffiths living in Stanley Street, West Melbourne, after he had robbed the firm of Clarke and Adams at the corner of Elizabeth and Collins streets. Griffiths' operation, a family business, now unravelled. He had used Thomas jnr, one of his sons, to break into buildings with him, and his wife Ann disposed of the goods, selling them door to door in Toorak. On 22 January 1870 he received eleven years. In 1872 Mrs Griffiths, who worked as a nurse and stole from her patients, was again convicted of theft and receiving and was sentenced to eighteen months. She later opened a small hospital in Carlton.

Garrotting during a street robbery was prevalent, particularly before electric lighting was installed in Hyde Park. In July 1870 John Moore and Thomas Bourke, who worked Little Bourke Street, each received ten years after garrotting the elderly Arthur Harvey while robbing him. Twenty years later the authorities were still keen to show that violence would be severely punished. On 11 May 1888 at the Collingwood Court, Thomas Donoghue and Henry 'Long Harry' Towerson each received twelve months' hard labour after being convicted of being suspected persons. Towerson was then hauled off to the Central Criminal Court for bag snatching and the robbery of a watch, and received a further seven years' hard labour and fifteen lashes to go with it. There was no question of rehabilitation, however—at least so far as Towerson was concerned. He was back housebreaking in April 1893 when he received two years to run consecutively with another twelve-month sentence. He was still operating a decade later when in November 1902, then aged forty, he was found with a revolver and charged with having housebreaking implements.

The next generation of garrotters and robbers included wharfer Thomas 'Chopsey' Hayes, who received five years for shooting at a policeman in September 1905, and his offsider the diminutive redheaded Allan 'Ginger' Moore, who stood a bare five feet. In 1907 in Sydney, Moore received five years for the burglary of Lady Burton at Darling Point and in September 1912 he was sentenced to death for the attempted murder of householder Geoffrey Syme in a burglary in Kew. His sentence was remitted and in April 1928 he was released into the care of the Salvation Army.

The fighting gangs, or Pushes, that ruled parts of the city for so long were formed in the late 1870s, and in 1880 Melbourne was in the grip of a crime wave. Invasions of homes and licensed premises were common, with the gangs swarming over them like locusts. The Hoddle Street Lairies, including the notorious brothers John and Edward Peddy, specialised in taking over hotels and bakeries, where they would drink and eat for free and then demand money from the owners. When the police tried to intervene after an attack on the Victoria Hotel in Collingwood, they were stoned, and in February 1881 Constable Shortell suffered a fractured skull in another attack. In September that year John Peddy led a gang that tried to steal the till from the Highbury Barn Hotel, also in Collingwood, and in 1882 two of his brothers, William and Edwin, broke up the London Hotel. If the police tried to intervene they could expect to be outnumbered and given a beating, although in 1886, when John Peddy was on the rampage again, local shopkeepers came to their aid. Despite his long record Perry was only fined £15.

These invasions continued until the beginning of the twentieth century. In October 1904 Maurice Laycock (also known as Arthur Lewis), along with three others pretending to be drunk, started a blue, distracting a publican, John Walkeley, so they could steal his watch and chain, worth £40. Laycock then met with the landlord and sold the stolen goods back to him. Followed by the police, he escaped in Bourke Street where he was shot at by detectives. Later in the chase he fell and was captured. This was a common type of robbery. Newspapers reported that, after another supposed blue in the Curlew Hotel in Fitzroy, one of the men used the distraction to go upstairs and steal a medallion. He was not quick enough: his boots were seen sticking out from under a bed and he was pulled out.

The best known of the Pushes were the Bourke Street Rats, originally a collection of twenty or thirty harmless newsvendors aged six to ten, but the group gradually morphed into a gang whose weapons of choice were fence palings, and who operated on the south side of Bourke Street near the old Opera House. When the nearby Bijou Theatre was sold out, one of the tricks of the Rats was to sell old tickets to careless purchasers. Another was to make the victim stand on his head and take the coins that fell out of his pockets.

Towards the end of the nineteenth century the Rats were in decline. Their leaders were then said to be a man called Jack, along with William 'Gunny' Hughes. Jack lost total face after being very badly beaten by a plain-clothes officer simply for being rude to him. In September 1889 Gunny Hughes, who had turned fizz, was set upon by John Hamer and Patrick McGinty in a lane off Little LaTrobe Street. They received two- and one-year sentences respectively but then Hughes died in the December and the pair were charged with murder. The process did not appeal to the jury, who acquitted them in fifteen minutes. By 1910 the Rats was little more than a gang of pickpockets. By then, however, they had acquired their most famous member in Squizzy Taylor.

Another man who had worked with the Rats, stealing from shop tills before he went on to greater things, was Abe Benson (aka Wright and Godfrey). A man of all trades who worked the thimble and pea in Queensland, Benson had a flowing moustache and wore a top hat, frock coat and diamond rings. He would, said an admirer, 'have filled a quack doctor with envy of his style'. He affected an intimate knowledge of racehorse owners and put money from 'my flats' (or dupes) on 'good things' at meetings. In 1910 he took the Countess Wiser of Austria for £128 after he met the elderly woman on the *Orantes* at Colombo, and when the ship docked at Fremantle introduced her to his 'fiancée'. His fiancée was in fact his sister Nellie, whom he described as 'a lady interested in racing circles' and who was playing the part of the daughter of a wealthy banker. The trick was the usual promise to put bets on horses and keep the money. Benson, who by then had convictions in every state except Tasmania, received eighteen months. Nellie was bound over to be of good behaviour.

Other Pushes who came and went included the Fitzroy Forties, the Bouverie Street Push, the White Roses from South Melbourne and the Crutchy Push—a collection of one-legged men from North Melbourne who used their crutches in devastating fashion in gang fights. Their stock in trade, however, was pickpocketing with an occasional bar invasion. In August 1899 the Crutchy Push invaded the pitch at the Footscray–North Melbourne football game and it took mounted police to clear them. The Freeman Street Push terrorised the Chinese community, and the Fitzroy Forties were said to be as dangerous as any three other Pushes combined. Members of Irishtown, a thirty-strong Push broken up in the middle of the 1890s, stood and demanded a toll at the entrance to Chapel Street Bridge. At the turn of the century there was also the Bouverie Forty, the Stephen Street Push, the Flying Angels of South Melbourne (who beat a man to death in a railway carriage after a picnic in Heidelberg), the Woolpacks (named after the Carlton hotel they frequented) and the Fitzroy Checkers.

The Melbourne Pushes survived rather longer than their Sydney counterparts, with sporadic outbursts of serious trouble to mix with their Saturday night tormenting of the Salvation Army. In March 1910, a North Melbourne Push said to be around a hundred strong invaded Carlton, shouting 'Death to the Emus'. Arrests followed but there was no question of imprisonment and the fines were relatively small, ranging from £3 upwards. In 1919, instead of going to the Melbourne Cup, a group of Collingwood youths, who mainly worked in boot factories and were known as the Little Campbells Push, turned on their old rivals, the Roses from Rose and Brunswick streets. Two Campbells, fifteen-year-old William 'Porky' Flynn and Harold 'Dodger' Smith, a year older, shot and killed fourteen-year-old Ernest Worseldine as he was running away from them. They were found guilty of manslaughter and each received three months, to be followed by detention in a reformatory. Additionally, Smith was to be whipped.

In 1926 there was said to be fighting most weekends between rival Pushes in Footscray. In 1927, on the weekend that gang leaders Squizzy Taylor and Snowy Cutmore were shot, so too was Richard Dunstan. He and Ronald Pearce, who was with him, both of the Hawk Eyes Push, had been at war with the Chefs.

The Pushes confined themselves to street crime but there was something much more professional when one of Melbourne's most sensational crimes of the decade took place on Monday 19 August 1901. In the days when a headline story was lucky to run the length of one newspaper column, this was spread across four columns. Shortly after midnight, a horse-drawn tram was held up by three masked men in Hawthorn and the eight passengers onboard were robbed of their money and valuables. The driver lost about

£2.10 from the night takings and in all some £25 was stolen. The robbers were thought to have expected a man who usually carried a quantity of money to have been on the tram. One passenger hit out with his umbrella and was knocked down for his pains. He was searched again and a further £7 was discovered. All were told that if they turned their heads they would be shot. The bandits, who made off towards the river, were never caught; nor, it seems, did they strike again. One suspect was John Henry Sparks who, with John O'Connor, robbed the manager of the No. 1 Premier mine at Rutherglen in the following December. He received ten years with hard labour but in the January he escaped from Pentridge in early morning fog and was never positively seen again.

Infanticide was also prevalent, in both the city and the suburbs, with the Yarra said to be awash with babies' bodies. In September 1893 *The Argus*, which had been campaigning about trafficking in babies, reported a 'shocking discovery in Brunswick'. A man working in his garden in Moreland Road dug up the body of a three-month-old child whose skull had been fractured.

The following year two more bodies were dug up and later baby-farmer Frances Knorr stood trial for their murders. She was the wife of a waiter who had deserted her, after which she took up with an Edward Thompson. In prison she wrote a letter telling Thompson how to suborn a witness and how, if she received a long sentence, he was to look after her two children. At her trial she tried to put the blame on Thompson and also a man named Wilson, who she said brought a child to her for burial. He was a complete invention.

Mrs Knorr sang 'Safe in the arms of Jesus' followed by 'Abide with me' on her way to the scaffold, but there were suggestions that she had been so liberally dosed with brandy that she was drunk. Her hanging, along with that of John Makin in Sydney, are credited with putting an end to the deliberate killing of children by baby-farmers.

In recent years efforts have been made to rehabilitate Knorr's reputation, seeing her not as a scheming murderer but as an unstable young woman who looked after many of the children in her care. Ranged against that is the evidence that she murdered at least thirteen of them.

Just to what extent the police were benefiting from the abortion rackets of the time is not clear. The Birthrate Commission of 1903 was told there was evidence that the police were failing to prosecute but this was explained by the difficulty in obtaining compelling evidence. In turn the police blamed the medical profession for providing suspect death certificates and shielding other abortionists.

In early 1898 banks in Victoria were the victims of a 'gold brick' fraud, in which a plug of gold was inserted into a lead brick that was painted gold. While it lasted it was a highly profitable operation. The Bendigo branch of a Melbourne bank was taken for £700 and branches in Kyneton and Taradale were also targeted. Both top and bottom of the brick cake stood the test in Taradale but Nesbitt, the manager of the National Bank there, became suspicious and broke one open only to find that the inside of the brick was copper. He covered the vendor William Theodore (also known as Charles Johns) with his revolver until the police arrived and Walter Cartwright (or Alexander Rowlands) was caught outside. The team of four— two were never arrested—had been buying gold from the banks, melting it down, coating copper with it and then selling it back.

* * *

The undoubted king of working-class Melbourne in the late 1890s was John Wren. Today it is suggested that, rather than being a criminal, Wren was something of a financial Robin Hood. It is not immediately apparent how this rose-tinted view can be sustained. He may have enabled the working classes to bet like their richer neighbours and in later life to have been a great donor to charity, but with his fixed horse, running, trotting, cycling and greyhound races, and boxing and wrestling matches, he robbed them blind.

Wren was born the third son of Irish immigrants at Collingwood in 1871. In 1899 his elder brother, Arthur, was sentenced to death for the rape of his next-door neighbour, prostitute Emma Hamilton. Shortly before Christmas 1888 she had complained about his language, for which he had been fined £10. On 22 February 1889 she was with a friend near the Johnston Bridge, Collingwood, when she was approached by four men, including Arthur, who stole a brooch from her dress and stood by while she was being raped. She asked him to help and he replied, 'Serve you right, you bugger. I have my revenge. Do you remember Christmas time?' The death sentence was commuted but he received a flogging and served a long and hard sentence. After being released in 1898, he became involved in his brother's enterprises, and died in July 1935 worth £52 468. He was apparently 'known for many acts of kindness'.

John Wren began his working life at the age of twelve in a wood yard, where he augmented his wages circulating betting cards and as a small-time moneylender. According to his view of life he launched his totalisator with big wins on the horses, first on Carbine in the 1890 Melbourne Cup and then on other lesser races. There were also rumours that he had fixed the 1904 Caulfield Cup, netting £50 000 with Murmur's win. He worked in an illegal Two-up school and then opened his Tote behind a teashop at 136 Johnston Street in 1893. In 1903 he founded the illegal City Tattersall's Club and from then on he conducted a long and, for some years, successful war with the police and authorities.

In the first years of the twentieth century, to keep his Tote up and running, Wren's men literally fought the police led by the courageous and incorruptible Sergeant David O'Donnell, known as Big O'Donnell. The clerks in his Tote wore Ku Klux Klan hoods and only their hands could be seen through the betting and pay-out windows. By 1903, Wren was said to be netting £2000 a year, mostly from one shilling bets. That year the police 'occupied' the Tote for a nine week period beginning on the eve of the Melbourne Cup before they were finally evicted. The next year Detective Johnson, recognised as an undercover officer who had been spying on the Tote, was attacked and badly beaten as he stepped from a tramcar in Sydney Road. In turn, Cornelius Crowe, another police officer who was engaged in the war against the betting shops, was attacked and beaten by men with an iron bar. Crowe subsequently had a curious career. In 1906 he was acquitted of demanding money with menaces but was thrown out of the force. In 1916 he was sentenced to three years for criminal libel but the conviction was quashed and he was acquitted on a retrial. O'Donnell and his family were constantly at risk from Wren's henchmen. At 3.30 in the morning of 6 January 1906 a bomb—a stone ginger beer bottle stuffed with powder—was thrown through the front window of his home at 6 Royal Terrace, Nicholson Street, Fitzroy. O'Donnell, regarded as a man who 'if he cannot help a man in misfortune never unnecessarily oppressed him', said he had expected his windows to be broken but never to have been the subject of a bomb attack. While there was never any direct proof that Wren had arranged the bombing his name has always been linked to the attack.

Cases against gaming clubs could be tricked out by Wren's solicitor and adviser, the redoubtable David Gaunson, said to have kept more men out of Pentridge Prison than any number of lawyers combined. At the time O'Donnell was bombed, a summons against the Metropolitan Club in Bourke Street ran for two years with no end in sight. When, despite Gaunson's efforts, the *Lotteries, Gaming and Betting Act* was passed and Wren's Tote was closed, it was no longer a great financial concern to him. He was already a millionaire and now had many other business interests. At its height his Tote had brought him an amazing £20000 a year and he had taken great care to nurse the neighbourhood with donations to the Church and the needy.

Although Wren went from financial success to financial success there was always the smell of corruption about him. In the first decade of the century he fixed pedestrianism (mainly heel-to-toe walking races), boxing and cycling. In the 1910s it was trotting and in the 1920s he added the new sport of wrestling to his control. In 1930 a non-Labor government inquiry found that because proprietary racing in Queensland was controlled by Wren it was inherently corrupt. In 1950, in his wife's name, he brought an ill-advised and ultimately unsuccessful action for libel against Frank Hardy over his book *Power Without Glory*, a thinly disguised roman-à-clef of his life. Wren lost, possibly because neither he nor his wife, who was the one libelled, gave evidence.

A keen supporter of the Collingwood Football Club, he died aged eighty-three on 26 October 1953 after the premiership, having pushed his way through the crowd to stand behind Collingwood's goalposts for the last quarter. His obituary in *The Age* describes him as being 'beloved by the poor of Collingwood'. The *Australian Dictionary of Biography* was confident that, 'There is no evidence that Wren had associations with the murderous tout "Squizzy" Taylor'. A saying coined about the celebrated bushranger was that 'Ned Kelly was a gentleman'. Its full version was 'Compared with X, Ned Kelly was a gentleman.' Compared with Joseph Leslie Theodore 'Squizzy' Taylor, Wren certainly was.

Squizzy Taylor and Friends

2

Joseph Leslie Theodore Taylor, alias Leslie Grout, alias David Donoghue, sometimes known as The Turk and more often as Squizzy, was a murderer, robber, dobber, coward, blackmailer and 'Australia's favourite larrikin'. He was born on 29 June 1888 in the coastal town of Brighton, 14 kilometres south of Melbourne. His father was a coachbuilder and the family moved to the city in the depression years of the 1890s. Small enough to be apprenticed as a jockey to the trainer Bobby Lewis, Taylor rode at the Richmond racetrack but his opportunities dried up as he was considered too crooked even for those days. Some say more charitably that—even though at the time of his death he was still under nine stone—he had had weight troubles.

By the end of the century Taylor had been sent to a boys' home, and by his late teens he was a member of the Bourke Street Rats, who controlled crime at the top end of Bourke Street, in those days a home for variety theatres, clubs, pubs, Chinese cafés and third-rate hotels. During that time Taylor was taken on tour by senior members as an apprentice shoplifter and pickpocket.

In 1906 Taylor was convicted of assault, serving a week, and in January 1907 he tried to steal a gold breast pin in Ballarat. This time the fine was £2, with the alternative of seven days. He was in Bendigo the same year, charged with possessing housebreaking implements and given twelve months reduced on appeal to a discharge. He was then fined £10 or three months after stealing ten shillings from the till of the Cherry Tree Hotel in Richmond. When he gave the magistrate some lip, the offer of the £10 was withdrawn.

In January 1908 he received two years' imprisonment for pickpocketing at Burrumbeet racecourse near Ballarat. Sentencing him, the judge, Sir Joseph Hood, remarked that he was now a confirmed criminal, but in fact this was his one and only conviction of any substance. Over the years, with a mixture of false alibis, bribed and threatened witnesses, on charges of murder, harbouring, robbery and assault, he would almost always avoid conviction.

By August 1910, and well out of his apprenticeship, Taylor was indulging in a spot of blackmail, something to which he turned his hand throughout his life. His first recorded victim was an abortionist. When she did not pay him sufficient money he reported her to the police. She received five years and was discharged a broken woman on 27 December 1913. By then he was a thoroughly vicious standover man. If a potential victim was told 'Squizzy Taylor has sent for a twenty' then £20 was handed over without protest—at least an audible one.

Now, with a series of girls (including the long-serving Dolly Grey; Lena Carr; and Mollie Jarvie, later known as The Decoy Duck), he worked what was known as the ginger game. Once the male victim had been taken to a hotel room and the 'Duck' or another girl was down to her underwear, in burst one of Taylor's team as the irate husband, brother or uncle. A variation of the game was that, once in bed, a jimmer or lurker would emerge from a cupboard and steal the punter's wallet. He and another man would then bang on the door and the girl would advise the man to leave by another door or window. They rarely returned for their wallets. Even at this relatively early stage of his career Taylor had learned that he need not be at risk at the actual sharp end of the crime to earn the money. A schemer and putter-up, he almost literally made the bullets for someone else to fire.

Taylor was moving on to bigger (if not always better) things and he was suspected of, but never charged with, the murder in January 1913 of a commercial traveller, Arthur Trotter, who was robbed of £215 in the bedroom of his home at 405 George Street, Fitzroy. Trotter had been followed when he returned home late one evening and clearly there was inside information. The robbers knew Trotter brought money home with him and also where the light switches were in the rooms. Bravely, Trotter swung a punch at his attacker but, with Taylor hanging back, Harold 'Bush' Thompson (otherwise known as Bairstow) shot him in the face.

Thompson had a number of convictions by this stage—three months in Adelaide for assaulting police in 1906 and another three months in Perth for being a disorderly person. At the time of Trotter's murder he was on bail for a robbery during the Melbourne Cup meeting. He jumped bail and headed for South Australia and then to Western Australia where he was arrested.

The police identified the fingerprint of Thompson on a windowsill. The development of the science, begun in Europe and South America in the late nineteenth century, was still by no means perfect and somehow the print, initially identified against one taken in Adelaide, did not tally with the one taken while Thompson was awaiting trial. Thompson's girlfriend Flossie, who at one time was suspected of being the small person on the robbery, provided an alibi and Mrs Trotter was no longer so confident in her identification. After four hours' retirement, Thompson was acquitted. Surprisingly, Taylor was thought by the police to have been in Adelaide at the time of the murder.

In 1914 Taylor was in hiding in South Australia, where he had moved with the blonde Dolly Grey, then the temporary Mrs Taylor. She was living off the kindness of a John Conlon and handing the money from him over to Taylor. Eventually Conlon twigged what was happening and began to threaten her. She promptly applied to have him bound over. Conlon had given her £15 the previous week and it had gone straight to Squizzy. It was a question of the gang's all here because in cross-examination she admitted that both of Squizzy's henchmen, Snowy Cutmore and bulldog-faced Two-up proprietor Henry Stokes, had visited her Adelaide Street address, then not one of the better parts of the city. 'She lives in a locality that is not select; but even persons living in localities of that kind are entitled to the protection of the court,' said her lawyer WA Rollison pompously. Many might have thought that those in the worst addresses needed the most protection. Conlon was bound over in the sum of £100 and ordered to pay £4 costs.

With the danger of the Trotter murder over, Taylor and Dolly moved back to Melbourne. It is not clear whether he was involved in the shooting of Constable David McGrath at the Melbourne Trades Hall in 1915. In *Power Without Glory*, Frank Hardy created Snoopy Tanner, a thinly disguised version of Taylor, and placed him firmly at the scene. However, a contemporary journalist, Hugh Buggy, who followed Taylor's career with interest, took the view that this was one of the few occasions when he was not actually a participant. Whether Taylor was the putter-up is another matter. Whatever, on 1 October, John Jackson, Richard Buckley and Alexander Ward burgled the Trades Hall, stealing £30 from the safe. In a bungled police raid a passage light was switched on, leaving Constable McGrath exposed. Twenty-six shots were fired and McGrath was killed. Jackson, who claimed he had fired in self-defence, was convicted at the first trial and hanged; but, with Taylor's interference, two juries disagreed over Ward and also Buckley, whose defence was that he had merely fired in the air as a warning. Finally on the third trial, Ward and Buckley were convicted of committing a felony and received five and six years' hard labour respectively. After his release Buckley became a Taylor stalwart.

There may have been doubts about Taylor's involvement in the Trades Hall robbery, but there is no doubt that on 29 February

1916 Taylor and another of his gang, John Williamson, hired a taxi driver, William Patrick Harries, for a drive in the country on which they took false number plates, suitcases and glasses as a disguise. The intention was to rob an employee of a bank in Bulleen. It seems that Harries would not go along with their plan and, for his lack of cooperation, was shot. At about 11.45 that morning his body was found inside his cab covered with a blanket. Nearby was a partly dug grave and found at a waterhole were false moustaches, dungarees, spirit gum and glasses. There were good descriptions by three witnesses who had seen the pair with Harries. Within days, Taylor and Williamson were arrested at Flemington racecourse on holding charges of 'being without means'. Now, with Taylor in custody, witnesses came forward to make positive identifications and it was a short step to a charge of murder.

At the trial in April, the three witnesses were in retreat and failed to make the necessary identification. Taylor had managed to get at them and he also produced an alibi. He was, however, temporarily inconvenienced when he was found guilty on the vagrancy charge and sentenced to twelve months' imprisonment. Within months of his release he was convicted of a warehouse break-in and received thirty days.

A man who joined Taylor's team shortly after the murder acquittal was Angus Murray, born Henry James Donnelly in Adelaide in 1882. By the time he was twenty-one Murray had not only burgled the home of the Chief Justice, Sir Samuel Way, but he had also robbed the State Governor at Government House. It was then that he was sentenced to seven years' hard labour for a series of robberies. He escaped from the fearsome Yatala Stockade Prison and was not recaptured for a year. His success as an escaper was not reflected in his intelligence for, after a number of successful burglaries, he boasted to the newspapers giving details of how he had executed the jobs, something that simply led to a further sentence.

He does, however, seem to have had some good points. While in prison in Fremantle he met up with Robert David Bennett, who was serving a sentence for the rape of a young girl whom he had infected with venereal disease. 'You are not fit to live in this world, because I have never heard a more horrible and disgusting story than that told in your case,' said Mr Justice McMillan while ordering Bennett to be flogged. Most men in prison can, to this day, make a good case for their innocence and Bennett convinced Murray who, on his own release, paid to have Bennett's claim investigated and also left money with the Salvation Army to pay his fare to join him in Melbourne, where in 1916 he had teamed up with Taylor.

On 18 September the next year Murray, Bennett and Taylor robbed the Middle Park branch of the ES&A Bank. Murray was to go into the bank while Taylor took the role of observer and organiser. In theory it was an easy raid. The bank teller was the only one on the premises and Murray, wearing a large pair of motorcycle goggles as a disguise, ordered him to lie on the floor. He bound and gagged the teller and was rifling through the safe when a messenger from another bank arrived, knocked and, getting no reply, looked through the letterbox slot, then ran off to find a telephone to call the police. Taylor had provided a horse and cart outside the rear of the bank that took Murray to a waiting car driven by Bennett. The next day the car was found abandoned in Albury and the police caught the pair in the local post office, where Murray was in the process of posting £380 to Sydney. On 15 October they each received fifteen years with hard labour. Naturally Taylor was never charged. Bennett served most of his term but Murray's confidence in him was sadly misplaced. After his release Bennett was hanged on 27 September 1932 for the rape of a four-year-old girl. The last person allowed to make a speech from the gallows in Victoria, Bennett addressed the spectators for nine minutes.

By the end of the Great War, Australia had instituted licensing arrangements that would provide a source of income for organised crime for the next sixty years. To prevent excessive drinking, hotels were closed at 6 p.m. and in consequence what was known as the sly-grog market opened up. Taylor was able to organise protection for the grog shops and supply them with stolen liquor.

Taylor was now expanding his organisation. Aside from Snowy Cutmore, Henry 'Long Harry' Slater was also added to the team. After his first conviction in 1910 for larceny from the person, for which he received eighteen months, Slater had gone to America where under the name of Henning Campbell he beat a vagrancy charge before being convicted of burglary and deported. In July 1918 diamond rings worth £2000 disappeared from Kilpatricks, a leading Melbourne jewellers. In a simple but effective diversion, an accomplice returned a ring to the shop, bought something more expensive, handed a banknote which required change and left with a companion who snatched a tray of jewellery. When the assistant, Henry Harburton, returned with the change he found himself padlocked in the shop. This time the 'sporting man' Matthew Daley and Cutmore were Taylor's partners in the raid.

If there had been anything of the notion 'honour among thieves' then Taylor might have lived a lot longer, but he was incapable of letting his right hand know what his left was doing. In keeping with his double dealing, he arranged that Daley should be the fall guy. He was sent to a Henry Collins in Sydney to sell some of the jewellery and the police were informed. Word was sent to Cutmore that Daley had been betrayed and he gave his share to a friend who returned with it to Sydney.

By the time Daley's trial took place, Collins had metamorphosed into Taylor's henchman, Henry Stokes, and become a prosecution witness. Stokes, born in 1887, a one-time horse dealer and book-maker, began his working life in a store before becoming a clerk in a Two-up school. By World War I he had progressed to running the biggest of those in Melbourne, eventually taking the game from backyard gambling sheds to somewhere society would go when out slumming. On 6 August 1918, along with a co-defendant John Dean, Matthew Daley was unexpectedly found not guilty and Stokes and Taylor were attacked as they left the court. There is a story that Stokes and Taylor were both tried in an unofficial underworld court and were themselves acquitted. After the Kilpatrick raid they were certainly long-time loose associates if not formal partners, with Taylor providing protection for Stokes's gambling in return for an investment in his own grog shops.

What followed became known as the Fitzroy Vendetta, a feud that lasted more than two years. Slater was now setting himself up as a serious rival to Stokes, and Taylor naturally wished to find out how the land lay. Taylor appears to have employed his brothel-keeping girlfriend, Dolly Grey, who was then running a house in Little Lonsdale Street, to spy on the organisation. She was sent to Ted's in Little Napier Street, Fitzroy, which was owned by former boxer Ted Whiting, one-time middleweight champion of Australia and now Two-up school proprietor. Whiting had been in a curious case back in June 1912 when Arthur Skirrett, who made a living as a street singer, was convicted of carrying a bludgeon and received four months. He said he only had it to protect himself from Whiting, who had previously knocked him out. Whiting was called and said it was quite correct and he would do the same again next time he saw him. What the quarrel (if indeed there was one) was about was never apparent.

Unfortunately for her (and indeed almost everyone else), Dolly the spy fell asleep at Ted's and when she awoke found she had been stripped of her furs and jewellery and left half-naked on the sofa. Things could not be allowed to stand as they were and within a matter of weeks five of those thought to be responsible had been either shot or beaten. It began with Hugh Hanlon, who was shot twice in the chest in Gertrude Street, Fitzroy, on 15 January 1919. Naturally, he declined to help the police, saying variously that he had been shot in the street and while sitting in a chair in a house.

On 14 February, Ted Whiting was shot in the head but survived. Next, Matthew Daley thought he was at risk and engaged his friends William Thorson and Frederick Lewis to protect him. Unfortunately, they were arrested carrying a variety of guns in East Melbourne and so Lewis went down for three months and Thorson for six.

On 6 May, Taylor attempted to organise a truce, travelling to Fitzroy to do so. He failed when, during the negotiations, Francis Counsel, described as a racing man, was shot seven times, taken to St Vincent's Hospital and dumped in the casualty room. His explanation was that he had been shot by mistake while he was in a motor car. It didn't fool the police, particularly when Counsel told them, 'If I die the secret will die with me.' They thought the shooting had been in a sly-grog shop in Fleet Street. Two days later Whiting was shot outside his home in Webb Street but again he survived. This time, when he was told by a doctor he had had seven bullets removed he replied, 'There must be another one somewhere. If I remember rightly I counted eight hit me while I was being shot. Have a look under the left shoulder blade'. Interviewed by the police he added, 'I know the chap of course. I hate to be disobliging but I can't tell you.'

In the meantime, he was charged with keeping a house frequented by reputed thieves.

The matter was resolved when Stokes and Slater, who was then on bail for wounding Albert Lewis as well as shooting at a Police Constable Cooper in Fitzroy, became involved in a gunfight in Melbourne's city centre. They met by accident when on 12 May, Stokes, who had left a hotel in Little Collins Street and had crossed into Swanston Street, saw Slater approaching him. There is no suggestion of pre-arrangement; it was one of those chance, and nearly fatal, meetings.

Slater probably shot first and missed, and Stokes returned the fire. In the exchange a tram was hit by two bullets and Stokes then reloaded and hit Slater five times in the shoulder and elbow as he backed across the tramlines. He collapsed against the wall of what was then the Café Français in Swanston Street. Slater behaved well. Asked his name, he swore at the officers and said, 'Get me some brandy.' In those few moments the feud was over and a few court visits later Taylor and Stokes were left in control. A month later Slater was out of hospital and on 17 June, in a very truculent mood, refused to saying anything about the shooting. For his troubles he was remanded in custody. By July he had been acquitted of shooting at Constable Cooper and his memory of events had improved slightly. He could recall fighting and being shot but not by whom.

In the wash-up Stokes received a six-month sentence for discharging a firearm in a public place. It was suspended on the undertaking that he exile himself to Tasmania for a short time. Slater, recovered from his injuries, retreated to Sydney and Cutmore went with him, although the pair spent some time in Adelaide when Slater was on the run for the Surry Hills murder of Thomas Monaghan on 19 June 1921. Slater had been trying to take over Monaghan's gaming club. After three trials he was acquitted of that shooting as well.

For the next few years Squizzy Taylor was the undisputed king of the Melbourne underworld, emerging as an almost acceptable figure in the public's eye. The likelihood is that the true mastermind was the far more intelligent Stokes, always happy to sit away from the spotlight.

* * *

Described as having a dark complexion and piercing eyes, Taylor dressed fashionably, usually wearing a bowler hat and an enormous diamond tie-pin and carrying a silver-topped walking cane. On 19 May 1920 he married a waitress, Irene Lorna Kelly, at the Congregational Church, Fitzroy. They first lived at a boarding house in Epsom Road, Flemington, and then he paid £1100 for a house in Station Street, Caulfield. They had two children: a son Leslie, and a daughter June who died aged seven months, but the marriage didn't last, partly because he was still involved with both Mollie Jarvie and Dolly Grey but particularly because he took up with a Miss Ida Pender, whom he had met at the St Kilda Palais de Danse and by whom he later had a daughter, Gloria.

It was thought that Taylor became involved in the cocaine trade but this didn't mean he devoted all his time to it, for his career suffered a minor hiccup on 15 June 1921 when he was caught in Scales' bond stores in King Street. His initial explanation was that he had simply walked in off the street, later elaborated to being chased into the shop by a rival, Louis 'The Count' Stirling, who generally worked as a commission agent as well as a receiver. Why the Count had chased him up to the third floor and then left him beside a pile of fur coats was never satisfactorily explained.

Indeed, quarrelling with Taylor was not really The Count's game at all. Born in 1900, he was more regarded as a dealer in stolen and counterfeit goods known as the 'shoddy drop'. In 1919 he had received three months for obtaining money by false pretences. He had duped a man into believing that for £100 he could settle income tax penalties. In June 1920 he was acquitted of stealing 600 yards of lace when the principal witness failed to appear.

Two years after Stirling was used as an excuse for Taylor's visit to the fur warehouse, The Count seems to have moved into a different league. He and Taylor's one-time offsider, the war hero William Macdonald who, it seems, actually did earn the Croix de Guerre, robbed two women of their jewellery at knife point in Randwick, an early version of a home invasion. They both received ten years.

Retrieved from the warehouse, Taylor was charged with breaking and entering. Bailed to appear on 2 August at General

Sessions, he promptly absconded his £300 bail. For a year he continued his career as safebreaker, thief and robber of successful gamblers. He also found time to write to the papers and when the Melbourne *Herald* asked in an article where he was, he wrote back, 'I cannot understand what all this bull is about.' Other letters said he would surrender when he had completed some outstanding business and would be pleased to take whatever punishment was coming to him. For a time he became a folk hero. During his year on the run he left Melbourne to go to the seaside at Frankston, moving about the city sometimes disguised as a schoolboy.

On 3 October 1922 Squizzy Taylor was shot in the right leg as he got out of a car in Bourke Street. A Slater man, Joseph 'Brownie' Cotter, was acquitted but was then given two months' imprisonment for being in possession of a pistol. Cotter was one of the more fortunate of the gunmen. In August the previous year he had been fined £10, again for possession of a firearm, after shooting The Decoy Duck's friend Arthur Bazley, who courteously declined to identify him. In November that year he had also been acquitted of the murder of John Thomas 'Jack' Olson in Regent Street, Fitzroy.

Lorna Kelly petitioned for divorce in February 1924 and Detective James Bruce gave evidence that when he had seen Taylor with Ida Pender and asked him about his marriage the reply had been, 'Oh, Lorna is a fair-weather friend. I'm going to stick with Ida.' He had paid the estranged Lorna £3 a week until before Christmas. Now she asked for £1 more but, as her lawyer freely admitted, no one knew exactly what Taylor had in the way of capital or income. As for Ida (known as Jazz Baby or Babe), the *Victoria Police Gazette* of 30 March 1922 described her as: 'Sixteen and a half years, five foot four in height, medium build and active appearance, bobbed, brown hair and shapely legs, fond of jazzing and skating'. Perhaps the pictures of her do not do her justice because she seems to be somewhat stout in appearance. A lively dresser, she could sometimes be seen wearing a silk top hat in the street. When she met Taylor, she was working on the hosiery counter at Myer. In a curious way Taylor seems to have been her Pygmalion. After a short time with him, out went the quirky dresses and with them her rough speech.

On 6 March 1922 she was arrested for breaking into Rita Moore's shop in Flinders Street and stealing a georgette frock, five sponge cloth frocks and a number of blouses valued altogether at £221. It was, however, merely a police ruse to question her about Taylor. She remained staunch, laughing at the questions, until she was finally bailed with two sureties of £100. Four days later the charge was withdrawn.

Taylor wrote defending her: 'In reference to the article in Friday's *Herald* referring to Miss Pender, I think it is only right I should deny the young lady is sharing my hiding place. It is taking me all my time to keep myself "in balk" without having to look after a second person.'

When he finally decided to surrender on 21 September, Taylor made sure he was dressed in his best and had notified the newspapers of his impending appearance at Russell Street Police Headquarters. He was once more released on a personal bond, backed by Richard Loughnan, organiser of the Builders Labourers Federation, and gave interviews saying that he had surrendered because his mother was ill and his friends were being continually pestered by the police.

While on bail he attended a race meeting at Caulfield and was promptly warned off. In another example of his spite and bravado, at 4 a.m. on 21 October, the night before the prestigious Caulfield Cup, he torched the Members' Stand, causing £9000 worth of damage. Despite rewards totalling £1000 and a free pardon to any accomplice who shelved him, no charges were brought against anyone. When Taylor was finally tried for the fur warehouse offence he was acquitted and now he moved into big-time robberies— including one of £2750 from the Victorian Railways payroll—in which the planning was done by Stokes, and Taylor was usually the getaway driver.

Meanwhile, Taylor's old friend Mollie Jarvie, The Decoy Duck, was now swimming in new ponds. Also known as Alma Murray, the Duck earned her soubriquet not from the ginger game but from her part in a robbery in Toorak Road on 4 September 1921 when the shopkeeper Alexander John Howard was relieved of jewellery worth £500. She had knocked on his door at 8 30 p.m. and asked to use his lavatory. When he opened the back door he was knocked down and kicked by three masked men who then stole trays of jewellery. Howard had recognised her as having been in the shop earlier to have a ring repaired. When the matter came to court, the judge said, had the men been in front of him, he would have given them several years and a flogging. The jury recommended mercy, and Jarvie, as a cleanskin, received twelve months suspended for three years, but there was much more to come from her. Another woman, Ella Watson, was also known as The Decoy Duck. She worked rather downmarket with 'convicted Chinese of the lowest class', luring men she met in cafés into the lanes where they would be robbed.

Jarvie took up with the burglar John Michael Mulligan and in January 1927, together with Arthur Bazley and George 'The Midnight Raper' Wallace, they were charged with a series of jewel robberies committed in 1922. Jarvie was found not guilty but the others received up to three years. Later Bazley worked with the forger John Gilligan who, in the 1940s, would fall foul of standover man Freddie Harrison in a fight for control of the gaming clubs.

The press and public may have idolised Taylor but he was not wholly popular with his peers. Apart from anything else, he was now recognised as a dobber. Shortly after he had been re-bailed he was shot in the leg. Nor, unsurprisingly, was he popular with the authorities. A racing film, *In Emergency Colours*, in which he was due to star as a jockey and of which several episodes were actually shot, was banned in Victoria as not being in the public interest. It was eventually released in Brisbane in 1925. It was then the wife of Sir Arthur Stanley, former Governor-General of Victoria, had the mistaken idea that she could reform Taylor. They took tea at the Menzies Hotel at a meeting arranged by a social worker. He promised to mend his ways and later presented her with a silver jewel box inscribed, 'To one who understands, from one misunderstood.' It is not recorded from where he obtained the box.

Any gang needs a tame doctor to patch up wounds that there is no need for the police to know of, and Taylor had the services of Dr Shirley Francis, whose son Charles became a barrister and parliamentarian. Taylor had a holiday home between Ferntree Gully and Upwey and from time to time Dr Francis, who lived nearby, would be called on for his services, no questions asked. Taylor was apparently a good payer—always in cash. He was also polite and, contrary to the opinion that he was a rat and a shelf, Francis thought him brave and indeed rather admired him. 'I think it was an error on my father's part but he found him friendly, charming and good to deal with,' Charles Francis QC would recall.

* * *

In the winter of 1923 Taylor decided it was time for the release of his old friend Angus Murray, then in Geelong Gaol, and set about plans for his escape. On 24 August, Murray made his break. A rope with a hook had been smuggled into the prison, along with a fretsaw and money, and Murray cut through the bars to his cell and hooked the rope to the outside wall. As he scaled it he touched an alarm wire but he nevertheless managed to get away and, as the *Victoria Police Gazette* reported, he was soon on his way to a safe house carrying a travelling rug and a small brown case. The police thought he would return to Melbourne and roadblocks were set up, but instead he remained at Geelong for a week before he was driven to the city.

Although Taylor lived for a number of years after the robbery of the Commercial Bank in Glenferrie in 1923, it marked the beginning of the end of his career. Murray had been at large for less than two months when, on 8 October, he and the lame Richard Buckley robbed bank employee Thomas Berriman as he followed his usual Monday routine taking a bag of notes to the Glenferrie Railway Station, something he had done at 11 a.m. for the previous six weeks. The plan was simple. Berriman would be attacked as he walked up the ramp to the platform. The bag, together with any gun he was carrying, would be snatched, and Murray and Buckley would jump into the waiting car. The driver was to be Taylor but, when it came to it, our hero preferred to skulk outside the police headquarters in Russell Street, so setting up a cast-iron alibi.

Buckley, now sixty years old and with a long record for violence, was on parole at the time of the robbery. Over the years he had regularly been placed in solitary confinement, and for one earlier robbery—of which he claimed to be innocent—he had received the lash. He walked with a limp, something he blamed on a beating by the police. As Berriman came down the ramp Buckley asked him if he could carry his bag, which contained more than £1850, and Berriman replied, 'No thank you, old man, I can carry it myself.'

When Buckley tried to take the bag from him the brave if foolish Berriman refused to hand it over and was promptly shot. Murray helped Buckley as he limped along to the getaway car, from time to time turning and waving his revolver at pursuers. Two days after the robbery two women telephoned the police to say they had seen two men burning a briefcase in a yard at 443 Barkly Street, St Kilda. In the early hours of 11 October the police broke through the doors of the five-roomed detached cottage. When they called out 'Hands up', Murray replied, 'They are up.' Taylor was in bed with Ida Pender but of Buckley there was no trace. It was thought he had been staying with Taylor but that night he had been out 'tomcatting' and on his return, seeing the police, he disappeared. Berriman had been taken to a private hospital where he died at 8.45 a.m. on 21 October 1923. As he lay in bed he positively identified Buckley as the gunman and Murray as being with him. The coroner returned a verdict of wilful murder against Murray and Buckley and, perhaps somewhat speculatively, a charge of accessory before the fact for Taylor.

The trial was scheduled for November but Murray wanted an adjournment to February and the police were happy because they thought it would give them more time to find Buckley. On 11 November, Taylor was granted bail with two sureties of £500 and went to live at the Queensland Hotel, Bourke Street. He did at least have the courtesy to try to assist his former employee. He had attempted to have Murray rescued from prison almost immediately after his arrest and now, out and about himself, he tried again, on 31 January 1924. This time a warder, who was to be bribed with an offer of £250 and £7 per week pension if he should be dismissed, told the police of the approach. In turn they seized a car outside the prison, arrested the four men in it, including Taylor's brother Thomas, and confiscated a rope ladder. There were, however, suggestions that Taylor was not being wholly altruistic in his efforts to free Murray; it was thought Murray might crack and divulge details of the Melbourne underworld. The weekly newspaper *Truth*, for one, thought it was rather fortunate for him that the escape attempt had failed.

The trial was a foregone conclusion. The prosecution alleged that the information about how easy it was to rob the bank came from a former employee who had met Murray in prison and, although Murray denied it, there is no doubt it told against him. After a retirement of an hour and a half the jury returned a verdict of murder and Murray was sentenced to death on 22 February 1924. His appeal was heard before the full court on 6 March.

'When death's wings fluttered over gloom of Criminal Court', head-lined *Truth* when it had previewed the trial. Now the wings flapped furiously. Meanwhile the evidence—as opposed to suspicion—against Taylor was very thin indeed and really relied on the fact the pair had stayed in his home. On 3 March the charge was withdrawn.

On 5 June 1924 all the men found in the car outside the prison were acquitted of conspiracy to release Murray, and Taylor was found not guilty of harbouring. He had given a virtuoso performance claiming he was being hounded by the police: 'I receive no credit for my good deeds, to say nothing of the charitable institutions I have assisted and the woman I tried to save recently and the Soldier Boys I got jobs for …' And so on, *ad nauseam*.

Along with anti-hanging groups, Taylor also tried to organise a reprieve for Murray, and a petition signed by some 70 000 was presented. A march was organised in which Taylor drove in an open car, graciously receiving the tributes of the crowd who respectfully doffed their caps. He was with Ida Pender and their baby. *Truth* reported that he provided his handkerchief to be used as a nappy.

None of it did Murray any good. Despite the petitions and a last-ditch attempt to show that he had a child who was a 'congenital idiot' and that his father, uncle and an aunt had all committed suicide, the authorities did not believe this added up to his being of unsound mind. He behaved as well in the death cell as he had done on the outside, writing to the man—certainly not Taylor—who had financed his appeal to apologise for presuming on him. When he broke his dentures the prison doctor, Clarence Godfrey, offered to make him a replacement as a matter of urgency but, according to *Truth* or legend, he declined, saying, 'Doctor do you really think it worthwhile?'

The thought of Murray in the death cell did not stop the underworld continuing its daily or nightly business. Shootings continued apace. Watched by the police at 2.35 a.m. on 10 March 1924, Archibald Fletcher was shot in Exhibition Street. He had been dealing in cocaine and at the time was on bail on a vagrancy charge. While he was on the ground, a longstanding criminal, Percy Dowdle, who had already served one indeterminate sentence, attacked him with a bottle. An officer pulled Dowdle off by the hair and arrested him. Clearly disorientated by the incident, Fletcher thought he had been attacked by a foreigner. They both lived to fight another day, so to speak. The vagrancy charge against Fletcher was dropped but in 1928 he received an eighteen-month sentence for housebreaking. His co-accused on that occasion, George Ellis, received three years, to go along with the sentence he was already serving.

On 20 March another Taylor associate, Albert Macdonald, also known as Kohlman or Grimes, was shot by a policeman in Exhibition Gardens. Macdonald dropped a rifle, another double-barrelled gun and a suitcase and took off. He stopped running after he was shot in the leg, and the police took him to hospital where he was kept under guard. He was allowed to go to the lavatory and promptly escaped through a window to a waiting car. He surrendered a fortnight later.

Murray was hanged at 10 a.m. on 14 April 1924 in Melbourne Gaol. He is reported to have said from the scaffold, 'Never in my life have I done anything to justify the penalty passed on me. I have tried to forgive those who have acted against me and I hope those I have injured will forgive me.' When the noose was put over his head he is said to have added, 'Pull it tight.' Another version, said to have been obtained from the lips of the hangman himself, is that the words were 'Carry on, Dig, not too tight.' Outside there was a mixed crowd of recalcitrants being surly towards the police — mounted and on foot, curious bystanders and abolitionists who sang hymns. 'As a distant clock chimed out the tenth hour an enfeebled old man led the gathering in the Lord's Prayer,' observed *The Age* a trifle unsympathetically. Earlier, *Truth* had been at its sanctimonious best: 'In the Great Beyond there is a whole army of men who have gone forth from the earth through the gibbet and the gallows. Angus Murray will not lack for company of this land.' Now it thought he had been game:

> So he died
> Give him his due
> Poor, wretched, wayward, careless, dangerous
> criminal Angus Murray knew how to die.

Murray would be the last criminal to be hanged in Melbourne Gaol—unless Buckley could be found quickly. He was not. There had already been suggestions that he was 'in permanent smoke'. If he was not, in theory it should have been easy to spot him for he was covered in tattoos—a cross on his right forearm, a dancing girl with a wreath on his lower inside right arm, and a woman's head on his inside right upper arm. A coat of arms was on his inside left lower arm and a vase of flowers on the inside upper left. But he must have kept his sleeves down. Known as the Grey Ghost, there were reported sightings of him in the United States, in Europe and in other states of Australia. One story had him dying in London under the name of Henry Freeman, an early alias. At first *Truth* had him dead and then, within weeks, unblushingly published an interview with him.

In fact, Buckley had never travelled very far. When he was arrested in 1930 he was found to have been living in Richmond and then Collingwood before moving to Bowen Street, Ascot Vale, with his granddaughter Pat, taking occasional exercise at night dressed as a woman. There have been stories that over the years he was supported by John Wren, but there seems to be little, if any, foundation for the rumours.

A Labor government was now in office and Buckley's death sentence was commuted to one of life imprisonment. In 1946, suffering from dropsy and not expected to survive more than a few months, he was released. Like so many other early-released criminals, Buckley found life on the outside much healthier and lived on, surprising everyone. He died aged eighty-nine on 15 September 1953.

Murray's passing may or may not have been mourned, but life had to go on, as did the weekly round of thefts and robberies. And Taylor was just as tricky as before. On 15 June he, along with his brother Tom, Murray Davis and Charles 'Prat-in' Allsop, nominally a bookmaker's clerk but regarded by the police as a gunman and 'one of the worst criminals in the State', bailed up a card game at a barber's shop in Glenhuntly, stealing cash and jewellery. One of the players, the racehorse trainer Charlie Caylock, recognised Allsop and arrests followed. Then came a series of delicate negotiations. Some of the players wanted the return of the jewellery, which had some sentimental value, and it was arranged at a meeting between Caylock and Taylor that the jewellery would be returned if he watered down his evidence. The trial was duly stopped but Taylor never returned the jewellery, saying that Ida Pender had become rather attached to it. One good thing to come out of the case was that Caylock was named in a newspaper as a defendant and received £800 in libel damages. The error was repeated in a number of other papers and in turn he sued them.

A month after Murray's execution, on 5 May, Taylor killed Daphne Alcon in a hit-and-run accident on St Kilda Road. But it was the same old story and, although he was committed for trial, on 18 June that year the Crown dropped the charge of manslaughter after witnesses changed their minds. However, he was later convicted of harbouring Murray and received six months' imprisonment. There were also stories that he had been kidnapping young girls and injecting them with cocaine before turning them out to deal the drug on his behalf. He was almost certainly involved in the abduction of one young woman who was returned to her family a week later in a dazed state after she had been injected with drugs.

While Taylor was serving his six months, Ida went out dancing with a young bookmaker back at St Kilda's Palais de Danse. On his release Taylor turned the liaison to his advantage by blackmailing the man. In 1925 he tried to buy Gorry's, a tobacconist and hairdressers, but the deal fell through when it was discovered who the purchaser would be. It was thought he had continued to be a police informer and now there were also rivals for his empire and for control of the burgeoning and lucrative cocaine trade. It was also thought Taylor was involved in a number of robberies, which included the Brighton Yacht Club on two occasions and a jewellery shop in Inkerman Street in which a young girl was shot.

Shortly before his death, Taylor was suspected, along with a series of interestingly named companions including 'Mush' Burns and 'No Toe' King, of the bombing of the Middle Park home of a man named Elchorn. Nothing came of the complaint, which was all part of the waterfront pay and conditions disputes that year.

On 22 June 1927 another of Taylor's henchmen, Norman Bruhn, was shot and killed in Sydney and then, at the end of October, Snowy Cutmore returned to Melbourne, ostensibly to pick up a horse. He must, however, have expected trouble, because he brought with him as a bodyguard the hulking standover man and bludger Herbert Wilson, then going under the name of Roy Travers. He stayed with his mother and wife but that did not stop him getting about of an evening.

Out on the town, the violent Cutmore (it was said he had once branded a girl with a hot iron) was drinking heavily at a brothel in Tennyson Street, St Kilda, which was under the temporary protection of Taylor, when he smashed up the premises and, pulling a young girl out of bed, stripped her naked before turning her onto the street. It was not something that Taylor, even in decline, could allow to go unpunished. On 26 October the pair met at Richmond Racecourse where there were high words, and in the afternoon Cutmore was warned off the course for life.

The double killing took place the next afternoon. As far as can be pieced together from the very mixed statements by witnesses, Taylor and two men took a cab, driven by John Hall, outside the Melbourne Hospital. From there they toured the hotels in Carlton—'getting Dutch courage', suggested Cutmore's uncle Frank McLaughlin—until at six o'clock they told the driver to stop in Barkly Street, Fitzroy, near Cutmore's house. There at the time were Mrs Bridget Cutmore snr, a tenant John 'Scotty' King (who later sensibly told the police he was in bed asleep) and Cutmore (who was also in bed, said to be suffering from a sudden attack of bronchitis and influenza). Out in the backyard cutting wood was Roy Travers/Wilson.

Describing the scene of the shooting, *Truth* was at its most lyrical, anxious to show its readers that the mothers of even the top standover men did not live in palaces:

> A wan light, even on the brightest day, filters through the rickety window to light the room where the death duel took place ... A tiny room, crowded with furniture, its pale pink walls showing dingy and grotesque ... its furniture cheap and tawdry ... family photographs, cheap fantastic vases, and ornaments litter the mantlepiece while, on a small table in the corner, old musty books jostle each other.

Taylor walked in and shot Cutmore who, with a pistol under the sheets, returned the fire. Between them they fired fourteen times. Cutmore died on the bed, shot through the right lung. Mrs Cutmore ran into the room and was shot in the shoulder. Taylor then staggered out, to be taken to St Vincent's Hospital. One man got in the cab with him until, at the corner of Brunswick and Johnston streets, he told Hall, 'Here, you do the rest on your own,' and jumped out. Taylor, like so many of the Melbourne underworld before and after him, died at St Vincent's.

When reporters from *Truth* went to see Cutmore's widow, there was Henry Slater, back from his Sydney exile, lounging 'moodily about the house'. The first wreath to arrive at the house had come from the parents of Norman Bruhn—which, said Cutmore's widow, showed they did not believe her husband had anything to do with that man's shooting earlier in the year. Arrests followed, including the Sydney standover men Siddy and Thomas Kelly and Norman Smith, along with Roy Travers, who was found a few days later in Albury making his way home. They were all charged with vagrancy and held in custody. Vagrancy was simply a holding device and after the completely ineffectual inquest the charges were dropped.

Although the police accepted that Cutmore and Taylor had shot each other, different versions of the killings have since emerged. One is that Cutmore was killed by Sydney criminals over the death of Bruhn; fortuitously Taylor happened to be there and was killed at the same time. Another is that somehow Cutmore shot Taylor first and then was shot by Taylor's companion. If this version is correct it was almost certainly set up by Henry Stokes who by now realised that Taylor was an untrustworthy little monster who might turn on him at any given moment. Whichever is correct, Mrs Bridget Cutmore was quite unable to help the police, apart from saying she had heard a quarrel. A further complication to the official version is that Eibar 'Destroyer' .32 calibre bullets of the type that killed Taylor were found under a picket fence some 200 metres from the house. It is possible that Travers, hearing the shooting, picked up and threw away Cutmore's gun. Taylor's gun was found on him at the hospital. There is another theory: that Cutmore's mother, seeing Taylor shoot her son, took a gun and killed him.

In the days before Taylor's funeral, some of the Bruhn brothers stood outside the Bookmakers' Club soliciting donations. When they told Charlie Caylock they had 'put him down' for £50 he replied, 'I'll give you £50 for a kick at his coffin.' Taylor's funeral left Darlington Parade on Richmond Hill watched by a crowd of thousands, women holding their children in the air and boys climbing lampposts to see their fallen hero. They had begun gathering an hour before the cortege—with Taylor in a gold-plated coffin—moved off to St James's Congregational Church, Fitzroy, and on to Brighton Cemetery.

* * *

Whether he had arranged the shooting or not, Henry Stokes now assumed the mantle of undisputed king of the Victorian underworld, a position he would hold for nearly twenty years. Naturally enough there were some hiccups along the way.

On 1 December 1928 the premises of one of his main rivals, the Greek Club in Lonsdale Street, was blown up and sentences of up to fifteen years were handed out. The evidence against Timothy O'Connell, Alexander McIver and Francis Delaney was not that strong. They were seen together around 9.40 that evening when the club was bombed. McIver then left them and reappeared with a parcel for O'Connell. They again separated and O'Connell and a man thought to be Delaney were seen to run out of the club shortly before the explosion. Their appeals in April were heard by the full court, one of whose members had been the trial judge. One judge thought the evidence against McIver was insufficient but he was out-voted by his colleagues. The convictions and sentences were upheld.

In July 1929, Stokes was charged with conspiring to pervert the course of justice over the case. It was alleged that he had paid Madge Vaughan, who had come to Melbourne from Brisbane for the Spring Racing Carnival and had stayed on, to produce perjured evidence in the appeals of the three men. Stokes was put on trial with McIver's brother Norman. Vaughan gave evidence that Stokes had met her in Lonsdale Street and afterwards she had gone to

a flat in East Melbourne. Stokes had let her in and she had had
a discussion with Taylor and Norman McIver, which would have
cleared the men. She was not believed. Not guilty, my Lord. Madge
Vaughan reappeared shortly afterwards, this time when she
brought an action for libel against the magazine *Smith's Weekly*.
The paper had claimed that she was one of the most notorious
women of the Melbourne underworld. Her associate, Percy 'Snowy'
Jenkins, who had earlier been shot and had his shop bombed, was
said to be in smoke and she had taken up with the French boxer
Fernand Quendroux, who had served time for robbery and assault
in Queensland. The *Weekly* also claimed — something she denied —
that she was a licensed public woman in Brisbane.

In January 1932, Stokes was shot but declined police assistance,
saying he would take care of matters himself. In 1935 he put
together an audacious robbery from the Commonwealth Bank at
Ballarat. Stokes approached a young constable, Rex Byrne, with
the proposition that he would receive £10000 — ten per cent of the
estimated take — if he arranged that neither he nor any other officer
was near the bank on the night when Stokes and his partners broke
in. Byrne reported the matter to his superiors and Stokes and his
crew were caught almost red-handed. They escaped, dumping
the oxyacetylene cutters near Melton, and hightailed it back to
Melbourne, where they were arrested. Stokes received four years.
He was then fifty-three.

The great turnaround in his fortunes came after he had
completed his sentence. His first gaming house had been The
Temple of the Kip in Goodwood Street, Richmond, over which
he had been fined the massive sum of £500 back in 1919, but
in 1938 he promoted Australia's first illegal casino. It must be a
matter of speculation which bank financed the enterprise but it
was based on the American concept of the floating casino, with
the *Alvina* — which had once been a gift from the Prince of Wales
to Lily Langtry (complete with hand-carved oak panels and deep

pile carpets) — sailing nightly around Port Phillip Bay. In December 1938 he was fined £150 after a raid by the Gaming Squad and from then on the *Alvina* had a marked deck, so to speak.

Stokes had an immediate solution. The next year he opened his first baccarat club, the Ace of Clubs, on the first floor of 2–7 Elizabeth Street near Flinders. Up two flights of stairs, the club was a heavily carpeted room with eight dummy tables with cards scattered on them in case of a raid and the baccarat table itself. There could be up to 150 fashionably dressed men and women in the club at any time.

There was naturally competition but once again Stokes showed his business acumen. Instead of waging war against Simon Kemelfield, a well-known Melbourne gambler, Michael Pitt, another turf identity, and the Palestinian-born gambler Hymie Mayer, Stokes engineered an amalgamation. *E pluribus unum*, or perhaps that should be the other way around for, from then on, the profits were enormous.

As for the long-dead Squizzy Taylor, after his death his brain had been sent for examination and, according to *Smith's Weekly*, showed the same kink as that of the late Kaiser.

Ida Pender was twenty-two years old when Taylor died. Always a keen dancer, she returned to be a regular at the St Kilda Palais. Later she met and married the dancer Mickey Powell but the marriage ended in divorce.

Sex in the City

3

By the 1860s the criminal class in Melbourne was said to be around 4000, out of a population of 140 000. The lanes at the end of Bourke Street, where Charley Wright's Coliseum Music Hall was thought to be the 'rendez-vous of thieves and the lowest-priced prostitutes in town', were dangerous. When night fell criminals stalked the bars and the vestibule of the Theatre Royal. One bar where prostitutes could be found for a modest charge was known as the Saddling Paddock. Higher class girls worked Collins Street. Both ends of Little Bourke Street, where garrotters lurked, were seriously unsafe and thieves prowled both the town and the suburbs. Bella Wright's residence was the 'lowest brothel in Melbourne'.

The city's brothel area, known as Little Lon, had sprung up in the 1850s and was roughly bordered by Lonsdale, Spring, Stephen (later named Exhibition after the Great Exhibition of 1880) and La Trobe streets. The better-class houses, among them two run by Scotch Maude and Biddy O'Connor, looked onto the main streets. The lower-class houses, which operated from the narrow lanes and a variety of shops, could front small one- and two-girl brothels. One was run at 17 Casselden Place by a Chinese girl, oddly named Yokohama, until the 1920s. Another, owned by Rita Milini (also known as Rita Cooper), was run from a confectionery shop in Lonsdale Street. Then, as now, brothels and drugs often went hand in hand, and her establishment was frequented by Ada Matlock, one of the major distributors of the period.

By 1883 Melbourne's brothel district was now contained, mainly in a square bordered by Elizabeth and Spring streets and La Trobe and Bourke streets, with the heaviest concentration of houses between Russell and Spring. Shortly after, the city began the destruction of the back slums and the women who worked there were moved on. By 1893 the girls worked Exhibition Gardens and Nicholson streets. There were assignation houses, hotels where the girls met their clients and took them to brothels and 'providers', which let out beds to prostitutes and their clients. With the inner-city clearance there were expensive brothels in Carlton and some girls moved to a house in Acland Street, St Kilda, but they were promptly moved on. It was very much a case of NIMBY.

In 1917 the Anglican clergyman John Good, giving evidence at the Royal Commission on Housing, displayed less than Christian charity, saying he wanted the girls moved out of residential districts; that is, out of his parish. He felt it did not do young boys any good having to ask their fathers or, worse, their mothers who were these painted ladies walking up and down their street.

Sex was also available at the highest level. When in 1867 the twenty-two-year-old Duke of Edinburgh, HRH Prince Alfred, arrived in Melbourne, Captain Frederick Standish, the dilettante Commissioner of Police, who liked to place naked white women on black chairs, took him to Sarah Fraser's very high-class and tastefully decorated brothel in Stephen Street. When Standish ushered in one of the Queen's children, Mother Fraser must have thought she had died and gone to Madam Heaven.

Fraser was succeeded as the queen of the city's brothels by the German-born Caroline Baum, known as 'Madame Brussels'. She had married Studholme George Hodgson in England in February 1871 and the pair sailed for Australia five months later. He joined the Victoria Police and was posted to Mansfield, leaving her behind in Melbourne where she put her talents to good use. By 1874 she was running a high-class brothel from her home in

Lonsdale Street. Two years later her seven-roomed house at 32–36 Lonsdale Street was well furnished with marble bathrooms, the carpets were 'like meadow-grass' and guests could pay £10 to £12 per day without wine or girls for board and lodgings. At the other end of the tariff, parliamentary visitors had a key to a door opening off Little Lonsdale Street and appointments in her special boudoir could cost up to £2000. She maintained her occupation for more than three decades.

In 1878, Sergeant James Dalton, giving evidence at a Select Committee upon a Bill for The Prevention of Contagious Diseases, was asked about Madame Brussels' brothels.

Q. How many brothels does Mrs B. keep?

A. She has two splendid houses in [Lonsdale] Street that cost her 1300 pounds, and those two houses are her own property … and then she has two cottages in —— Street and she has in —— Street too.

Q. Do you know of any other brothel of the same character as Mrs B.'s?

A. Not so extensive.

She was then described as a 'magnificent pink, white and golden maned animal'.

Her first husband, Hodgson, developed tuberculosis and died in 1892. Her second and possibly bigamous husband was the German engineer Jacob Pohl, fifteen years her junior, who disappeared from view in 1896, and she may also have had a child by the composer and critic Alfred Plumpton. In his 1891 treatise *The War between Heaven and Hell*, the wowser reformer Henry Varley angrily wrote of Madame Brussels walking on Collins Street with a girl under twenty who had a white feather (signifying virginity) in her hat. Varley thought that 'maiden virtue was to be had for a price in her gilded den'.

Early one morning in October 1891 after the House had risen, the Parliamentary mace—five feet of silver gilt and weighing 217 ounces—disappeared. Legend was that it had gone to Madame Brussels but when a board of inquiry into the disappearance sat some sixteen months later it specifically named as the beneficiary the equally popular Boccaccio House, run by Miss Annie Wilson, also in Lonsdale Street. That brothel had one of Melbourne's first telephones installed for the benefit of a member of parliament who lived there. In 1891 one of the first call-girl networks in the world operated from the brothels catering for the businessmen and parliamentarians who did not wish to roll up unannounced. Now the houses booked appointments for their favourite girls to be available, the reverse of the present system of outcalls for girls, which seems to have developed in the 1930s in the United States.

Towards the end of her illustrious career, Madame Brussels suffered at the hands of the new moralists of the era. In 1889 she was targeted as the 'pin-up girl' by those who were crusading to close brothels and the vice industries. Tried on charges instigated by the moralists, she was found not guilty of procurement and to be in charge of a house that was well conducted.

In 1898 she was again brought before the courts, this time with her Lonsdale Street neighbours Maude Miller and May Baker. The three women were tried for 'occupying premises frequented by persons without lawful means of support', a forerunner of the consorting laws of the twentieth century. The charges came courtesy of the Wesleyan Methodists, and the police must have felt they were between a rock and a hard place. They were obliged to pursue the complaints of the God-bothering moralists and to prosecute but they then had to concede, once on oath, that the 'houses were well conducted'. Dismissing the charges against the trio, Chief Magistrate Malcolm McEachern, who also happened to be mayor, made his feelings on the subject very clear: 'Do you think that Melbourne would be improved if a large street like this were filled with Syrians, Hindus and Chinese?' The Supreme Court quashed the verdict and on the retrial McEachern thought he must bow to their opinion but that justice would be done by imprisoning the women until the court rose that day.

At the beginning of the twentieth century the campaign against Madame Brussels and her colleagues intensified. The crusading *Truth* editor, John Norton, saw her as 'an immoral monster' and 'the wickedest woman in Melbourne'. In March 1906, at yet another court hearing, she was described by the paper:

> Madame certainly was quietly attired ... The spectacled, middle-aged woman with her rectitude on her arm, and her fan languidly waving, had more the appearance of a benevolent midwife than the keeper of a notorious brothel ... but the rest were bobby dazzlers ... She was quite a performer and the court was awash with her tears both before and after the presiding magistrate said he would discharge her.

But the wowsers were winning. In April 1907 Henry Pallenberg successfully sued her for £150, the amount of a cheque he had paid for settlement of his bill for a five-day period in the brothel. He said he had been drunk when he wrote it. Later that year Brussels closed her doors and, ill with chronic pancreatitis and diabetes, she died on 12 July the next year. She was buried in her first husband's grave in the St Kilda Cemetery, but the grave has not survived.

Another wowser determined to clean up gambling and vice in Melbourne was the Methodist reformer William Henry Judkins, along with his brother George Alfred. A wisp of a man, described alliteratively in *Truth* as 'a gospel-grinding, gammoning ghoul', William had a florid style in the pulpit and attacked gambling, prize fights, racing, drinking, dancing and barmaids with equal enthusiasm. In May 1906 after he had effectively closed down John Wren's illegal Tote, Judkins turned his attention to Sir Samuel Gillott who, as chief secretary in the administration, held responsibility for illegal off-course gambling, claiming it was prima facie evidence of collusion between the administration and the police. Now Premier Sir Thomas Bent, himself no straight arrow, instructed Gillott to promote a bill that would effectively outlaw off-course gaming.

But worse was to come. In a sermon on 16 September 1906, Judkins told his congregation, 'If I were to tell you all I could, you would hold your breaths; matters are so serious in some departments of our public life you would shiver.' He was offered a Royal Commission but backed down. On 29 November *Truth*'s very-often drunken editor John Norton wrote an open letter alleging that Gillott had been financing Madame Brussels since 1877. Three days later Judkins disclosed that Sir Samuel also held the mortgage on her brothel at 36 Lonsdale Street. Pleading ill-health, Gillott resigned from office and returned to England, where he remained for a year. As Madame Brussels' biographer Leanne Robinson points out, although Gillott 'freely acknowledged his role as Caroline's mortgagee, he claimed ignorance as to the nature of [her] business—despite the fact that, as a parliamentarian, he'd been instrumental in framing legislation against gambling and licensing and had chaired public meetings on the suppression of vice'.

Even at the lowest end of the scale, prostitution in the early twentieth century might have appeared attractive as a way of life, partly because it offered women both the chance to work from home and an easier and more flexible way of living. A shop worker might have respectability but the part-time prostitute was infinitely better paid. Two shillings and sixpence was the going rate for a short time, and with one client a day the woman would earn far more than a typist who worked all day.

By the early 1920s much of the prostitution in the centre of Melbourne was in the hands of a group of brothel owners, one of several known as The Combine, who paid substantial sums of money to police officers both to avoid prosecution and to stop them hanging about in front of the houses, scaring away potential customers. Between them, Ruby Lynch (aka Jackson) and Maud Gunther ran twenty-eight places, including fourteen in Little Lonsdale Street alone. Sarah Brenner (also known as Sal Redan) ran the Poplars, a somewhat higher-class 'supper joint' in Exhibition Street, which catered for senior police officers. Even so, she was still expected to pay £50 a month to them for protection.

Maud Gunther had worked her way up from the Chinese brothels around Little Bourke Street. She had been found in one in September 1904 and was given the option of a year or exile to Wagga Wagga. Ruby Lynch had also been around for some time. In June 1908 she told the court that she had been in a café with Edward Gardiner and was his alibi for a housebreaking and assault in Drummond Street, Carlton, on 8 April. From then on it was onwards and upwards. On 16 November 1912 she was involved in a shooting in Newry Street, Prahran, when she went to a party with a man she knew only as Jack whom she had met that afternoon. The party was given by an Alice Morgan who was living with Robert Barklay McGrindle. Quite what it was all about the coroner was not able to discover. It seems that after supper the front doorbell was rung. Ruby Lynch told Alice that the man, Jack, had a gun and he had been following her. Three shots were fired into the hallway and then Robert McGrindle fired at Jack, who now fired three times, killing McGrindle. As he lay dying McGrindle said, 'A fellow with curly hair who had a gun did it. Ruby's boy is the man I suspect. The shots were not intended for me. I went up the passage and ran into the bullets.' Lynch said that she had last seen Jack at around 1.30 in the morning when he said he had had enough and was off. Jack, who was the John Thomas Olson killed in 1921 by Joseph Cotter, said he had left the party before the shooting and was in bed when it occurred. Quite how he would have known was never disclosed. The following morning he had gone to Bendigo with Ruby. 'In my ten years' experience this is the worst case before me, there being no evidence that can be believed, except that of the police and the medical man. There is no doubt someone is guilty of murder.' The coroner thought there was some evidence against Olsen but he was never charged.

One of the most talented of all the high-class girls of the time was Vera Purdy (born Hannah Garnett in New Zealand and also known as Bobbie Mason or Barry), who was also a talented pickpocket and shoplifter. A genuine queen of the underworld with a one-woman house in La Trobe Street, Purdy was a friend of Sydney's Nellie Cameron and Squizzy Taylor's long-time associate Dolly Grey. In 1930, at the age of twenty-one, she married the welterweight boxer Charlie Purdy. He divorced her in April 1935 after a stormy marriage, which began on their wedding night with her throwing cups at him when he complained about her flirting with an old boyfriend. He admitted that over the years she had knocked him out five times.

Before then she had led a rackety life, often working the ginger game with her friend Margery Astor as well as with Leslie Faure and his wife Irene, the former wife of standover man Norman Bruhn. In September 1933 she and the Faures were acquitted of possessing unregistered pistols. The previous year she had been very busy. On 11 May she gave evidence against a Peter Costello in a razor slashing case and the same day was herself acquitted of robbery in another courtroom.

She was also acquitted in September 1933 of a consorting charge. In April 1935, when she was arrested for theft, she ate a series of banknotes she had stolen from a client and then claimed the unfortunate man had stolen her furs. Two years later she successfully appealed against a police refusal to grant her a driving licence because she had been convicted of consorting and soliciting. She had been driving to Collins Street, where she collected her clients. The law was changed after she had won a High Court action that held that a one-woman brothel was legal.

By now she had consumption. In 1939 she absconded her bail in Melbourne and went to New Zealand, where she also absconded on a charge of stealing diamonds.

Early in 1940, Purdy was named in a divorce case brought by one Pearl Shannon against her husband Patrick. The previous year she had been acquitted of assault after Pearl had been to Purdy's flat enquiring after her husband. She then told *Truth* that she was going to Toowoomba to be a teacher, adding, when some surprise was expressed by the journalist, 'I'm going to teach 'em a thing or two in that little Queensland one horse town.' Purdy was indeed working in the Sunnyside brothel in the town when she died on 21 December 1940 following an overdose of cocaine. There were suggestions she had been given a hotshot, but these came to nothing. After her death, Patrick Shannon appeared, claiming he was her husband and wanting her belongings, but she had in fact married the career criminal Horace Clive Robinson in 1936 and they had never divorced. In May 1937 Robinson received three years for what was known as the 'Little Flemington' kidnap case when a bookmaker was held up by Robinson and his offsider Jack Kain, posing as policemen, on his way home from the Maribyrnong races. Robinson would go on to greater glory as one of the men accused of the attempted murder of Dr Reginald Stuart-Jones in Sydney in 1945. He was acquitted.

Purdy's near contemporary, Tasmanian-born Jean Beaumont, was regarded as one of the most beautiful of Melbourne's street walkers. On 17 June 1945 she walked into Windsor Police Station to say she had shot her pimp James Varney eight times in self-defence. She and Varney had had a long and stormy relationship. On their better days they gave parties for the underworld at which guns, knives and razors had to be left on the hall table of their Raleigh Street flat. On their bad days he gave her terrible beatings. She was acquitted of the murder after telling the jury she had shot Varney when he was about to attack her again.

On 27 April 1952 Beaumont was slashed on her face by another woman at St Kilda junction and had eight stitches put in the wound. She gave as good as she got, and when the women were seen by the police they told them of an attack by an unknown man. Six years later, her looks gone as a result of the scar, as well as suffering from lung disease, she lived penniless and in squalor in St Kilda. In her heyday she had chewed £10 banknotes for show. She died on 31 January 1958.

Aside from illegal gambling clubs, prostitution was the feature of St Kilda. By 1948 the Vice Squad was called on to deal with the increasing number of prostitutes who could be found in Fitzroy Street. The war had set the scene for what was regarded as the 'virtual immunity from prosecution of organised crime leaders'.

In 1949, St Kilda was described in *Truth*, which had clearly not lost its purple touch, as 'the haunt of harpies, hooligans, drunks and perverts, to say nothing of teenagers who are willing converts to the vicious lawlessness that thrives there', and Acland Street was said to be 'the spawning ground for crime and mob violence'. Would-be St Kilda Councillor Jim Duggan campaigned on the basis that St Kilda, once the showcase of Victoria, had become notorious as the stamping ground of Melbourne's underworld, where one could be 'accosted by prostitutes to say nothing of the thieves, rogues and bash men who accompany them'.

In the same year in which *Truth* had made its pronouncement, Melbourne-based prostitute Jean Lee became the last woman to be hanged in Australia. Also known as Smith, White, Brown, Duncan, Marjorie Brees and Marie Williams, Lee, an attractive redhead, was born in Dubbo in 1919. After leaving school she worked for a milliner, then as a waitress, then as a clerk and finally in a factory. At the age of eighteen she married a man from Sydney and had a daughter. When, at the beginning of the war, her marriage broke up, she became a prostitute working in Kings Cross. She acquired a number of convictions and, realising she needed a minder, took up first with Morris Dias and then with Robert Clayton, both known bludgers. It was only a matter of time before Lee and Clayton latched on to the ginger game as an easier and more profitable form of work. She would go with men to hotel rooms or the back seats of cars only to be 'discovered' by Clayton who, as the aggrieved husband, naturally demanded financial recompense. When Clayton found that some of the victims were prepared to fight it out with him, it was necessary to recruit another member to the team. In 1949 Norman Andrews, whom Clayton met in a bar, joined as 'husband's friend' and he supplied the strong-arm stuff when the men showed any reluctance to pay. Unfortunately one of the victims went to the police and reported the beating and robbery he had suffered. Doubly unfortunately, although the police were able to identify the trio from the descriptions—Andrews had a number of convictions for robbery—they did not arrest them immediately.

On 7 November 1949 the trio went to a bar in Lygon Street, Carlton, and latched on to the small and fat William 'Old Bill' Kent, a seventy-three-year-old local bookmaker. It was only a matter of drink and time before he was persuaded to go with Lee to his flea- and lice-infested rooming house in nearby Dorrit Street. She told him her stage name was Valez and wrote it down for him. She then got him more drunk and, while performing oral sex, tried to pick his pocket. When he would not let go of his wallet she hit him on the head with a bottle and a piece of wood and, joined by the others, tortured him. Kent was placed on a chair with his thumbs tied together with a bootlace while for over an hour he was repeatedly kicked and beaten. Finally he was strangled and left tied to the chair. With the money, Clayton bought tickets for a flight to Sydney and while waiting for the plane the three went to a club to celebrate. After their night out they returned at 4 a.m. to their hotel room to find the police waiting for them. Lee had been traced by an astute officer who linked her to the name Valez, which she had used in Sydney. It was Clayton who broke first, blaming the others.

When the jury announced its guilty verdict, Lee threw her arms around him, screaming, 'I didn't do it.' The convictions were quashed by the State Court, which excluded some of the police evidence, whereupon Lee began kissing Clayton and had to be physically separated from him before being led from the dock laughing. The High Court reversed the State Court's ruling and restored the death penalty sentence. Lee could not believe that the government would hang a woman, but she was wrong.

The Sydney standover man Chow Hayes wrote of them, 'I'd been in jail with Norm Andrews, who wasn't a bad bloke... It was never revealed in the newspapers, but the whisper was that they'd cut off their victim's penis and stuffed it in his mouth.' Which would account, at least in part, for the government's reluctance to grant a reprieve. That was partly confirmed by the veteran reporter Alan Dower, who wrote that Kent's penis had been bound with a bootlace and repeatedly stabbed. According to *Truth*, Clayton made one last effort to save Lee. He offered a warder £25 to allow him into her cell so that he could try to impregnate her—expectant mothers were always reprieved. His offer was rejected. At 8.01 a.m. on 19 February 1951, Lee was hanged at Pentridge Prison. Heavily sedated, she was carried to the gallows wearing khaki pedal pushers, a white shirt and sandals, and was hanged sitting in a chair in which she had to be supported by the hangman's assistant. There was a story in the underworld, put about by standover man Joey Turner, that she had actually died of fright in the cell the night before. Two hours later Clayton and Andrews were hanged in a double execution. Outside the jail, part of the crowd sang 'Nearer my God to Thee'.

Bludgers, like any other form of criminal, adapt to changing circumstances, and with the arrival of 'New Australians' in early 1958, a mobile vice ring operated in and around West Melbourne where girls, minded by several men, worked from luxury caravans charging £2 a time. They avoided the police by staying only two hours in each place. Known to have operated throughout New South Wales, Victoria and Queensland, the unit moved about in areas frequented by New Australians, particularly Italians.

Victoria was the first state to adopt a policy of regulation, rather than suppression, of prostitution. The 1970s had seen the arrival of massage parlours—the rub and tugs that provided a front for prostitution—and 1984 saw the passing of the *Planning (Brothel) Act* followed by an inquiry that recommended steps to avoid some of the problems that had occurred in New South Wales following the licensing of prostitution. The *Prostitution Regulation Act 1986* was the result. In 1994 the *Prostitution Control Act* legalised and regulated both brothels and escort agencies in Victoria. Now brothels were made subject to local council planning controls and required a permit. However, street prostitution (by both males and females) continued not only to be illegal but to flourish, particularly in St Kilda where, along Grey Street, on the corners of Dalgety, Robe, Greeves and Barkly streets, soliciting remains rife to this day. Other suburbs where sex was offered on the streets included Dandenong, Footscray and the city centre.

The 1997 Dixon Report into the legalised industry included tabletop dancing among its main terms of reference. 'Tabletop dancing' included close contact with or touching of men, double acts with other women or men (showers, oil wrestling) and personal or lap dances where the dancer sits on a man's lap 'gyrating, twisting and generally stimulating his groin area, or rubbing her breasts in the patron's face'. It seems that a regular feature has been the insertion of objects such as mobile telephones into the dancer's vagina or anus. In 2003 it was estimated that the four large strip clubs in and around King Street in the city employed between 60 and 130 women a night.

By the end of the twentieth century it was estimated that each week 60 000 Victorian men spent a total of $7 million on prostitution, with the legalised industry turning over more than $360 million a year and drawing on some 4500 sex workers.

One of the objectives of legalisation was to eliminate the criminal connection to the operation of brothels. Whether this has actually worked out is, however, open to question. There are continued suggestions that organised crime has at least partial control of some legal brothels. Victorian sex 'businessmen' have become involved in the lucrative international trade run by crime syndicates, which is worth an annual $30 million in Australia. An Australian Institute of Criminology study estimated that Australian brothels earned $1 million a week from this illegal trade.

Some examples came to light in 1999. One Melbourne sex trafficker brought forty Thai women into Victoria as 'contract workers', holding their passports and earnings until their contracts were worked off, something called debt bondage. The women had to have sex with 500 men before receiving any money and were effectively imprisoned by the businessman. He received only an eighteen-month suspended sentence and a fine. In another case, twenty-five Asian women were found in similar circumstances in one of Melbourne's legal brothels. These incidents are likely to be just the tip of the iceberg, and there have been reports that a number of legal brothels are known to contain such 'contract workers'.

Another long-term trafficker, Singapore-born Fred Lelah, settled in Melbourne and was involved in the industry from the 1980s. Although once described by his barrister as 'a benign, non-threatening type of individual', he had convictions in 1986 and 1989 for living off the earnings of prostitution and managing a brothel, in 1994 and 1997 for entering into an agreement for the provision of sexual services by a child and in 1997 for being an unlicensed provider of prostitution services. In the 1990s barrister Dominic Hickey joined forces with Lelah and Rosa Brcic, who ran Sasha's, a licensed brothel in Fitzroy. Hickey's role was to recruit prostitutes to work either at Sasha's or privately for other clients. Sadly he was not particular enough about the ages of the girls he recruited or whose services he used. The girls, while not children, were, the court said, 'vulnerable by reason of their youth and their addiction to heroin'. Lelah and Hickey would offer the girls, very often from St Kilda, the drugs they needed in exchange for providing their services. In 2000 Hickey and Lelah pleaded guilty to seventeen counts, including making an agreement for a child to act as a prostitute, inducing persons to engage in or remain in prostitution, supplying drugs, and taking part in acts of sexual penetration of a child between ten and sixteen years. Lelah was sentenced to a minimum of three and a half years. Hickey received six years with a minimum of four.

It was not only Thai women who were being imported. In 2003 the preliminary report of Project Pierglass, a review of the illegal sex industry in Victoria, found there was also a traffic in Russian women who paid up to $50000 to marry Australian men and were then forced to work in brothels to repay the fee. Once repaid, they then divorced and could remain in the country.

Until 2003, women found without work permits in brothels were deported, even those who told police or immigration authorities about the crimes committed against them, something which no doubt proved to be a disincentive for the women. To its credit, the Howard government then stopped the mandatory detention and deportation of trafficked women and brought in a support scheme for victims, who were given access to a variety of residency visas. It also strengthened the law on trafficking as well as the Australian Federal Police's capacity to prosecute sex slave traders.

The changes made a difference. Some women were given support to help them recover from the violence they had experienced and prosecutions went ahead. In 2009 the High Court found Wei Tang, a brothel owner, guilty of slavery. Wei Tang, who had herself earlier been imported for sex, received a total of nine years with a minimum of five. And while Tang was being dealt with, four men were on trial facing allegations that they had brought five Thai women to Australia and forced them to work off their fares of a staggering $94 000 by servicing between 500 and 750 men. Two of the men were sentenced: Kam Tin Ho received thirteen years with a minimum of ten, and his brother Ho Kam Ho ten years with a minimum of seven.

Estimates of unlicensed brothels operating in Melbourne continue to vary. In 2002 it was suggested there were 400 unlicensed brothels to 100 licensed. A 2006 study in which advertisements from Melbourne newspapers were analysed, based on the language used, in order to identify premises likely to be unlicensed brothels, estimated that the number in Melbourne was seventy at most, with thirteen at the least. In 2009 a survey thought there were forty unlicensed brothels, but it is often the case that when one door shuts another one opens.

Unhappy Families

4

Blood is thicker than water. If you really must have partners in a life of crime—and this is not generally regarded as advisable—then it is certainly a good idea to keep it in the family. In contrast with criminals in other states such as New South Wales, where until the rise in ethnic crime there was no tradition of family groups, over the years Melbourne has seen some outstanding crime families, starting with the Bruhns from Fitzroy who, from the early 1920s, went on to found what amounted to a dynasty.

The ugliest and nastiest of the family was Norman who served, albeit sporadically, in the 46th battalion and was court-martialled in 1916 and 1919. His criminal record ran the gamut from cruelty to a horse, larceny, vagrancy, shop- and housebreaking to indecent exposure, the last for which he was sentenced to six months in prison in July 1923.

But it was the serious crimes for which he was not convicted that made him so dangerous. In the winter of 1926 it became highly desirable for him to make an interstate move. He had raided a sly-grog shop cum brothel in Melbourne run by Dot Patrick, stripped and assaulted the girls and taken around £1000. While a prosecution was unlikely, there would almost certainly be reprisals from his rivals, whom he had seriously upset. In the underworld these things could often be sorted out through intermediaries such as his brothers, but a spell away never hurt and for the moment Sydney seemed a much better option.

For a time he worked on the Sydney docks under the name Noble, joining the wharf labourers' union, but the job didn't last and his wife returned to her family in Melbourne. Not that Irene Bruhn née Wyatt was any cleanskin. She had worked the Melbourne hotels as a prostitute and often worked the ginger game with her husband. In June 1921 she was acquitted of receiving £200 worth of blue twill, which, she said, a man she neither knew nor could describe had handed her through an open bedroom window. Bruhn was very fond of blue serge; all his suits were made of it.

During his months in Sydney, Bruhn ran prostitutes (including the gorgeous Nellie Cameron), dealt in cocaine and the standover, put together a little team of his own, cut boxer Billy Chambers (one of Sydney's top receivers) to ribbons over a prostitute Florrie Masters and generally upset as much of the rest of the local talent as he could manage in a short time. On 22 June 1927 he spent the day drinking in the Courthouse Hotel, Darlinghurst, with racehorse trainer Robert Miller and two other men. At some point there was a disagreement, and Bruhn and Miller split from the others and moved on to Mack's, a sly-grog in Charlotte Lane. Later that evening, when Bruhn was refused free drinks, he threatened to shoot up the place, but he and Miller eventually left. The local working girls usually sat soliciting on doorsteps or in armchairs in the doorways of the lane. But on this night there was a sea mist and the girls were indoors when two men pushed Miller aside, saying, 'You're not in this,' and shot Bruhn five times, killing him. Not that the girls would have dared say a word, even if they had been outside.

The possible motives for his killing were limitless. There was speculation that it involved cocaine; either that or Bruhn had failed to divvy up the proceeds of a robbery. It could have been a personal quarrel, Billy Chambers' revenge or that Bruhn had robbed a friend of standover man Snowy Cutmore. Or it could have been because he was a dobber or police informer, something that has never appealed to the underworld. 'Pentridge is half full of men Bruhn betrayed,' said one Victorian detective. A number of arrests were made and identification parades were held. But, unsurprisingly, no one was willing to finger the gunman, generally thought to be the Sydney standover man Frank Green.

In 2007, when Bruhn's grandson, Noel William Faure, was on trial for murder, a court was told that Irene had gone into hiding after Bruhn's death. However, this may have been a bit of rhetoric for she appeared in and out of the papers and courts over the next decade, notably when she, her new husband Leslie Thomas Faure (whom she married in 1932) and the highly talented madam, Vera Purdy, were found not guilty of possessing pistols found at their mutual home.

Over the next decade Norman Bruhn's younger brother, the diminutive Roy (he stood barely five foot three)—who had started his criminal career in a reform school after a conviction for warehouse breaking—generally led a charmed life both in the courts and out on the street. On 21 January 1929 his long-suffering prostitute girlfriend Margaret Ellen 'Mona' Ryan was shot in Nicholson Street, North Carlton. In July the previous year she had been attacked with a bottle in Essendon. *Truth* thought her to be 'an exceptionally good looking young woman brought up in the country'. She first became friendly with Irene Bruhn in about 1926 and from then on it was downhill when the pair began soliciting in various hotel lounges.

This time, Mona had apparently been walking with her landlady, who turned out to be Bruhn's sister Agnes Genoa, at about 5 p.m. one day in January 1929 when Genoa claimed she heard what she thought was a car backfire. Mona stumbled but said nothing. Genoa said they went back to the house where Mona collapsed on the floor. She was taken to hospital where it was first reported she had died, but she survived readily enough. The real story was, of course, quite different. Mona and Bruhn had been in her room when they quarrelled and he shot her. The twenty-four-year-old Bruhn was charged and alleged to have admitted the shooting but at the trial Mona maintained there had been three men whom she had just met in a hotel and she did not know which one had shot her. On 19 April, Bruhn was triumphantly acquitted and the unfortunate Mona received a month's imprisonment for contempt of court.

The following year was another busy one for Roy Bruhn. In June that year he was found not guilty of assaulting his sister-in-law Irene, by now married to Leslie Faure, at a party in Port Melbourne. According to Irene she had quarrelled with Mona Ryan and had then been forced into a cab and taken to Port Melbourne lagoon, where Bruhn tried to push her into the water. Clearly family relations were at a low ebb. When asked by the police if he had assaulted Irene, Bruhn replied, 'I should have killed her.' He called two witnesses to say that all he had done was carry her from the beach to a taxi. The charge was dismissed.

Just a few months earlier, Mona had gone into smoke after being accused of stabbing Hilda Lane. When she re-emerged she was found not guilty, principally because Hilda would not give evidence. Mona's brother forfeited £300 bail money.

On 3 October 1930 Bruhn was himself shot in the chest at his home in Abbotsford Street, North Melbourne. Again, it was never quite clear what had brought this about but the probability is that it was a dispute with his one-time offsider Arthur Mackay over the proceeds of a robbery the previous week. A taxi driver collected Bruhn from his home, took him to Palmer Street, Richmond, and then returned with him to North Melbourne. Bruhn left the cab and went into the house. The cab driver heard a shot and, shortly after, Bruhn returned to the cab and told the driver to take him to hospital.

He did just that, dumping him at Melbourne Hospital and saying to the staff, before disappearing, 'You know who he is. He is Roy Bruhn.' Bruhn's first words to the police were, 'I've got it. I'll take it with me.' Later he said he had heard a noise at the back of the house and had been shot as he went to investigate. Since the gun had been pressed against his chest, leaving powder burns on his waistcoat, the police said they were not pursuing that particular line of inquiry. Bruhn survived and poor Mona was once more hauled in for questioning. The papers thought the shooting had been 'in connection with the recent sensational arrests', which referred to a bank robbery in Brunswick a fortnight earlier.

Arthur Mackay went to visit Bruhn on his first evening in hospital and was promptly arrested as a vagrant. At a short trial on 17 October, Mackay produced a bank book showing that he had deposited £20 on 29 September. He had already shown it to the police but had refused to say where the money had come from. Now he said it was money he had won coursing. The stipendiary magistrate said that while the police case was thin it nevertheless amounted to a *prima facie* one and he did not accept Mackay's explanation. He was given six months. The next day, against medical advice, Bruhn discharged himself from hospital. And that was the end of that little matter. In November the next year, after claiming that the jury had been out drinking with a prosecution witness, Bruhn was sentenced to two years for receiving at Wangaratta. The next week he received another two years to run consecutively, again for receiving—this time a leather overcoat and women's stockings at Ballarat. He had been charged with breaking and entering but was acquitted. Mona Ryan and her sister Alma had been on the expedition, probably as lookouts, but were never charged,

Another problem with Roy Bruhn was that he did not always pay his debts. Money had been put up for lawyers who secured an acquittal on a robbery charge at Bright Magistrates' Court in December 1930. Two months is a long time to wait for repayment and on 16 February 1931 twenty-seven-year-old Patrick Shannon and Ernest Lionel Reid came looking for Roy at his father's house in Station Street, Carlton. It was the right place, because there was Roy as well as Mona. When Roy was threatened, his father Oscar bravely intervened and was shot in the thigh for his pains. Brave Mona also went to fight off the attackers and took a clump around the head in response. Shannon and Reid were charged, the latter with shooting with intent to murder. But by the time the trial came up in April, peace had been restored. Neither the Bruhns nor Mona were prepared to identify the men.

Perhaps Roy Bruhn's most challenging time came in the summer of 1937. At about 4 p.m. on Monday 11 October that year a semi-trailer driven by John Thomas Demsey was sent from Carlton to Bendigo. For the return journey it was packed with bales of wool to be delivered to Essendon that evening. After Demsey was seen with the lorry around 9.20 p.m. he was not seen alive again. On 3 November his body was found in a shallow grave in a gully at Kinglake West. He had been shot three times in the heart, liver and lungs. The vehicle was recovered but all the wool was gone. The wool was no doubt the second prize; it was thought the load was to have been gold from the Bendigo mines.

Bruhn (now calling himself Roy McFarlane) and three others were arrested and the trial was eagerly awaited. There were no eyewitnesses and the Crown called more than a hundred others in an effort to prove guilt by circumstantial evidence. Bruhn ran an alibi that he had been sleeping at his mother's home near the abattoir in Coronet Street, Flemington. He had told her, 'Mum I'm going to take on the vealers.'

At the trial Bruhn's mother disclosed some information about her offspring. Roy was the youngest of ten, born on 21 January 1910. His elder brother Stanley had died on the first morning of the trial. Stanley had been a sergeant in the 6th battalion along with Norman. Billy and Oscar jnr were on the troopship *Ballarat* when it sank in the English Channel after it had been torpedoed on

25 April 1917 but they survived. McFarlane was her maiden name. Roy changed to it by deed poll when he wanted to make a fresh start. In fact it had not stopped him being convicted of taking a motor car, for which he was fined £20. Sadly, by now Mona had been replaced by a factory girl, Lilian Vera Chrystobel Brown, who also gave Bruhn an alibi, but she sensibly added she was not convinced she was going to marry him when it was all over.

On 1 March the trial judge directed the jury to acquit all four men, adding that this did not necessarily mean they were not guilty; simply there was not sufficient evidence to convict. Bruhn was immediately rearrested and charged with having stolen rails and side tip trucks to the value of £470. A *nolle prosequi* (a formal notice of abandonment of an action) was entered.

Bruhn then stayed out of the limelight until March 1947 when there was a curious article in the *Canberra Times*. A man had been chased and caught in Sydney. He told the police his name was Morrison and he was a baker, but they thought it was Bruhn who was apparently wanted for two murders and fraud in Melbourne the previous year. No other newspaper carried the story and in fact all he was wanted for at the time was passing off some dud cheques, but that too faded away. He died in the winter of 1951.

As for Mona Ryan, discarded by Bruhn, she continued life as a prostitute until she married a John William Coffey. She died in 1945 and was buried in Botany cemetery. Coffey was later found with a fractured skull on a tram after being badly beaten in a residential block in Erskine Street, Sydney, in circumstances that were never made clear. Observing the rules, he told the police he would settle things his way. Apparently he would place flowers on Mona's grave every month but on this occasion he had gone out drinking with the money.

* * *

The Bruhns themselves may have faded away but the new generation continued to fly the family flag. Noel Ambrose Faure, son of Irene and Leslie Faure, became a high-class safebreaker, generally working on commission, and a high-ranking member of the Melbourne branch of the Painters and Dockers' Union. In later life he worked in a Footscray abattoir. A criminal's criminal who never lagged and wouldn't talk to the police, he suffered from diabetes and died in 1999 at the age of seventy-eight, leaving behind him sons with whom to be reckoned.

In June 1984, Norman Leslie Faure, a cousin of Noel Faure's sons, gaoled for eight years in 1977 over the shooting of a police constable in a robbery, asked his cellmate Vincenzo Delouise, due for release, to look after his de facto Darlene until his own release a few weeks later. Darlene, a heroin addict from the age of nineteen, had had a chequered career and Faure had forgotten the old maxim, 'Never introduce your donah [girlfriend] to a pal.' The highly sexed Darlene immediately began a relationship with Delouise. Unfortunately, it continued after Faure's release in the November, to the extent that she was sleeping with the men on alternate nights. Faure discovered he was not the only man in her life when he went to the Templestowe house where she and Delouise were living. Delouise hit Darlene and the men then stabbed each other to death with knives that had apparently been hidden under cushions in the living room. At least she had the courtesy to repent her ways, even if only on a temporary basis, telling a casualty officer, 'It's all my fault, I play games with them.'

She then hid from the families of both men until she found safety when she married John 'Piggy' Palmer, one of Melbourne's high-class robbers with whom she went on a spree in 1986, threatening to cut the throats of children during a robbery in Moonee Ponds; a friend of Palmer's had died of an overdose and he believed the parents were responsible. But all was not well on the matrimonial front either and Darlene glassed a woman she believed was having an affair with Palmer. After that she dobbed him in for the robbery. She was given limited indemnity to give evidence against him and, largely thanks to her, he drew a fifteen-year sentence.

That left Darlene exposed on all sides and in 1987 she took up with a cleanskin, Raymond Andrew Johnson, a former security guard who took to carrying a sawn-off shotgun as a defence weapon. Unfortunately he was with her in a Coburg shopping complex when the police tried to arrest her for shoplifting. He intervened and was shot by the police in the shoulder and upper arm for his pains. To add insult to injury, in August 1988 he was given a twelve-month suspended sentence for using a firearm to prevent an arrest. He continued to visit Darlene on a weekly basis when she pulled a three-year sentence for the Moonee Ponds home invasion. Unfortunately, there seem to have been other distractions for her in Fairlie Women's Prison and one male officer resigned when he was transferred after developing what was described as a 'close relationship' with her. At least Johnson was there to meet her at the gates when she was released on 16 August 1989.

On 5 August 1997, Noel Ambrose Faure's son Leslie Peter, named after the high-class robber and standover man Les Kane, shot and killed his girlfriend Lorna Stevens at her home in Dromana, apparently while playing Russian Roulette. The prosecution claimed she had been shot in an argument over whether she might have AIDS. Faure said he told her, 'You can die here,' and she had replied, quite accurately, 'You gotta die some time.' He was convicted of her murder but the conviction was quashed and shortly before the retrial began he pleaded guilty to manslaughter and was sentenced to fourteen years with ten to be served.

Before and in between prison spells, another son of Noel Ambrose, Noel William Faure, a master butcher and plasterer who had worked with his father in the slaughterhouse, faced a murder charge in 1992 and his wife Toni gave evidence against him.

Ultimately, the death of Frank Truscott in 1990—something that, according to a witness at the trial, Faure likened to killing a sheep— ended in a conviction for manslaughter. In 2005 he received three years for possessing an unregistered firearm while a prohibited person. Then in February 2007 he suddenly and unexpectedly pleaded guilty to the contract murder of Lewis Moran and the wounding of his mate Herbert Wrout in Brunswick in 2004 during the Melbourne Gang Wars. Although the gunmen who shot Moran and his offsider were masked, Noel Faure had been caught on CCTV and recognised by a tattoo of a bird on his hand. This time he was jailed for life with a twenty-three-year minimum.

As for Toni Faure, she subsequently married Joseph Vodopic and in 2002 was involved in a most curious case. In the 1990s she had become something of a society figure, running a fashion boutique in Toorak. However, she never quite divorced herself from her past. She was an associate of the drug dealer Terence Hodson and a failed business scheme to import petrol cost her around $800 000. It was then that she devised a scheme to kidnap millionaire Dean Kenneth Reilly to force him to sign over $3 million. In August 2002 he was bundled into a car by her husband outside his business premises in Mitcham and she abused him until he signed the necessary papers, which, quite properly, the bank refused to honour. She received a minimum of six years and Vodopic a more modest three.

Aligned with, if not as well known as, the Bruhn family but just as dangerous were the Cartledges, an extended Fitzroy family whose notorious leader was the standover man Leo Clinton, and whose criminal career lasted throughout the 1930s and into the early 1960s. Back in May 1931, two of the brothers, Henry and David Lawrence (known rather dangerously as Dopey), were acquitted of housebreaking, a verdict with which the judge thoroughly disagreed. The next week, however, the pair were convicted of assaulting a police officer. David was in trouble again when he was sentenced to an indeterminate term for assaulting two youths on Boat Race night and on 5 May 1932 he managed to escape while he was being transferred from Castlemaine reformatory. He successfully stayed out until July that year when he picked up an additional twelve months for his escape.

Their brother, six foot four Kenneth Roy Cartledge, worked the ginger game with his sometime de facto Blanche Harris and Rayon Clarke, his sister-in-law. In July 1939 he was shot by Norman McAllister and William Grosvenor as he walked in Fitzroy beside his brother David and Blanche. With a bullet in his brain, his condition was described as critical, but that was not a matter to worry a Cartledge. Grosvenor was later arrested in Sydney. There had been bad blood between them. Earlier McAllister had told Blanche he was going to shoot Cartledge on sight and if she 'coppered' he would shoot her as well.

At the trial in the October, Grosvenor made an unsworn statement saying the brothers had attacked him and McAllister and he had let a bullet go to defend himself. McAllister's version of events was that Blanche had told him he was going to get a good kicking from the brothers and when he saw them near Exhibition Gardens he heard her call out, 'Here they are.' The brothers rushed at them and McAllister was hit on the head with a bottle. As he lay on the ground he heard a shot fired and saw Grosvenor with a gun in his hand. Fearing his friend was trying to commit suicide he took the gun from him and put it in his pocket, which was where the police found it. On the face of things it was not one of the more promising explanations and on 18 October, after a six-hour retirement, the jury disagreed. In December 1939, Grosvenor, now described by the police as a 'notorious gunman', was back in court in Sydney, charged with the murder of Thomas Brennan, whom he had shot in the chest. Convicted and sentenced to death, he was reprieved after the full court of the Supreme Court of New South Wales dismissed his appeal.

The Cartledges were very often acquitted. As with the Bruhns (and later Freddie Harrison, Norman Bradshaw and Harold

Nugent), witnesses failed to appear or repeat what they had originally said. There were, however, setbacks. In 1944, Kenneth Roy Cartledge received twelve months for actual bodily harm. The next year he was acquitted of housebreaking.

All in all, the first few months of 1945 were good ones for brother Leo. In the March he was acquitted of the murder of a black American serviceman, Raymond Theodore Combs, whose body had been found in the Yarra River on the previous Christmas Eve. Out of the kindness of his heart, on 19 December, Cartledge had taken the lonely man to his home for a meal where Combs had behaved thoroughly badly, cuddling Mrs Cartledge snr and picking up his steak with his fingers and smearing it with butter. Cartledge remonstrated with him over this ungentlemanly conduct, telling him 'not to behave like a pig' and, as the great lawyer Robert Monaghan later told the jury, 'The negro became incensed and the inferiority complex of the negro race swayed up within him.' Unwisely, he attacked Cartledge with a 'long bladed' knife. He needed rather more. Cartledge beat him with a beer bottle, fracturing his skull—in self-defence of course. Combs, not yet dead, was put on a horse cab and rolled into the Yarra near Fairfield, where he drowned. Cartledge explained that since he had seen only one dead person in his life, he panicked. Quite rightly, his mother Adeline and brother Gerald, who were in the house at the time, refused to give evidence against him. On his acquittal, Cartledge was promptly rearrested and charged with unlawfully disposing of Combs's body, but in April the prosecution entered a *nolle prosequi*.

Things continued to go well. In the June he and another Fitzroy resident, Molly Morva Moran née Lloyd, who had married American Master Gunnery Sergeant John Michael Moran in June the previous year, were found not guilty of standing over Ishmael Ymer, the owner of the Kamel Café. She had threatened to wreck the joint unless he gave them £10 and cashed a US$50 cheque.

However, it had not been too good a time for some of the other members of the family. In February 1943 Kenneth and his red-headed wife Phyllis (Blanche had gone by now) had been acquitted of robbing two American servicemen, but in July that year she went down for three months for theft—she had three previous for soliciting and one for perjury. In December 1944, Kenneth and David Lawrence, who had previously been whipped, received twelve months apiece for robbery. Luck held for Leo and Mrs Moran when, on 13 June 1945, they were acquitted on four counts of obtaining money with menaces, but Leo's luck ran out when he and David Lawrence went down later that month for a total of ten months for consorting. The next year there was another three months after Leo and Ray Abbott attempted to escape from the Brunswick lockup.

Worse was to follow. On 10 May 1946 Leo Cartledge and Mrs Moran were found guilty of wounding Emanuelle Miscelli in Russell Street. It was their third trial on the charge. He received four and a half years and she got two. When Cartledge asked if the sentence could be made concurrent with the ones he was serving, the judge declined. It was the Court of Appeal that came to his rescue, quashing his conviction in June. He still had to serve an eighteen-month sentence for having unlawfully damaged a plate glass window.

In 1950 various members of the Cartledge extended family were involved in ex-bantamweight boxer Stanley Shaw's trial for the murder of his de facto, prostitute Sylvia Holmes. The principal witness against him was the brothel keeper, Ada Cartledge (also known as Adkins or Maddocks). Ada had lived with David Lawrence Cartledge until he went to prison and then took up with Cartledge's friend Lachman, a seaman, as well as Shaw. On 3 May 1950, Shaw had been drinking with Ada at the Standard Hotel, Fitzroy. According to Shaw, he left at 5 p.m. and went home, where he found a note for him from Sylvia Holmes saying she had gone out; then it was back to Ada and when he returned home again at 6 p.m. he found Sylvia dead. Ada vanished, presumed to have gone interstate, and in June that year the coroner returned a verdict of murder by persons unknown. Then, in August 1951, she reappeared to say Shaw had told her he had hit and killed Holmes. The reason Ada had gone interstate was because Cartledge had been due out of prison and was threatening her. Shaw claimed he found Holmes dead but the jury retired for only thirty-five minutes before convicting him. During his appeal in December he ran out of court, saying on his recapture minutes later he had wanted to go and see his mother. The appeal was dismissed but he had better luck with the full court in March 1952 when a retrial was ordered. In May 1952 he was sentenced to seven years' imprisonment for her manslaughter.

In June 1951, Leo Cartledge was charged with shooting at barman Richard Cassidy after he had been thrown out of the 'women's parlour' of the Champion Hotel, Fitzroy. He was duly acquitted but his powers were clearly not what they once had been. In October that year he and his offsider, Raymond O'Connell, made the mistake of trying to hold up ex-commando Herbert Smart in Carlton. He took their gun away from them and gave them what he told the court was a 'reasonably good hiding'. Rather piteously, Cartledge and O'Connell told the jury they had been 'savagely attacked' by Smart. In addition to the beating, they each received thirty months.

Leo reached the nadir of his career in November 1951 when, at the age of thirty-one, he received a year for indecently assaulting a two-year-old girl on 23 July. He had quarrelled with the child's mother Iris Mendoza and broke into her house in Condell Street, Fitzroy. Iris and another girl left the house and Cartledge then attacked the child. Real standover men do not indecently assault babies. The jury retired for a bare half-hour before dismissing his claim that it had been an accident. Six months of his sentence were made concurrent with the thirty months. In August that year, despite his please that he would be ostracised in prison as a rock spider, his appeal against a nine-month sentence for possessing a pistol had been dismissed.

In September 1958 he was up for trial with Judy Maher, Robert Field and William Sylvester Barrett and four years later, on 19 April 1962, he added a further five years to the total of twenty-two years and three months in prison sentences since 1939. This time, while on parole, he had broken into a shop and stolen a large number of rifles and shotguns.

But as the years went by the Cartledges faded into respectability.

* * *

Other friends included a pair of standover men, the McCubbin brothers—Benjamin and Ambrose—as well as the infinitely more sinister Burles brothers—Richard 'Shanghai' (known as Jack Lee) and Tassie-born John. For some time the police confused them, believing they were one and the same person.

In January 1942, John Burles, who admitted to nine previous convictions, and his forty-three-year-old mother-in-law Peggy Thomas, who admitted to sixty-three, each received two years for larceny from the person. Peggy Thomas and Burles's wife Margaret had thrown their arms around a member of the RAAF in Burke Street and stolen his wallet. Since Margaret had only two previous convictions she received a bond on her undertaking to leave Melbourne and the suburbs for two years.

Shanghai Burles, the last man sentenced to death for rape in Victoria, was a much more sinister kettle of fish. In September 1930 he was acquitted of a charge of robbery under arms but on 5 December 1933 Burles, then twenty-three, was sentenced in Melbourne to five years and twelve strokes of the lash for robbery with violence. Kenneth Milne had met Burles at a club and offered him a lift home. When Burles got out of the car he pointed out to Milne that there was a flat tyre. Milne bent down to repair it and Burles hit him over the head with a bottle and robbed him of £23. He was convicted of theft at the Geelong races in 1939, by which time he had amassed ten previous convictions. In 1947 he was sentenced to death for the criminal assault of a Sydney woman on her honeymoon. He had gone drinking with the pair and after hitting the husband over the head with a bottle he dragged the girl into a room and raped her. The Court of Appeal dismissed his appeal but, as was the custom, he was reprieved and a six-year sentence was imposed consecutive to a four-year sentence for robbing the husband. He died in 1960.

Among their other contemporaries the Maloney (sometimes Moloney) family from Fitzroy, regarded by local residents as people worth a detour, was led by father Michael and mother Evelyn who ran a boarding house in Palmer Street, an establishment that the police claimed was a brothel and which they denied. Sons and daughters included James 'Red' Maloney, a former Victorian welter-weight boxing champion; his brother Tom, charged with armed robbery in 1940; Michael jnr; and sisters Violet (alleged by the police to be a prostitute soliciting outside the brothel, something she denied) and Eva. All except Red, who lived with a Phyllis West, lived together in the Palmer Street property.

The police regarded the troupe as a menace and court appearance followed court appearance. In March 1938, Evelyn was in court as the victim after she had been attacked by Michael Sullivan, her lodger, in Palmer Street. Percy Nicholls who went to her defence was also badly slashed. Sullivan was sentenced to a total of four months. Nicholls was sent to the cells after he was found to be too drunk to take the oath.

In July 1941, Michael Maloney, jnr and Violet brought an action against the police for false imprisonment and harassment, a claim that was swiftly dismissed in the county court.

But it was Red Maloney and his girlfriend Phyllis who would feature in one of Melbourne's big criminal cases of the 1940s— that of James 'Paddles' Anderson, on trial for murder of John James Abrahams.

World War II

5

In the early days of World War II, the then relatively small-time Sydneysider James 'Paddles' Anderson—so called because of his large feet or his childhood passion for swimming—travelled to Melbourne where he stayed for six weeks in a boarding house in Murdoch Street, Brunswick, with a woman, Mary Eugene. It was during this time that he was arrested for the killing of local identity John Charles Abrahams in Johnston Street, Collingwood, on 16 June, 1940. That night Abrahams and Anderson had been out on the town along with James 'Red' Maloney.

During the evening they met up with Leonard Foster and two women—Phyllis West, with whom Maloney was living, and Christina Henderson. At some time Anderson and Abrahams scuffled in a car but things quietened down after Maloney spoke to them sharply. Then, according to the prosecution, Anderson left the group, saying he was going to meet a woman described as 'a mysterious and intriguing blonde, Dulcie'.

Later the party, minus Anderson, all went on to a gambling club in Johnston Street. As Abrahams and Maloney were leaving around 2.30 a.m. Abrahams was shot through the neck by a man who ran away, gun in hand. Maloney took Abrahams to hospital, where he died. That night Anderson was arrested in the boarding house along with Mary Eugene. She was charged with vagrancy. She was in fact the prostitute 'Pretty' Dulcie Markham, who had used that name years earlier when she had given evidence at the inquest on her early boyfriend Cecil 'Scotchy' McCormack, stabbed to death in a fight in Sydney over her favours or earnings.

Naturally Maloney, Foster and the club's doorman were unable to identify the tall man who shot Abrahams, although the doorman did say he had seen Anderson outside the club at a time when he was meant to have been off with Dulcie. As for the women, Christina Henderson also had a spot of night blindness but Phyllis West, who thought the police were about to arrest Maloney, told the coroner the shooter was Anderson.

Time often dulls the memory, particularly in gangland murders. At court in the September, West downgraded her evidence, claiming she was no longer sure; she could have made a 'grave mistake'. Pressed in cross-examination by the prosecution, she changed her mind again and said she was sure it had been Paddles.

Anderson gave evidence, telling the court he had left Dulcie and gone to a skillball game in Flinders Street. He then produced an alibi in the form of a taxi driver whom he had treated to a steak-and-egg meal at a diner in Bourke Street and who had taken him home. One of the problems for the prosecution was that it could not ascribe a motive to Anderson but it is possible that the quarrel was over Dulcie Markham, whose favours both men were enjoying; that or who was to control the gaming in Collingwood. The jury took only a short time to acquit him.

Outside court Anderson, who had described himself as a caterer, told his barrister Maurice Goldberg, in one of those 'Winning the Melbourne Cup is better than sex' remarks, 'God, that's better than winning the lottery'. Then he promised him a present on each anniversary of the acquittal and also indicated that this was the last time he would be associating in unsuitable company. It is not recorded whether he did send presents to his lawyer, but he certainly failed in his intent to avoid undesirable company. Four months later, now back in Sydney and described as a machinist, he appeared on a charge of consorting with criminals in William Street, for which he received a month. He was acquitted of standing over a bookmaker and fined for assaults on two police officers and obtaining a motor licence and registration documents by false pretences. From then on his career was onwards and upwards as he graduated to being a senior member of Sydney's so-called Double Bay Mob, second in command of a crime empire run by Detective Inspector Ray Kelly. Many years later he would say that he had carried a gun into the court and would have tried to shoot his way out if the verdict had gone against him.

For her pains Pretty Dulcie received a month's imprisonment on the vagrancy charge, quashed on appeal after she told the court Anderson had given her a regular weekly allowance. For the moment, she remained in Melbourne working in a brothel.

* * *

At the outbreak of the war, two other men came to notice. Although neither was involved in particularly sensational cases, in different ways the pair would have an enormous influence on the Melbourne crime world during the next twenty years.

Harold William Sydney Nugent, twenty-two, of South Melbourne, spent the first few days of the war in prison. He and his year-younger offsider Lawrence Tiffen were charged with armed robbery. The court was told that on consecutive nights in July 1939 the two men had lined up the customers at the International and Bohemia clubs and forced them to put money in a hat they passed round, in true gangster fashion threatening to 'get them' if they 'squealed'. Nugent called an alibi and complained that not only had he been the only man on the identification parade wearing an overcoat but also he had been bricked by the police when a pistol was planted on him. It did him no good. He received five years for the robberies with three months concurrent for the pistol. Tiffen, who had sixteen previous convictions, was also given five years.

A year later, on 28 June 1940, Charles Edward 'Inky' Wootton, possibly pound for pound the best street fighter of his generation, was charged with manslaughter the day after a fight in the Bookmakers' Club in Elizabeth Street. Thomas Leslie Dorter, described as a clerk—who, in a tribute to the old bare-knuckle fighter, had boxed as Tom Cribb—had died. In fact Dorter, who had been the Western Australian middleweight champion in the 1930s, was a standover man and was probably looking to take over control of the club. According to the spectators it was Dorter who started the fight, after Wootton had called him a bludger. The pair tangled, wrestling each other to the ground three times as the others in the club stood back to give them a fair go. Death had been suffocation caused by the inhalation of blood from the nose. This, thought the pathologist who examined Dorter's body, could have been caused by the impact of a hard object but could not have resulted from a punch.

The coroner thought Wootton had done rather more than just defend himself but he refused to commit him for trial. It was the spectators who came in for his criticism for not stopping the fight, but there again coroners rarely have had a firsthand experience of a bookmaking club blue.

Charles Wootton had a son named Charlie, who would go on to be the king of Melbourne's illegal gambling scene and the most influential figure of his generation on the docks. And Charlie's stepfather happened to be Harold Nugent.

As the war went on, Harold Nugent and his friend the drug addict Leslie Francis Eugene Xavier 'Lair' Brown (who suffered from cysts around his testicles) could often be found in the Blood House in St Kilda, the name given to the Court House Hotel in Barkly Street. The habitués there were a motley collection including 'Nigger' Clarke, a friend of armed robber Tony Martini, who often worked in women's clothing, and Mona Beatten, Clarke's prostitute girlfriend. *Truth* thought the hotel barber (sneak thief)

Percy William Smith, known as the Midnight Rover, was the king of them all. And if Percy was the king, who was the queen of the Melbourne underworld at the time? None other than 'Pretty' Dulcie Markham, who was once arrested outside the hotel wearing only her underwear and wielding an axe as she chased a client down the road in a dispute over her charges. For her pains she was fined £5.

Percy aside, in terms of sheer survival, the seventeen-stone wharfer 'Big Moocher' Stanley Keith Birch seems to have been something of a neglected hero. When shot in the thigh in Fitzroy in July 1941, Birch, who had been acquitted of rape ten years earlier and again in 1937, 'could offer no explanation' as to who might dislike him so much. Possibly those he had robbed in early 1939 with Leslie Ernest Walkerden, known as 'Scotland Yard' because of his penchant for detective novels rather than his bad habit of dobbing in his rivals. He didn't have much luck around the time because, in July the next year, he was not expected to survive after being shot in the liver in another blue at a Two-up game in Surry Hills, Sydney. Albert Bayley was duly found not guilty of attempting to murder both Birch and Eugene Ryan, who had been shot in the arm. Birch clearly had a strong constitution, because he had recovered sufficiently to be suspected of a shooting in St Kilda on Christmas Eve that year. But his luck ran out again in 1945 when he was shot in the stomach by an American merchant seaman, Earle Joseph Andry, once more in Sydney. That November the Attorney-General dropped the murder charge against Birch. At the time, Birch was on bail for yet another shooting, on 30 June in Paddington. And before his death, Walkerden gave his one-time offsider a bad beating because he would not pony up for a collection he was having for a colleague's legal expenses. Apart from local working girls, other habitués of the Blood House included an ex-detective from Sydney named Preston, whose hotel had been closed because of an incidence of venereal disease (perhaps Lair Brown had been a patron).

In December 1943, despite his claim that there was no criminal motive behind his association with Lair Brown and that he was merely changing a car battery for the man, Harold Nugent received nine months for consorting.

On 27 July 1943, pretty nineteen-year-old Pearl Lilian Oliver, a waitress from Bacchus Marsh, was shot in the back as she tried to run away from a boarding house on Brunswick Street, Fitzroy. The bullets passed through her body between her shoulders and her waist, exiting through her chest. As she fled, Pearl dropped her handbag in the middle of the road. She made it to the gutter, ten metres from the steps of the notorious Rob Roy Hotel on the corner of Gertrude Street, where she collapsed. Whoever had shot her was taking no chances to be identified. He (or they) went over to where Oliver was lying and clubbed her with a pistol, fracturing her skull in two places. She died five minutes after admission to St Vincent's Hospital.

In the same incident, wharf labourer Joe Fanesi, a one-time light-heavyweight boxer from Western Australia, was shot in the legs and allied sailor Peter Croft was also shot in the legs, arms and body. They were both clubbed but survived. Fanesi told police he and Pearl had just walked along Gertrude Street and into Brunswick Street, where both lived, when shots were fired as they reached the front of their apartment house. On 3 July the *Herald* reported that a woman 'well known in the underworld' was seen with a male near the scene of the murder, suggesting jealousy or an underworld feud could be the motive. Why Croft was shot was not known, but he had been seen earlier in the day with Fanesi. The police believed that the killers were lying in wait for their victims.

On 31 July the same newspaper called for assistance to locate a light blue–coloured naval truck seen parked for several days in the area around the time of the murder. At that stage police were still searching for a motive but they now had a clearer picture of what they thought had happened. They believed Oliver, Fanesi and

Croft had got out of a car in Brunswick Street and were about to enter a house when they were approached by Nugent and another man. After some discussion shots were fired at Fanesi by Nugent and his companion.

Then, on 19 August, the *Herald* published photographs of two men wanted for questioning. They were Lair Brown and Harold Nugent. On 29 August, Nugent was arrested by armed detectives in a raid on a Geelong house and charged with Pearl Oliver's murder. John McKenzie, another wharf labourer, was charged with having harboured him. Police also issued an alert for a third man to help with their enquiries. He was forty-five-year-old Cecil Bobbs. At that stage police were still looking for Lair Brown.

The case was argued on the basis that there had been a blue because Nugent had been paying Pearl unwanted attention. A so-called domestic matter usually called for less punishment than one involving a standover. But it really was more a question of establishing a pecking order. In November 1943, after a five-day trial, Nugent was acquitted of Pearl's murder but in April 1944 he was sentenced to three years for unlawfully and maliciously wounding Fanesi. By then he was already serving another six-month sentence for consorting.

Lair Brown was eventually found hiding under a bed in a St Kilda flat in April the next year and was duly acquitted of the murder at the end of June. He received three years with hard labour for the Fanesi wounding. By then Brown had acquired convictions for assault, larceny and carrying an unlicensed pistol. 'I can't conceive a more serious case,' said Mr Justice Lowe. That month Nugent also received six months for being found with a loaded gun in a car belonging to the redoubtable Moocher Birch.

By then Nugent, described in the *Victoria Police Gazette* as 'five foot seven, brown, wavy hair, hazel eyes, fresh complexion, medium build, usually wears sports coat and grey trousers, or brown suit and grey shoes', had become one of the Big Five of the postwar

Melbourne underworld. 'Nugent was very serious. Not too many people wanted to give evidence against him,' recalls a former barrister. And for the next ten years, with the odd exception, they didn't.

The war was a good time for conmen, particularly those posing as military gents, and there were few better (at least so far as gullible women were concerned) than Kenneth William Korrington-Willis, also known as Kid Stranger when he was posing as an American boxer, and sometimes as scientist Kenneth Ricardo. Although he always worked with an American accent, he had been born in Holbrook, New South Wales, in May 1910. Early in his career, posing as a jockey 'in the know' which enabled him to get information on certainties in the then notoriously corrupt Sydney hurdle racing, he took nearly £100 in five days from one businessman.

In 1939 Korrington-Willis persuaded a Heidelberg woman that he was a professional parachutist due to earn a large fee demonstrating a jump from an aeroplane. He needed and obtained £100 to make the necessary preparations. He had, in fact, yet to make a jump of any kind. In 1941 he was between bouts as Kid Stranger, staying at a Sydney hotel and passing dud cheques. It was about this time that he became a scientist and military man, claiming he was from Denver, Colorado, the son of an officer in the Marine Academy, California, and that after school he had served as a Marine Ensign in Texas. Then it was back to parachuting and a move to Melbourne. Between September 1943 and August 1944 he took over £700 on the pretence that he owned a parachute factory at Kensington and needed the money to expand to fulfil government contracts. But his greatest moment was yet to come. He persuaded officials of the Lord Mayor's Hospital Appeal that he was an expert parachutist and he would make a charity drop from a Royal Aero Club plane onto St Kilda beach near the swimming baths on 23 October, 1944. A crowd of 50000 waited in vain to see their hero. At least Korrington-Willis would have looked the part. Before the plane took off he was arrested at Essendon aerodrome kitted out in white cord breeches, a white sweater embroidered with a parachute and wings, black knee boots, white flying helmet and black gloves and goggles. When questioned he first claimed to have made over 350 drops in Europe but later admitted he had no parachuting experience, no factory, no bank account and, worst of all, no prospect of repaying the money. This time he received two years with hard labour.

Naturally, visiting American troops were targets for crime but occasionally they retaliated. In February 1943 a taxi driver, Francis Phelan, suspected of ripping off soldiers over fares and women, was found shot three times in a Prahran gutter. His cab was found abandoned half a mile away. A soldier's cap was found in the cab but the man explained he had lost it some time some time earlier. No charges were brought.

And, of course, in times of rationing and shortages there were endless opportunities for the conman. Korrington-Willis's days as a parachutist may have been over but he was by no means finished. In April 1948 he obtained £300 from a Melbourne businessman, George Douglas, pretending he could get him a car—something then worth its weight in gold. This time Willis was Captain Barry K Le Grand of the United States Department of Justice. When Douglas suggested they should see a solicitor, Korrington-Willis/ Le Grand, who was at the time fresh from interviewing Hitler, was dismissive, saying, 'My stamp "Department of Justice" is sufficient.' When Douglas queried why Le Grand was not in uniform, he was quickly put in his place. The captain was working undercover 'investigating Italian Communists'. For this crime he received twelve months.

During World War II there was a black market in almost everything, from motor cars, potatoes, wheat, meat, fish—whiting was particularly popular in Melbourne—to taxi licences, petrol, cigarettes, silk stockings, shirts, pyjamas and firewood. In December 1946 potatoes, which should have been sold for one shilling per

10 pounds, were fetching sixpence a pound. Ration coupons changed hands for 30 shillings for fifty-six. In March 1945 there was a thriving trade in stolen cars and car parts run by nineteen-year-old James Beaumont, who collected four years, to be followed by time in a reformatory at the Governor's pleasure. His offsider, seventeen-year-old Charles Phillips, received two years.

Any war provides enormous opportunities for crime, and when the Commonwealth Government deemed dock work to be essential labour and exempted those employed from conscription, the underworld and SP bookies quickly hid behind the shield of the maritime unions in order to escape more strictly supervised war work or, even worse, the call-up. The waterfront became a refuge for naturalised enemy aliens, grafters, spielers and the riffraff of the sporting world. *Truth* thought it had also become a safe haven for the sons of rich men who, for suitable payment, could get a card. Those sheltering there included 'bookmakers, jockeys, boxers and young men, sons of fathers high in the Melbourne business world', said *Truth*, adding, in a reference to Harold Nugent, that 'notorious men in murder cases and men involved in robberies', as well as those dealing in stolen goods and sly grog, held permits to work on the waterfront: 'Everyone knows the majority of pseudo waterside workers had rarely attended a pickup.'

Also out and about on the docks was the very shadowy figure of Alfred Charles 'Lou' Wright. Apart from a few convictions for illegal gaming, he was convicted of offensive behaviour in 1927 and went on to bigger and better things. In July 1928 he was jailed for four months for stabbing a man in a fight in St Vincent Gardens, Albert Park. He was out for only a few months before he was jailed again, this time for the carnal knowledge of a girl aged under sixteen. In May 1935, he was acquitted of the murder of his offsider Timothy O'Sullivan in West Melbourne after a drinking bout, having pushed him down a flight of stairs then kicked him in the head and face with what the police report deemed 'unbelievable savagery'. Wright then dumped O'Sullivan in a lane off Ireland Street to die. He was convicted of manslaughter.

Sentencing was adjourned when Wright's counsel argued that his client was mentally sub-normal and once he had started drinking he did not know right from wrong. The judge agreed that Wright's cerebro-spinal fluid should be tapped. On 7 August, Wright, who by now had three convictions for assault, one for wounding and three for offensive behaviour to go with the carnal knowledge, was sentenced to twelve years with hard labour. Nothing more was said about his mental condition. In the November he was refused leave to appeal against his conviction.

Released just before Christmas 1943 with any possibility of mental sub-normality long forgotten, he was back to the docks, where he assumed the position of *éminence grise* for the next thirty years. At the time of his release the police thought of him as 'a murderer, sex offender and violent criminal ... a brutal bully who for some years has terrorised a section of the West Melbourne community'.

In June 1945 the baccarat king Harry Stokes died following a heart attack suffered while sitting in a chair in his club. Earlier, Stokes, financed partly by the store-breaker Arthur Bazley, had teamed up with Gerald Francis 'Frank' Regan and Lou the Lombard running games at the Canton café in Swanston Street. Opposed to them were Kim Lenfield, Charlie Carlton, Hymie Bayer and Abe Trunley at the Ace of Clubs, Elizabeth Street. Ralph Pring of the VRC financed the Kim Syndicate, which also ran games at 52 Collins Street. The old-time confidence man Harry 'Dictionary Harry' Harrison, who had worked Europe with gambler and conman James Coates for many years, had also returned to Melbourne and become involved in the baccarat schools.

With Stokes's death, jockeying began for control of the increasingly lucrative gambling scene. One tenet of business is to eliminate the opposition and this is just what happened, although perhaps not quite in the way business management degree courses teach. On 9 September that year the standover man Freddie 'The Frog' Harrison and his offsider Norman Bradshaw, working for Cristos Paizes (aka Harry Carillo and also known as The Old Greek), began harassing customers outside the Ace of Clubs. Admittedly with some help, the now-balding standover man Scotland Yard Walkerden administered a bad beating to them. Walkerden, known as Australia's first 'two-gun man', mostly worked for club owner Frank Regan, but he also helped out at the Ace of Clubs as both bouncer and chauffeur, ensuring that winning punters, who had been recruited from the corner of Little Collins and Spring streets, were not waylaid on their way home.

Two nights later, at about 2.30 a.m., when Walkerden left a baccarat school that was run by George De Sanctis in Waltham Street, Richmond, he found that a tyre had been let down on his black Buick. As he changed the flat, he was shot. He should have been on guard—there had been an earlier puncture, which he had passed off as genuine—but perhaps his mind was on other things. After all, Pretty Dulcie Markham was back in the city after war duties in a Queensland brothel.

With his stomach torn out, Walkerden staggered back to De Sanctis's gambling club, yelling for another friend, George Newman, to take him to St Vincent's Hospital, where he refused to talk to Detective Senior Constable Joseph Lewis, telling him, 'You mind your business and I'll mind mine.' Walkerden survived until eight o'clock the following morning.

During the inquest into her husband's death, Walkerden's wife Gladys sat calmly reading a racing paper. There were newspaper reports that Dulcie Markham, who wasn't named 'for her own protection', maintained that she did not know he had been associated with baccarat games (her name does not appear in the inquest depositions, unless she was masquerading as the much younger Lorna Carol Maddox). Described as a 'monitoress' at the State

Theatre, the young woman told the coroner she was also stepping out with Walkerden at the time. His killer was never officially identified, but there was little doubt in the underworld that painter and docker Freddie Harrison, with an assist from Bradshaw, was responsible. That did not in any way stop the pair trying to shift the blame onto their rivals John Gilligan, Bob Brewster and the thoroughly unpleasant gambler James Coates, who wanted control of the baccarat scene.

The Combine

6

After World War II, organised crime in Melbourne was run largely by a quintet collectively known as The Combine who were, in theory, members of the Federated Ship Painters and Dockers' Union. How many of them actually turned up for work as opposed to collecting a pay packet or two is a completely different matter. Harold Nugent, by this time regarded by the police as 'a reckless and dangerous criminal who may resort to firearms if cornered', was probably the most senior. The others were Freddie 'The Frog' Harrison, his mate Norman Bradshaw (aka Cornelius) and the former boxer Jack Eric Twist. Standing slightly apart from the others, mainly because he was in prison most of the time, was Joseph Patrick 'Joey' Turner, also known as Monash. It was Turner with his 'dead' blue eyes who seemed the most frightening, but *Truth* journalist Brian Hansen thought Harrison, Bradshaw and Twist all displayed 'suave arrogance and absolute brutality'.

Their regular court appearances and reputations for shootings, standovers and armed robbery earned them yards of hot metal in many senses of the term. Notably unsociable, the five of them made occasional public appearances—for example, by turning out together for the first night of a Hollywood gangster film. But generally photographers were not welcome to take pictures and their cameras often hit the ground split seconds before their owners. One jockey-like *Truth* photographer, Johnny Ellison, was bitten by Harrison's then girlfriend, Beryl Holland, when he was trying to take a picture of one of Harrison's many arrests by the extremely dubious detective Fred 'Bluey' Adam. Perhaps sensibly, Ellison took himself off to hospital for an anti-tetanus shot.

The best criminal is the one who is never charged or who, if he is charged, is acquitted. Freddie Harrison was one of those. Born at Moonee Ponds on 23 August 1922, and standing five foot seven, he faced seventy-five charges, ranging from abusive language to attempted murder, throughout his career. He was rarely convicted and the longest sentence he served was fifteen months. Harrison joined the Royal Australian Navy at the age of seventeen, just after the outbreak of war in Europe in 1939, and his criminal career began with a conviction for desertion from HMAS *Lonsdale* in 1943, for which he received ninety days' imprisonment.

After he was discharged from the navy in 1946, he copped several fines for street betting in St Kilda, where he was a regular at the Peanut Farm, the weekend home of bookmakers and Two-up near Luna Park. But his career took off after the death of Henry Stokes when he was recruited to work in the Elizabeth Street clubs. He and his offsider, Norman Bradshaw, were always on hand to do some dirty work or clean up after someone else.

Good-looking and always well dressed, Bradshaw intensely disliked his nickname The Chauffeur—given because he generally drove Harrison on jobs and acted as backup. Not that he was not formidable in his own right. His first case of armed robbery came at the age of seventeen and by 1946, at the age of twenty, he had eight previous convictions when he received fifteen months after the jury had added a recommendation for mercy after finding him guilty of store-breaking. Later he was regarded by Interpol as one of Melbourne's Big Three. In 1954 there was a charge of wounding with intent to murder the prossie Joan Dobbin, shot through the door of her Punt Road flat. But then a key witness took off to Queensland and that was the end of that. By 1962 the *Victoria Police Gazette* thought Bradshaw to be 'a gunman, gangster, garage and store-breaker, sly grogger, arsonist and vicious assailant. He is seldom without a firearm and should be searched wherever practicable'.

The battle for control of the baccarat clubs continued, with Harrison and Bradshaw up against John Francis Gilligan (who sometimes described himself as an industrial chemist but who, along with Lance Skelton, had served four years for forgery back in 1927) and his offsider Bob Brewster, another high-class forger.

On 22 May 1947, Gilligan and Edward Ellis, the latter for once a genuinely innocent bystander, both survived a shooting near one of the Fink's Buildings in Elizabeth Street, where Henry Stokes had once run his baccarat game. The previous night, Gilligan had set fire to a car belonging to Scotland Yard Walkerden's mate, George Henry Newman, a man who was then a cleanskin in terms of convictions but who had poor taste in associates. Now Newman effectively called Gilligan out and a meeting was arranged in Elizabeth Street. Gilligan later maintained that angry words had been exchanged between himself and Newman and as he was walking away he was shot in the back. Ellis was shot in the knee. Brewster, who was with Gilligan, helpfully called out to the crowd, 'Kick him to pieces, he shot my mate.' Three passing American soldiers disarmed Newman and held him in a headlock until the police arrived. 'It was just like Chicago,' one said happily. Harrison, who had been with Newman, disappeared into the crowd.

When Newman stood trial for attempted murder he told the court that, in the quarrel, Gilligan had said, 'I should have done you when I done Scotland,' and had told him to get out of the state. Newman had carried a gun only because of his fear of Gilligan and, the night he shot him, thought he himself was going to be killed. The judge, handing Newman two years, took the view that, while Gilligan was 'a worthless person', it did not entitle Newman to shoot him—especially if he was unarmed at the time.

Harrison went into smoke and, while there, took on the contract killing of James Coates, the generally disliked confidence trickster, principally because, as well as being a dobber, he was a man who would neither repay a kindness nor forget an insult. Coates also went by the name of Mark Foy (rhyming slang for boy). He had claimed he was only a Mark Foy when he was caught by a steward rifling a cabin on a liner and the name stuck. Born in Perth, Coates worked with 'Dictionary Harry' Harrison on the liners to Europe where, in London in the early 1930s, he paid for deportment lessons and joined the thirty or so other talented Australian confidence men working the European capitals and the Riviera. On his final return from Europe at the end of the war, Coates turned his attention to baccarat and joined the struggle to take over Henry Stokes's schools. It was this that may have finally killed him.

Around 7.30 p.m. on Saturday 22 July, Coates left his now heavily barricaded flat, telling his wife he was going to buy a copy of the *Sporting Globe* from a shop in Punt Road, a mile from his home. He did not return. At 8.15 p.m., several shots were heard in the vicinity of Union Street and Punt Road, and immediately before that several car doors were heard to be slammed simultaneously. At about 10.40 a.m. the following day, Coates's body was found on an allotment near a baccarat club. He had been shot at least four times.

Although there appeared to be numerous potential independent witnesses, no one was ever charged with the hit. One witness, however, spoke of the killer wearing a smart coat and it was generally accepted in underworld circles that Harrison had carried out the hit for a fee of £600. Another suggestion is that he was killed because he had made off with the defence fund raised for George Newman who, at his trial for shooting Gilligan, had had to rely on legal aid. This would have been quite within Coates's character and he would not have been the first or last to do so. Coates's burial at Melbourne General Cemetery was poorly attended.

The Gilligan–Brewster/Harrison–Bradshaw tag match continued over the next three years, mainly over control of gambling.

On 28 January 1950, with Bradshaw in his usual role as driver, Harrison shot at Gilligan and Brewster as they sat in a taxi in St Kilda. Then things took a nastier turn. On 6 February, with Bradshaw again at the wheel of a grey Holden car, Harrison opened fire on Gilligan and Brewster with a machine gun. Gilligan was hit in the right arm, and, more seriously perhaps, eight bullets hit the gates of the Melbourne Cricket Ground. This vandalism could not go unnoticed and the next day the Holden was found with its windscreen blown out. It did not require the best brains in Melbourne to work out who was involved and Harrison and Bradshaw were arrested and charged. At first Brewster was prepared to say that he recognised the pair as they opened fire but Gilligan, quite properly, would not.

When the committal proceedings began on Friday 17 February, Brewster failed to appear and there were fears he had been kidnapped, but he had not gone far. He was retrieved by the police from a house in Ormond the following week. His explanation was that he had received threats that his house would be bombed if he gave evidence. Harrison and Bradshaw were duly acquitted after Harrison called an alibi to say he had been with his aunt. It was back to court again for the first shooting and another acquittal. After that Gilligan realised he was no match for the pair. Meanwhile, twenty-one-year-old Gavan Walsh received fifteen stitches after being involved in a fight with Brewster and his brother in a Prahran hotel. In September the next year Walsh would be killed in a quarrel over missing bail money when he was with Dulcie Markham at her flat in St Kilda.

Initially, Harrison was modestly described in a police file as 'associating with gunmen and street women; frequents baccarat schools', but by 1952 the *Victoria Police Gazette* said he had reached 'maximum menace and nuisance value'. He was 'trigger happy and suffering from a persecution complex'. In that year alone he faced fourteen charges, ranging from possessing an offensive weapon and larceny to attempted robbery under arms. He and Jack Twist, pretending to be policemen, were also charged with robbing a jeweller of £1200 worth of gold bars. Their lawyers successfully argued that the jeweller had no proof he owned the gold. The next year Harrison's wife divorced him while he was in Pentridge and he later married his longstanding girlfriend, Beryl Holland.

Out of court, Harrison did not have things all his own way with the police. Nor, for that matter, did other Melbourne hardmen. After the thoroughly nasty Shanghai Burles took a beating from a consorting squad officer, Jack Manley, Harrison was offered £1000 to throw a bomb through Manley's window. He withdrew from negotiations after he himself was given a beating by Manley's boss, Frank Holland.

There was a good deal of interstate travel for the standover men. Over the years, Sydney identities finding New South Wales 'hot' (with the police after them) often travelled to Brisbane, but sometimes in the search for easy pickings they came to Melbourne to stand over the bookmakers there. One man who would have been better off staying in Sydney was twenty-stone 'Big' (or 'Tiny') Percy Charles Neville whose criminal career began in 1928 when he received probation for stealing. It then followed the traditional route of malicious damage, breaking and entering, demanding money with menaces and, during the war, failing to report for the call-up. There were the usual acquittals. In April 1949 the Sydney brothel keeper Kate Leigh failed to appear to prosecute him for the theft of her fox furs, and his career reached its peak the same month with his acquittal after two retrials on charges of murdering his partner Francis John Allard, a standover man and confidence trickster since childhood. Allard's body was found in a storm canal in Alexandria, south of Redfern in June 1948. He had been seen being bundled into a car in Lidcombe and driven off with his legs hanging out of the window.

In the autumn of 1951 Neville was looking at the Melbourne club scene as a potential money spinner but it was not straightforward.

First, he was shot at in a gambling den in Little Lonsdale Street and retreated to Sydney. When he thought the time was right he returned to Melbourne and booked into the New Treasury Hotel on the corner of Bourke and Spring streets. It was not a good career move. Almost immediately he was visited by Detective Bluey Adam, who charged him with illegally possessing a Lüger and a .38. Bailed on 9 April 1951, Neville went to stand over a baccarat game run by Lou the Lombard on the corner of Elizabeth Street and Flinders Lane and as a result a call was made to Norman Bradshaw.

Neville left the game with another man shortly before midnight and was in Flinders Lane when a car came down the street the wrong way. Neville pulled out his gun but he was not quick enough. Before he fired, the passenger shot him in the shoulder and lungs. Neville fell, picked himself up and ran across Elizabeth Street in pursuit. His companion put him in a taxi to be taken to the Royal Melbourne Hospital, where he died. Neville was unlucky. If he had sat on the pavement and waited for help he might have survived but his chase had aggravated his injuries.

Unsurprisingly there were no witnesses except for two clean-skins—a soldier and his girl standing in a doorway—who initially identified Bradshaw as the shooter, placing him as firing while standing in Flinders Lane. The man who left with Neville was never found, nor was the driver of the car. Identification evidence, particularly at night and in exciting or frightening circumstances, is always suspect and although the judge praised the soldier for coming forward, Bradshaw was acquitted on 10 July on the direction of Mr Justice Barry.

Later Bradshaw told the journalist Alan Dower that he knew he was going to be acquitted the moment the soldier said he had been on the pavement. He had fired the shots, but from inside the car. Bradshaw's driver was undoubtedly Harold Nugent's old mate Lair Brown. Bradshaw was said to have killed Neville himself to show that he was rather more than just Freddie Harrison's chauffeur. By the spring of that year when they were fined £2 each for directing insulting words at the police in the High Street, St Kilda (now St Kilda Road), he and Harrison had apparently become pastry-cooks.

In August the next year Beryl Holland, now described as Harrison's de facto of three years' standing, appeared on nine charges of consorting with reputed thieves, including Harrison, Bradshaw, Leon Bazin and Lair Brown. They were all living at Bradshaw's mother's house in Victoria Parade, Collingwood. Harrison, temporarily in Pentridge, came to court to say he gave her as much money as she needed. Obligingly the stipendiary magistrate dismissed the charges. In 1953 Bradshaw skipped his bail and went to Canada with the aim of slipping across the border into the United States either to work for a gambler in Florida or to go to South America to be a bodyguard for the dictator Juan Peron. He was immediately deported.

The fourth of The Combine was the elegant Jack Eric Twist, who in 1948 regularly appeared in twelve-rounders at the Melbourne Stadium, winning a fair number, usually on points. Unfortunately, his career suffered a setback when in December 1949 he was shot in the shoulder before breakfast at a Sassafras guesthouse in the Dandenong ranges. Twist's arrest and acquittal record was rather more impressive than his boxing. In a five-year period from July 1946 he was convicted twelve times, but he was acquitted or had his conviction quashed on appeal on no less than twenty-seven occasions. Twist's one-time mother-in-law was Miriam Rischin from North Carlton, a brothel keeper and perjurer. Back in 1934 she was convicted of falsely declaring she owned a house when she stood surety for Robert George Bailey, who had appealed a conviction under the Licensing Act. With the help of her son-in-law she ran much of the prostitution in and around St Kilda.

In 1951, Twist was acquitted of a £2000 payroll robbery from Mayne Nickless after the eyewitness picked out the wrong man on a lineup. In August 1953 he and Freddie Harrison were acquitted of the theft of gold bars and later that year he was charged with standing over Leonard Flynn and shooting Flynn's de facto, Nancy Lowe. This led to all sorts of complications. First, Flynn went to the solicitor Frank 'Mr Frank' Galbally, who defended the top villains in the city for three decades, to say it was he who had shot his wife accidentally. That should have been enough to gain an acquittal but, just to confuse things, once in court Nancy said that neither he nor Twist had shot her; it had been a man standing at the gate when she answered the door. Not guilty, my Lord.

In July 1953 Twist had nine appeals adjourned. Earlier that month he was accused of standing over the Bohemian Club, wanting £10 a week for its protection, but this time the club proprietor, Edward Honkys, stood up to him. Although Twist called an alibi that he was babysitting at Tecoma in the Dandenong Ranges, he received five years. The newspapers were ecstatic. The *Herald* wrote, 'Success of the crime and the possible commission of further crime had been frustrated by the courage of a Pole and a Czech and a pianist who had rung the police.' Perhaps, but not for long. The conviction was quashed on appeal and at the retrial the next year Twist was acquitted. Even when Twist was convicted of a crime, the penalties were often negligible. He never served a sentence longer than eighteen months. And life in Pentridge was not all that uncomfortable for him. He protected the warders against other prisoners and possibly because of this his extracurricular activities were not investigated too closely. In 1955 he lost £300 and a stash of tobacco that he had hidden in the prison library.

Never really as close to the others was Joseph Patrick 'Joey' Turner who, although he held a Painters and Dockers' Union ticket for two decades, often claimed to be a miner. Although a talented thief and planner, he was also a thieves' ponce. If you did a job in Melbourne then Turner usually had his cut. The journalist Tom Prior, meeting him for the first time, described him as wearing 'a well cut grey suit, smart yellow overcoat, cream sharkskin shirt, grey tie, hat and shiny black shoes'. He had a diamond in a front tooth, a feature he shared with his good friend Kath Pettingill, who always spoke well of him. 'Flash as a rat,' says a Melbourne barrister who knew him. Another regarded him as one of the three greatest criminals he had ever met. Turner was reputed to sleep with a sawn-off shotgun under his pillow. This was certainly the case on one occasion when the police raided him and his home resembled an armoury.

Born in 1918 and another diminutive criminal who boxed at bantamweight pretty badly—seven bouts, seven losses—Turner always maintained that he did not know where Pentridge was until he did his first job after a night out in his early twenties. For a time in his early days his associates were said to include the talented thief, ex-boxer and theoretical wharfer Harold Whitford, also known as Summers, whom he later shot. On 28 November 1947, Turner was acquitted of killing the Sydney standover man George Barrett (also known as John Paul), who himself had been acquitted earlier in the year of shooting Keith Hull, who, in turn, had been acquitted of killing the standover man Donny 'The Duck' Day in Sydney. Barrett had driven to the Melbourne home of the unrelated Leslie Thomas Day and threatened to take him to Coburg and kill him over a £2 debt. When Joey Turner arrived by chance, Barrett shot and wounded Day and then pointed the gun at Turner, who shot him dead and shot Harold Whitford, who was with him, in the lung. At the December inquest Barrett's red-headed girlfriend, Mavis Helen Miller from St Kilda, helpfully told the coroner that Barrett had 'shot a few people in Sydney and the odd one in Melbourne'. Self-defence, said the coroner.

A former Victorian lightweight champion, Whitford was going through a bad patch. Fifteen months later, on 6 February 1949, he was shot in the stomach outside his home in Hoddle Street. Again, he survived. Later the same gunman was believed to have fired shots through a window in a Richmond house where Whitford had been involved in a blue the previous night. His brother-in-law George Pearson, another longstanding criminal, went into smoke and did not reappear until just before Christmas that year. Pearson was shot and killed at his sister's home in Abbotsford on Christmas Eve 1949 and Whitford surrendered at Russell Street Police Headquarters. Charged with murder, he was acquitted the following February after telling the jury he did not think Pearson was the one who had shot him and that he had no quarrel with his brother-in-law.

In 1952, Turner received three months for consorting with Norman Bradshaw, Miles Patrick O'Reilly, the docker Leon Bazin and Stanley 'Moocher' Birch; twelve months for possessing a fire-arm; eighteen months for armed robbery; and then, in July, a further two years consecutive to the current sentence for stealing around £2000 from a Mayne Nickless truck in Collins Street. His mate Bazin, who was doing twelve months on yet another consorting charge, picked up eighteen months. It was the first time in a non-capital case that the jury had been kept together throughout the trial to defeat any attempt at nobbling. The first trial had been aborted after the jury foreman was paid a visit. Now Turner was warned that he was well on the way to being declared a habitual criminal.

In September 1956, Turner was accused of the attempted murder of hardmen Bernie Hargreaves, Stan Beckwith and ex-middleweight champion Jack Kirkham, who all did the unforgivable and told the police Turner had shot them. By the time the case came before the committing magistrate they had corrected this communal slip of the tongue and said they didn't know who had held the gun. 'Someone put the Chinese burn on them, I think,' Turner told reporters Mike Ryan and Don Greenlees some years later.

After serving his sentence for the Mayne Nickless job, Turner ran one of the first car-wash businesses in Melbourne. For a time he made a go of Washland, near Collingwood Town Hall, but it didn't last long. Just as their predecessors had paraded in front of the 1920s brothels owned by a former Combine, so now the police took to parking their cars in front of the entrance, which tended to deter potential customers. When Prior and other journalists at *Truth* fell foul of another Melbourne identity, Turner was recruited as what might euphemistically be called a mediator. It was the same with Jack Twist. Frank Galbally used him to knock down another criminal who was causing a fellow lawyer trouble over fees. This help could work both ways. When the Melbourne consorting squad raided the Top Hat nightclub in Bourke Street, Turner and his friends passed their guns to the crooked barrister Robert Vernon, who was drinking with them, to hold while they were searched.

It is often difficult to tell exactly what was the true position in the underworld, and such an instance came in April 1959 when Turner's Collingwood home was raided by police. At the time there was no question of the police bricking Turner. Among the arsenal that was uncovered were a .30 American carbine found behind a chair in the lounge, a Japanese automatic wrapped in a facewasher in another chair, a Lüger pistol in a plastic bag hanging in that favourite hiding place the lavatory cistern, a couple more pistols, a homemade bomb, and a soup tin loaded with two sticks of gelignite packed inside moist sand, along with 130 two inch nails and twelve live cartridges in the roof. Turner was outraged and asked the police to fingerprint the guns and bomb to show he had not touched them. In February 1961 Senior Detective Booth told the jury that the police had raided Turner's house as the result of a tipoff. The question was whether the dobber had simply dobbed or whether he had planted the weapons.

Turner's defence was a plant. He had the reputation on the docks of being something of a dobber himself, and in court he named the man he claimed had done the dirty on him. He had quarrelled with the man over a £500 deposit for his car-wash business. The man had been at his home the day before the raid and the day after had telephoned Turner and gloated he had done more than £500 damage to Turner.

When it came to it, the jury returned something of a mixed verdict. Guilty on some charges and not guilty on others, which Judge Buller-Murphy said must mean they accepted some of Turner's defence. He was sentenced to seven years with a pre-parole period of forty-two months. Would Turner have risked storing the gelignite when he had his small son in the house? But even given that Turner said he left his back door unlocked, how could the man have planted all the weapons without anyone knowing? Years later, after his final release from prison, Turner claimed the police had planted the weapons to get rid of him as a serious identity. 'There was only one machine gun in town like that and it had last been seen at Russell Street. Can you imagine me leaving a machine gun under the blankets of my son's cot?' he asked reporters without any expectation of a positive answer.

Throughout his life, Turner remained good to his friends, particularly standover man Horatio Raymond Morris. Morris, who had a tattoo of a racehorse on his upper right leg and tattoos on his fingers that read TRUE LOVE when they were interlocked, was thoroughly fearsome. Off the job he was apparently quite likeable, but New Australians seem to have been something of an anathema to him. In July 1950, along with Moocher Birch, he was acquitted of shooting three of them in Carlton. Keeping up with his offsider, in September the following year Birch was acquitted of shooting at yet another New Australian and hitting him over the head with a pea rifle.

In 1946 Morris, whose grandfather Sam Morris was both the first Tasmanian and first black man to play Test cricket, had been extremely lucky to be acquitted over the murders of sly-grog dealers Ernest 'Ikey' Dew and William Sheargold. The pair disappeared some time after 21 June that year. When their bodies were found in a river near Geelong three weeks later, Dew had been shot in the eye and there was some medical evidence that he had been disembowelled, possibly to help his body to sink. Sheargold had been shot behind the ear.

The inquests in the September did not go well for anyone. Cherie Morris repeatedly refused to give evidence against her husband and was promptly jailed for contempt. For the prosecution, the medical evidence was not strong. It was thought the bodies had been in the water for a fortnight, and the contents of their stomachs, or what was left of them, could not be analysed. In the wash-up Morris merely received four years for wounding Sheargold.

In 1951 Morris went on trial for the murder of New Australian Stanislaus Socko, and his good friend Turner was on hand to help. Socko died during a sly-grog party in the backyard of the Morris residence at Orr Street, Carlton, watched by Horatio, Morris's wife and his mother Annie Marguerite, Morris's sister Lilian, Turner, a cook Leila Ethel Schultz-Trinus and possibly Socko's ex-de facto Louise Marks. 'You've killed him,' said Morris's mother. 'I've killed better men than him,' replied her lamb. After that it was all hands—except Leila's—to the pump. Mrs Morris went and found a revolver, knife and hammer and put them in Socko's pockets, thereby establishing the basic grounds for a claim of self-defence by Horatio.

Later that night Morris went to Russell Street to tell the police, 'Surely a fellow can do that in self-defence. He was attacking my wife with a knife.' Things got a bit confused because doing his bit, Turner told the police he had seen Socko trying to strangle Annie Marguerite, another good reason to shoot a man if ever there was one. Louise Marks told the jury that her ex drank neat gin and vodka, was violent in drink and had once stabbed her in the buttocks. Ranged against them was Schultz-Trinus, who remained staunch, saying she had been there and that Socko had been behaving perfectly well when Morris took him out.

At the trial in October 1951 the Morris contingent denied that Schultz-Trinus—who had over one hundred convictions for drunkenness, one for perjury and a number for forgery—was even at the house at the time of the shooting and they were supported by Violet Harkins, the former Violet Maloney, who said they had been drinking together in the Exhibition Gardens. After a six-hour retirement the jurors said they were hopelessly split.

Things did not go so well for Morris at the retrial the next year. In an unsworn statement he said he had fired in defence of his mother who was being attacked. The shot had been intended to merely frighten Socko. Morris received ten years for manslaughter. In June that same year, Kenneth Roy Cartledge was acquitted of threatening Schultz-Trinus in an attempt to persuade her not to give evidence. Losing his sight but back to standing over South Melbourne SP bookmakers, the increasingly alcoholic Morris was shot in the leg in 1971. The next year, on his thirty-ninth wedding anniversary, he was arrested after a car accident and taken to South Melbourne Police Station where he died. He was aged fifty-eight.

All good things must come to an end and The Combine was no exception. By 1958, Harrison was on the slide, thought to be running prostitutes in South Yarra. If he was, he was not making enough to keep up the rent and payments on his car and television. Although the police still regarded him as 'Maximum menace and nuisance value', his arrest rate had dropped dramatically—two charges in 1954, four the next year and only one in 1956—not necessarily an indication that he was being more careful or cleaning up his act. More likely the police were not bothering to roust him.

Inevitably the five fell out—well, three did—not about money but about the pecking order. At the end of January 1958, Harrison, Nugent and Twist borrowed a trailer from another dock worker, Robert Hayes, and headed off on a pig-shooting expedition on the Broken Hill side of Oxley in New South Wales. It was an ill-tempered outing: the trio quarrelled first with hotel staff who refused to serve them beer in the middle of the night and then amongst themselves.

On 3 February, they were still in the Oxley district, drinking, arguing and threatening to shoot each other. Nugent put a loaded gun in the back of his car and later, when they returned to the hotel, Harrison said he was leaving and the others followed him, driving to Balranald. For some reason they stopped at the side of the road and, in another row, Harrison told Nugent he was getting too big for his boots and shot him. Nugent managed to cover his stomach but as a result lost several fingers on his right hand. When Harrison tried to shoot Twist the gun misfired. Twist took the gun from Harrison and broke it. Harrison drove off leaving Twist to get Nugent to hospital. There he bravely told the doctors his gun had accidentally gone off as he was getting out of the car to shoot a kangaroo.

In the early evening of 6 February, Harrison was literally executed at 13 South Wharf with a shotgun blast to the back of the neck. That day he had worked a few hours until he went off drinking with union leader Jimmy Doyle in Richmond. On payday it was usual for foremen to be paid first, with the rest of the men then paid in alphabetical order. No one could agree who was near Harrison when he picked up his £11 at 4 p.m. and walked over to his Ford, which had the trailer still coupled to it. As he and Robert Hayes knelt to uncouple it from the car, Hayes heard a blast from a 12-gauge shotgun and Harrison collapsed in the gutter. The shot, which killed him instantly, hit him behind the right ear. Who the gunman was no one could even guess, let alone identify. For some dockers their views were obscured by the bulwark of the *River Murchison* on which they had been working; others paid no attention, thinking, as one might, that the gunshot was merely a car backfiring. At least twelve men said they were in the two-man lavatory. Lou Wright, who was thought by some to have set up Harrison for the killing—an allegation he denied—remarked of the collective bladder weakness, 'It was coincidence that nature took its course, that during the time Harrison was shot I was in the lavatory.' Wright himself had recently been under threat. At 2.15 a.m. on 27 September 1957 a bomb made from gelignite stuffed in a tin can exploded outside the front window of his home in South Melbourne. Some months earlier shots had been fired into his house. The attacks were probably connected with illegal gambling but no charges were ever brought. The cognoscenti thought Harrison had been the bomber.

One future Melbourne identity came of age that night. It was Charles Joseph Wootton, the seventeen-year-old son of Inky and stepson of Nugent. After the shooting a police officer noticed Wootton running away from the docks clutching a box of twenty-five 12-gauge cartridges under his cardigan. There were twenty-two in the box of twenty-five and Wootton had two more in his pocket. The shells contained the same no. 4 shot that killed Harrison. Questioned, he told the police he had seen a box of cartridges on top of some newspapers and picked it up. He was released and went straight into smoke. Unfortunately, by the time he reported voluntarily to the police some weeks later, despite intense pressure from detectives he could not recall anything much more of that day.

Barely three dozen attended Harrison's brief memorial service but about two hundred turned out to watch the coffin, topped by the collar of his favourite dog, as it left for Springvale. Of the eleven cars travelling to the crematorium, three were occupied by reporters and photographers. Eighteen months before his death Harrison had finally married Beryl. She sent a three-foot-high cross of red roses but did not attend. Norman Bradshaw sent a wreath of gerberas, lilies and orchids, 'In loving memory from Norm and Geri'. He went to the service but few of Harrison's old friends went with him. Twist merely sent a wreath. Nugent was still in hospital saying nothing. This was not the time to be counted.

Beryl claimed compensation from her husband's employers but she and Harrison were unlucky in the place and time of his death. The board said Harrison had collected his pay and left his place of employment, so he was not on company time. Nor was he on company property. It would have been different had he been twenty feet away on South Wharf or if the shooting had happened before he received his pay packet. While the *Herald* thought, 'One man would try to avenge his death but would judge his own time to move,' there seemed to be a marked reluctance among Harrison's friends to do anything. In particular Bradshaw made no move. A South Melbourne bookmaker offered 50/1 against the conviction of Harrison's killer and never came near having to pay out.

Both the press and police were convinced Jack Twist was the gunman. He was grilled for eleven hours at Russell Street Police Headquarters by the formidable trio of detectives Bluey Adam, Jack Matthews and Jack Ford, but most of the time his answer to their questions was, 'I have nothing to say.' Apart from the fact that he had been a friend of Harrison and indeed they had had breakfast together the day before the shooting, he hadn't been on the wharf when Harrison was killed. He seemed more interested in discussing the footy scores with them.

The trouble was that, while more or less everyone on the docks knew who had killed Harrison, the police had no evidence. Given the poor relationship between police and dockers they were not going to get help and indeed when they did go to question the men they received a hostile reception. A piece of paper found in Twist's car seemed to come from the box of cartridges found by Charlie Wootton but all that showed was that the cartridges had been in Twist's car at some time or another. After all they had been out shooting together within the last week. Although *Truth* signalled to its readers with the headline 'New Twist to Harrison murder', given the total lack of cooperation by the dockers the investigation faded. As for the wider picture, for the time being Twist was in control. Bradshaw clearly had no intention of taking things further, Nugent was recovering from his wounds and really it was little of Joey Turner's business.

Two years later Twist, Nugent—who was said to be making £250 a week in standover money on his own account—and Joey Turner were challenged by Terrance Clyde Sheehan. Collecting a debt Sheehan owed, they shot up his St Kilda flat only to find this did not faze him in the least. In retaliation Sheehan and a friend allegedly shot up Nugent's flat on three different occasions; the last time, it was sprayed with some twenty bullets. Then Nugent behaved thoroughly inappropriately for a lord of the underworld. He went to the police and ultimately Sheehan was acquitted of conspiracy to demand money with menaces—he had allegedly asked Nugent for £200 to go to Sydney. In the wash-up he was merely found guilty of discharging a firearm in a public place and was fined.

In September 1961, Nugent was stopped by the police while driving a newish Buick in Albert Park. Questioned, he told them he earned his money as a scrap metal dealer but he was promptly charged with possession of £50, suspected of having been stolen or unlawfully obtained. In court he was cross-examined by Detective Ray Tobin and asked whether he was 'standing over bookmakers demanding money for The Combine'. The correct, if lying, answer would have been 'No' but instead Nugent stupidly asked, 'Who are The Combine?' giving the detective the chance to reply, 'Twist, Bradshaw, yourself and Joey Turner when he is out.' Tobin seized his chance and went on to tell the court that the quartet were standing over SP bookmakers, club proprietors, prostitutes and Two-up schools in Footscray, Brunswick Street, Fitzroy and Prahran, as well as bookmakers at Moonee Valley racecourse and various secondhand-car dealers. How could that be the case, asked 'Mr Frank' Galbally for Nugent. Wasn't Turner in jail? Yes, but his share of the proceeds was going to his wife.

Twist's downfall came in 1962 when, after he tried to stand over the Iliad restaurant in St Kilda, he was stamped on once and for all. At the time the *Victoria Police Gazette* thought, with a clear reference back to Freddie Harrison, that Twist was:

> Shop breaker, gunman, and violent criminal … He has been involved in a number of shooting affrays, and is alleged to have murdered a criminal associate with a blast from a shot gun. The 'standover' methods of this hoodlum against prospective witnesses against him has enabled the offender to escape the proper penalty for most of his crimes of violence.

Not this time. He received a month and now Twist was effectively banned from entering Melbourne, the police permitting him only to return for weddings and funerals.

The cognoscenti believe that, with the death of Harrison, Bradshaw was never again the same man. In February 1952, during a weekend when there were four separate shooting incidents in the city, his home at Abbotsford was shot up seemingly without any reprisal and in 1954 (under the name Cornelius) he served fifteen months for fraud in Queensland's Boggo Road, where he was not popular with either inmates or staff. On 22 July that year he was stabbed in the throat, requiring twenty-one stitches, by two prisoners in the exercise yard. It was thought to be as punishment for dobbing in an earlier escape plot. On his release he fell foul of Miriam Rischin, Twist's mother-in-law, who went to the police saying she feared she might be shot. Bradshaw was thought to be trying to reclaim his lost control of sly-grog and small gambling dens. He was barely out before he was back inside again when he, along with fellow docker Leonard Patrick Flynn from the earlier shooting incident of his wife, served two years in Pentridge for demanding money with menaces from Flynn's uncle. The pair wanted £1000 to help them leave Australia. In Pentridge Bradshaw was not popular with the warders either.

On his release Bradshaw married Geraldine Kelly and ran a car repossession business in Richmond, but at the time of his death it is probable that he was trafficking in firearms—that, or planning to take part in an armed hold-up. In the spring of 1961 a small arsenal of guns was found in the security box of Richard Ross Le Gallien, for whom he worked as a repossessor, in the strongroom of the Commercial Bank of Australia in Richmond. Earlier in the year Le Gallien had been convicted of possessing rifles and automatic shotguns.

On Sunday 15 October 1961, shortly before 5 p.m., a Proctor light aircraft took off, did a loop the loop and within minutes crashed in the sea off Port Phillip Bay. On board were Le Gallien, Kenneth George Napier (who was the owner of the plane), thirty-four-year-old Bradshaw and his twenty-year-old friend Gail Connolly (who owned a ladies' hairdressing business). At the inquest the following year the coroner said he was satisfied Le Gallien had been the pilot. There was evidence that the men had been drinking at Bradshaw's home earlier in the day and, whatever people might speculate—sabotage, a fight on board, pilot error, drink—the coroner returned an open verdict.

Crime abhors a vacuum, and the Snowball gang—a team of standover men from Sydney—arrived to stand over the St Kilda prostitutes previously looked after by Bradshaw. In turn they were met by a team from Adelaide and another from Sydney. The girls themselves looked to old-fashioned Italian Victorian market interests for help and the Sydneysiders returned home both battered and bowed.

The end for Joey Turner came in 1970 when he led a gang of Melbourne dockers in a raid on the security company MSS. Information was provided by Charles Raymer, who had worked for the company for six weeks, and on 4 June an MSS security van was stolen from Camberwell. Inside was a bundle of about a hundred keys. On 10 June, thieves broke into the East Melbourne Police

Station and stole a police cap and coat. At 2 a.m. the next day, when a security guard at MSS answered a call on the intercom, there were two police officers wanting to return the stolen keys. He later identified the one in plain clothes, who said he was a detective, as Joey Turner because of his piercing blue eyes, something Turner bitterly disputed. The men threw the bundle of keys on a table and, as the guard was picking it up, a gun was shoved in his face. He was pushed to the ground and handcuffed. Turner and his offsider cut open the wire cage that held the payroll money and left, taking $289 233 with them.

Breaking out of prison is sometimes easier than staying hidden, and getting rid of the proceeds of a substantial robbery is sometimes more difficult than the robbery itself. It was thought that some of the money was in Hong Kong within twenty-four hours but the case was solved when Turner himself was caught because of his own carelessness. He had left a number of $20 notes in his trouser pocket. His wife had washed them and although he tried to iron the notes dry they were still wet when he bought a kangaroo skin rug in the souvenir store in the old Southern Cross Hotel. When the shop assistant took the notes to the bank, the cashier became suspicious and checked the numbers. Bingo.

It is always to a criminal's advantage to delay any court case as long as possible because it creates the opportunity to get at witnesses, some of whom genuinely begin to forget details as time passes. The MSS case took years to resolve. More or less everything that could go wrong did, and not always because of Turner. In July 1972, the first trial was aborted after a juror said she had been approached. At the second trial a month later Turner failed to appear; for his pains he received a two-year sentence for breach of bail. The third hearing in May 1973 collapsed after a juror took time off to go to a concert in Sydney. Hopefully he enjoyed it because he was fined $1500 on his return. In the fourth trial, which began in July the same year, the jury was deadlocked, apparently unable to decide whether it was armed robbery or simply a larceny. After nearly thirty-seven hours, then the longest retirement in Australia, the judge discharged the jury. 'The answers given by the lady forewoman reveal a staggering misconception of the issues in the case, which were put with great clarity by counsel,' he remarked, adding to the belief that jurors should not be allowed near complicated cases.

Finally, on 22 October 1973, Turner and five others were convicted. He and three others were given twelve years. 'You played for high stakes, you lost. The game is forfeit,' said the judge.

Time can be done hard or soft and Turner knew enough to do his sentence as easily as possible. He was also powerful enough to ensure that he was left alone by fellow prisoners and screws alike. He was released in July 1982 at the age of sixty-four but by then the heyday of The Combine was long gone. Turner gave a series of interviews to reporters from the *Sunday Press* and then left Melbourne to live quietly on the coast. Bored with that, for a short time he went prospecting for opals. He was killed when his car ran off the road and hit a tree at Nyora in South Gippsland in January 1995.

In 1977 Jack Twist was named in the Australian Royal Commission of inquiry into drugs, which heard that he operated a fishing boat from Williamstown to Sorrento and King Island and under this cover retrieved drugs that were dropped at sea. In later years he finally retreated to Tweed Heads in New South Wales. There it was said he had become a pillar of the community and a keen member of the local bowls association. However, evidence was given to the 1984 Costigan Royal Commission into the activities of the Painters and Dockers' Union that Twist was still at it, taking his boat out to pick up drugs dropped on airbeds offshore. He died from cancer in July 1988 aged sixty-one. In 1988, Turner's forty-one-year-old nephew John 'Beeper' Turner, a small-time career criminal, was stabbed to death in Sturdee Street, Reservoir. In

August the next year John Mark Jones and Frankie Waghorn, the latter a man Chopper Read thought highly of, were found guilty of the murder. Given a retrial in 1991, Waghorn was again convicted.

But now a new star was shining—the young Charlie Wootton was carving out a career for himself as the gambling king of St Kilda.

Melbourne Market Matters

7

Although there were plenty of Black Handers in Australia in the early part of the twentieth century, it was never a formal organisation such as the Mafia or the Camorra; rather a linked number of individuals who extorted money from their fellow Italians. Most of the initial immigrant Italian population of the pre-war era arrived in the 1920s and they totalled well over 40 000 by the end of the decade. The historian and author Richard Evans regards the suggestion of early organised Italian crime in Australia as an overrated concept. He believes that, at a time when the White Australia policy was an article of faith, the local population was bigoted and hostile towards a conspicuously male-dominated society in which few were married and most were law-abiding. There is no doubt, however, that as the years passed an identifiable Italian influence on organised crime developed.

The first of the modern Mafioso killings in Melbourne was probably the death of forty-year-old Giuseppe 'Fat Joe' Versace at a Fitzroy apartment house in October 1945. He had been stabbed a total of ninety-one times. He had allegedly been pestering twenty-two-year-old Dorothy Dunn, the sister of the woman with whom Versace lived. Michele Scriva, Domenico Demarte and Domenico Pezzimenti went to speak to Versace on the subject and fighting broke out. Versace, a known standover man, carried a fully loaded automatic but he had no opportunity to draw it. Pezzimenti agreed that he had stabbed Versace eight or nine times because he had a gun but no one ever explained to the jury how the dead man received the other eighty-plus wounds. The trial judge directed that Scriva and Demarte should be discharged and the next day the jury acquitted Pezzimenti. Despite the evidence that the fight was over a girl, the more likely view was that it was over control of Italian interests in the Queen Victoria Market.

In July 1950, Michele Scriva was charged with another murder, this time of a former veteran of the 6th Division AIF, Frederick John Duffy, who was stabbed to death after he tried to help a man Scriva was attacking. Scriva's daughter had been hit by the man's car in Peel Street, North Melbourne, and, armed with a long knife, he attacked the driver and passengers. Duffy went to help those in the car and the prosecution alleged Scriva, who was wearing a maroon jumper, stabbed him to death. Scriva claimed he had been working behind a vegetable stall that afternoon and had then caught a bus to Fitzroy. It was a hopeless defence for, as well as contradicting three witnesses who saw the attack, he denied that he was wearing a maroon jumper and grey trousers at the time of the fight, saying he only wore a suit to work. Scriva was condemned to death but, as was the usual practice, he was reprieved and served ten years of the commuted life sentence. His friend Antonio Romeo, who was with him, received a twelve-year sentence for attempted murder.

The same year Giovanni Cirillo, believed to be a member of *L'Onorata Società*, the Honoured Society, was deported after being convicted of the stabbing of Ilario and Domenico Roccisano at a wedding party at their home in Mildura. *Truth* took a close interest in the activities of the Society and on 7 April 1951 had an investigator on hand to say:

> The activities of this society must sound like fairy stories to Australians who have never experienced such victimisation. Most Australians could never calculate the terror and horror this band of scum produced among the Southern Italians in this country.

> The State and Commonwealth Governments must take actions
> now against the dreaded society. Already it has secured a
> stranglehold on a fear-stricken Italian community.

A decade later, Domenico Italiano, known as 'The Pope' and
regarded as a modern Godfather of Victoria, died peacefully in
West Melbourne on 13 December 1962. Italiano was seen as the
head of *L'Onorata Società*, which then effectively controlled the
Queen Victoria Market. To obtain work there it was desirable to be
Italian, particularly Calabrian. Shortly after Italiano's death came
that of his right-hand man, Antonio Barbara, a squat man known
as The Toad, also from natural causes. On 29 December 1936
he was charged with the murder of Edith May Pretz, or Walker,
who was found dying with a knife wound in her neck outside her
North Melbourne shop. They were said to have quarrelled over
his perceived maltreatment of the girl with whom he was living.
Barbara surrendered to the police after writing a letter to Detective
Bluey Adam:

> Sir, regards the Italian you are seeking for in connection with
> the Victoria street murder. I am impersonally writing to you.
> So you can rely I will call at head-quarters, Russell-street, not
> later than noon, Monday, January 4, 1937. Being a sport follower
> I would like to know how the third test, England v Australia,
> starts, as I hope Australia wins the toss, also the match. Wish-
> ing you a happy new year, with best respects,
>
> Barbara, Antonio.

He was acquitted of the murder and sentenced to five years for
manslaughter. In 1952 he was acquitted of forging migrant permits.

The deaths of Italiano and Barbara sparked a power struggle
for control and extortion of money from the decent stallholders
who worked in the market. At first it seemed that the transition of
power had gone smoothly. Into the breach stepped the very well

respected Vincenzo Muratore, together with Domenico Demarte, who had been acquitted of the killing of Versace. Their accession was, however, challenged by a former standover man from Calabria, Vincenzo Angilletta, who had a market garden in Kew and saw the opportunity to transform the operation into something more resembling the Mafia, leaning not only on the Italian community. His suggestions were rejected. Foolhardily he turned his back on Demarte and the market, declaring he would no longer sell his fruit and vegetables to the Society wholesalers. Asked to reconsider, he refused and was stabbed for his pains. He still refused to conform and was kidnapped and taken to Woodend where he was stripped and smeared with excrement as a final warning.

He still would not cooperate and went against all known rules, selling his market garden to a Greek family. Now he set up his own Society, *La Bastarda*, in opposition to Demarte and there must have been some widespread displeasure with the top brass of *L'Onorata* when he quickly picked up 300 members. Angilletta was clearly at risk. He was shot in the early hours of 4 April 1963 outside his home in Chapman Street, Northcote, with two barrels fired from a *lupara*, the sawn-off shotgun favoured first by Calabrian shepherds and later by the Mafiosi.

Six months later, 'the Market Wars', as they became known, began. First, Demarte was shot in the back and seriously injured on 26 November 1963 as he left his North Melbourne home for market. The shootings continued after the New Year and on 13 January 1964 Antonio Monaco of Lower Dandenong Road, Braeside, survived after he was shot in the shoulder and chest as he also prepared to go to market. It was not clear whether this was part of the power struggle or a domestic dispute. However, the death three days later of Vincenzo Muratore certainly was clear. He was killed at 2.30 a.m. by a masked gunman as he left his home in Hampton, he too on his way to the market. The shootings of

Demarte and Muratore were thought to have been in revenge for the death of Angilletta. Michele Scriva was a pallbearer at the funerals of both The Pope and Muratore.

On 23 January 1963, Jack Matthews, then chief of the Homicide Squad, had led a raid on the Queen Victoria Market halting every truck and lorry. The resulting searches produced a haul of weapons including daggers and flick knives as well as twelve shotguns, five rifles, two pistols and fifty-three detonators.

Domenico Cirillo was the next victim, shot and wounded in the early hours of the morning of 6 February as he left his home in Moonee Ponds. Once again the attack was thought to have had a domestic and financial motive rather than to be part of the power struggle. Later that year, market worker Francesco de Masi disappeared. His blood-stained car was found but there was never any sighting of him or his body. It was thought a contract killer had been imported from Italy.

Following the Demarte and Muratore shootings, the Victorian government brought in a mafia investigator from America, John T Cusack, who reported that there was indeed a Mafia-style operation dealing in extortion, prostitution, counterfeiting, gambling, smuggling, guns and office breaking: indeed, most of the things that make a criminal organisation worthwhile. He believed that, if things were left uncontrolled, in twenty-five years the Society would have branched into all facets of organised crime and legitimate business. Even then, there was a generally dismissive attitude among some members of the press and in government towards what was seen clearly as home-grown organised crime in the Italian community—at best fledgling and at worst fairly well structured—rather than any national or worldwide operation. In 1995 the National Crime Authority thought the mafia activities in Australia were in decline and indeed this view persisted until 2008 when the Anti Mafia Commission reported to the Italian Parliament that the Calabrian mafia in Australia was now a key player in a $38 billion cocaine trafficking operation. Even then the Australian Crime Commission said it stood by the 1995 report of its predecessor.

But, back in the 1960s, unsurprisingly the Society was not pleased with the unwanted publicity and investigation into its affairs, and its saviour was Liborio Benvenuto, then in his mid-fifties and originally from Calabria. Fearing a full-scale war, he negotiated peace and took over the Society's leadership. It was a situation that lasted for twenty years until, on 10 May 1983, his Toyota Landcruiser was blown up at the Melbourne Wholesale Fruit and Vegetable Market in Footscray Road. Gelignite had been strapped under the car. No one was injured but it was regarded as a sign that another power struggle was about to break out.

More trouble came nearly a year later when, on 6 May 1984, the mutilated bodies of Rocco Medici and his brother-in-law, Giuseppe Furina, were found weighted down in the Murrumbidgee River near Griffith. One had an ear cut off and both had apparently been tortured. It was never quite clear whether this was a revenge attack or the elimination of top brass prior to an attempted putsch. On 19 June the next year Giuseppe Sofra was shot in the legs in his Springvale Road shop, which actually belonged to Antonio Madafferi. This might have been related to a greengrocers' price-cutting war or to serve as a warning to Madafferi, who considered himself a man of influence. 'I am a man who is very respected at the market,' he told detectives.

However, not all attacks and murders of the period were market-related. On 18 July 1985, Dominic Marafiote disappeared from his home in Mildura and it was not until two years later that his body was found buried under a chicken coop. In fact he had been murdered by the sociopath Alistair Farquhar 'Sandy' MacRae, who was thought to have killed up to twenty-five people. On the pretext of a drug deal, MacRae had apparently lured Marafiote to his home, where he stabbed him. MacRae then drove to Adelaide and killed Marafiote's elderly parents, Carmelo and Rosa, for the money he expected to find on Carmelo. He was disappointed; later it was found sewn into Rosa's clothing.

Market-related trouble became much more serious in 1988. Before Liborio Benvenuto died of natural causes in June, there had been discussions about his successor. Benvenuto's son, Francesco ('Frank'), was not favoured and it was thought that his son-in-law, Alfonso Muratore, who had married Benvenuto's daughter Angela, was perhaps too inexperienced to take the reins just yet. Insurance broker and money launderer Giuseppe 'Joe' Arena, regarded as 'The Friendly Godfather', had been in discussion with Benvenuto as his possible successor but things changed dramatically within weeks when Arena was shot and killed in his own backyard as he was taking out rubbish bins in August 1998.

Now Alfonso Muratore took control, but unfortunately things did not work out either domestically or business-wise. On 4 August 1992 he was killed by a shotgun blast to the head outside his home. After his succession he had left Angela for another woman, Karen Mansfield, and his wife's family was not impressed. He had also been talking to retailers such as Coles Myer about price fixing by market identities. It was suggested that the Honoured Society had organised a ring so that payment was made to a preferred and therefore lucrative supplier. Muratore had been saying that better and cheaper produce could be obtained by avoiding the ring.

At the 1999 inquest on Muratore, Karen Mansfield told the coroner that Frank Benvenuto, who had taken over his brother-in-law's stall when he left Angela, had hired someone to kill her lover. For a time after Muratore's death, Frank Benvenuto took to using one of the notorious Pettingill crime family, Victor Peirce, as a bodyguard. Later, as things became even more blurred, he employed the uncontrollable standover man Alphonse Gangitano, who would in time be known as the king of Lygon Street.

Earlier that year, on 9 January, Vincenzo 'Vince' Mannella, who had been involved in a large cheese theft and was a friend of the founding member of the Black Uhlans biker gang, had been shot as he returned to his home in North Fitzroy. It was thought his killing had been contracted by a cocaine cartel. Seven months later Vince's brother Gerardo was shot dead in North Fitzroy. In August 2007, Vince's son, Giuseppe Mannella, who had no criminal convictions, along with Hayley Wood, the one-time lover of shot Russian Mafioso Nic Radev, were both found guilty of trying to obtain a shipment of ecstasy pills hidden in barbecues and said to be worth $7 million. Mannella was sentenced to a minimum of seven years and Wood was given a suspended sentence. In 2010 the Court of Appeal quashed Manella's conviction and ordered a retrial.

In the afternoon of Monday 8 May 2000, Frank Benvenuto was found shot dead in his car in Dalgetty Road, Beaumaris. It was parked away from the kerb and the door was open. His sister, saying the family would not forget the killing but would forgive his killer, 'because that's what my brother would do', described him as a 'good hard-working Christian who loved his family'. According to Victor Peirce's wife Wendy, Benvenuto was shot by Melbourne identity Andrew 'Benji' Veniamin because Benvenuto had ordered the killing of another identity. It seems that, as Benvenuto lay dying, he called Peirce on his mobile but was only able to groan. Some $64000 had been left in the boot of Benvenuto's car, so clearly the motive was not robbery. Some time later Peirce and Veniamin met in Port Melbourne and agreed there would be no reprisals for Benvenuto.

Out of the mainstream of the Melbourne Gang Wars, fifty-year-old Domenico Italiano, an alleged Mafioso and grandson of the old Domenico, died on 25 June 2005, hours after being granted a retrial on charges of blackmail and false pretences. In 2002 he had served a sentence for rigging the Youth Motor Sport Foundation raffles. Along with Thomaslav Dusko Kaladjic, he was said to have kidnapped a young man in Brighton and forced him to hand over a Mercedes car. Granted bail, Italiano had taken the opportunity to have too much recreation and not sufficient rest. He purchased a quantity of Viagra and, after a night with an old girlfriend, 'his heart packed in', a source told the newspapers.

Italiano had been suspected of hiring Philip Lander, also known as Matthews, to make and plant the bomb in the 1998 murder of mechanic and businessman John Furlan, killed on his way to work when his Subaru Liberty blew up near his Coburg home. It was thought that Furlan had discovered the raffle rigging and had been killed to ensure his silence. Lander, however, had died of natural causes on 23 July 2004. Italiano's funeral at St Mary's Star of the Sea, West Melbourne, included a mass and the traditional rendering of 'My Way'.

Antonio Madafferi has repeatedly denied his connection with organised crime over the past twenty years. He was reputed, again only with unsubstantiated allegations to back it up, to have been involved in two killings of greengrocers. A 1998 police report thought him to be 'involved in a substantial number of crimes, including murder, gunshot wounding and arson'.

Left: Squizzy Taylor—
Australia's 'favourite
larrikin' or a murderer,
bludger and blackmailer?
(REPRODUCED WITH PERMISSION
FROM THE COLLECTION OF
VICTORIA POLICE)

Left: Crowds queued for
hours to attend Taylor's
funeral. He was buried
with his infant daughter.
(COURTESY FRANKIE BATESON)

Above: Taylor's 'all weather' companion, the stylish Ida Pender.
(REPRODUCED WITH PERMISSION FROM THE COLLECTION OF VICTORIA POLICE)

Left: Multiple killer Dennis 'Mr Death' Allen looking young and fit before his drug habit took control.
(© NEWSPIX/NEWS LTD)

Below: The celebrity gangster Chopper Read, chronicler of the Melbourne underworld.
(© NEWSPIX/NEWS LTD)

Above: The man who effectively destroyed the Painters and Dockers' Union, Billy 'The Texan' Longley. (© NEWSPIX/NEWS LTD)

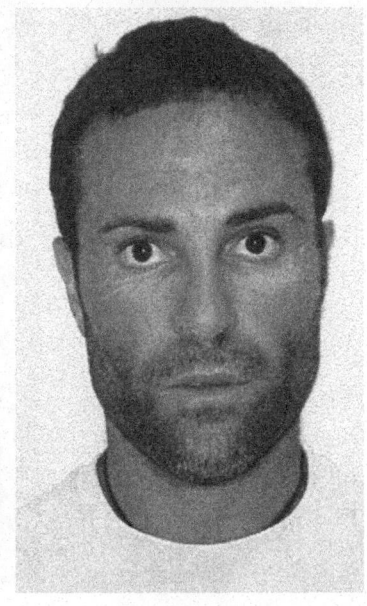

Above: Jason and Mark Moran, half brothers and drug dealers.
(© NEWSPIX/JAY TOWN, © NEWSPIX NEWS LTD)

Left: Jason and Mark's mother Judy Moran, on trial for killing Desmond Moran.
(© NEWSPIX/TREVOR PINDER)

Right: Alphonse Gangitano, the Robert De Niro of Lygon Street.
(© NEWSPIX/BEN SWINNERTON)

Right: Carl Williams, the man who brought down the Moran family.
(© NEWSPIX/JOHN HART)

Left: Family patriarch Macchour Chaouk, who was shot dead in his garden in the Melbourne suburb of Brooklyn.
(© NEWSPIX/FIONA HAMILTON)

Below: The once feared Pentridge Prison, often known by the nickname The Bluestone College, now a housing complex.
(© NEWSPIX/ANDREW TAUBER)

H.M. PRISON PENTRIDGE

Some Painters and Dockers

8

How many people died or disappeared in and after the struggle for the control of the Federated Ship Painters and Dockers Union's war in Melbourne during the 1970s depends on who is telling the tale. Certainly two dozen died or disappeared, including one woman, but there were possibly up to forty deaths. And how many were shot but survived is impossible to calculate. Of course, not all of the deaths related to the battle for control; some were over the division of spoils of robberies, some over women, some over respect; one child was an innocent bystander. But deaths they all were.

After World War II the leadership of the Melbourne branch of the union became increasingly corrupt. Those in control were the ones who benefitted most from the wholesale theft of cargos, the blackmailing of owners so their ships could leave port, 'ghosting' — the practice of requiring owners to pay for more men than were actually employed—tax rorts, SP bookmaking, standover, prostitution and sly-grogging, as well as the 'Lemon Tree', or the allocation of work in return for kickbacks. The proceeds were divvied up between council members and their cronies. For those in power or close to it the union was a gravy train. In 1957 Lou Wright, regarded as sub-normal at the time of his murder trial in 1938, admitted to walking around with £100 in his pocket. By the time of his death in 1980 he had acquired a small fortune of nearly $300000. One year he had under-declared his taxable income by

$67000. This was at a time when the average weekly wage of a docker was the equivalent of between $100 and $120.

Part of the problem was the composition of the membership. Working as a ship's painter and docker was a filthy way to earn a living, often carried out in freezing and insanitary conditions, and it was certainly not for the faint-hearted. It did, however, provide employment for those released from Pentridge who could not find work elsewhere, and so the prison and the union became a revolving door. Neither ex-policemen nor nightwatchmen were welcome. The punishing work aside, there were other fringe benefits. One of the bonuses offered by the union was that false identities were readily available to its members. As a result, criminals could easily stay in work while on the run, and false claims for unemployment benefits and multiple claims for workers' compensation could be made. All but two of the Victorian branch senior members in the early 1970s had at some time or another used aliases. One of its secretaries, Jack 'Puttynose' Nicholls, used at least four. Another benefit of membership was that it could be used to defeat a consorting charge. Union men found by the police hanging around in public houses with other criminals could rely on the defence that they were waiting to be picked up for work.

By the late 1960s it was estimated that seventy of the top 100 criminals in Victoria had links with the union and in 1970 serious troubles erupted after the secretary, Jimmy Donegan, died of liver disease. At the time of his death he was awaiting trial on a charge of receiving part of the proceeds of the $580000 robbery of a Mayne Nickless van in Sydney. After his death a bitter struggle broke out for control of the union.

On the one side, on the so-called Blue Ticket for the December 1971 election was Pat Shannon, a man with thinning hair, a bulbous nose, a schoolteacher wife and three daughters. He had once run a pub in Adelaide and was appointed caretaker secretary after the death of Donegan. Now he sought re-election and wanted his friends Arthur Morris as president, Fred Persson for vice-president and the banana-nosed Doug Sproule (who had a conviction for wounding a policeman with intent to murder) in the all important, if quaintly named, position of vigilance officer.

On the White Ticket was Billy Longley, who had joined the union in 1967 and was later convicted of the Mayne Nickless receiving. Known as The Texan, either because he carried a Colt .45 or after the character of the same name in a television western series, Longley had already been acquitted of the shooting murder of his first wife, Patricia, and then, after a retrial in 1961, of her manslaughter. He had also been acquitted of a charge of shooting with intent to murder in May 1959 and again after a fight in the Rose and Crown Hotel in Port Melbourne ten years later.

Longley did not oppose Shannon for secretary. He wanted to be president and have his own men: Burt Aspel as vice-president and James Frederick Bazley (known as Machine Gun because of his rapid speech) as the vigilance officer. On paper Bazley's early career did not really suggest he was suitable for the job. In 1947 he had been convicted of carrying an unregistered pistol while working as a bouncer at an illegal baccarat game in Lonsdale Street. Just before Christmas 1964 he was convicted of a robbery of $2970 from a bank in Collingwood. He escaped from prison twice and was finally released in 1969. Later he would be convicted of the murders of anti-drug campaigner Donald Mackay and Douglas and Isobel Wilson, two couriers for the Mr Asia drug syndicate. But given the union's penchant for violence, perhaps he really was suitable.

Now began a decade of violence. On 26 March 1971 docker Thomas Connellan was shot in the back as he was walking home past Preston Girls' High School. He survived. The violence intensified during the 1971 election campaign when, at the end of November, Robert Crotty, a Longley supporter, was involved in a fight behind a South Melbourne hotel. As he went to shake hands afterwards he was hit with a brick and then kicked and beaten. He was left with brain damage which persisted until his death seven years later. Witnesses told the police he had fallen over and hurt himself but the name of docker and standover man Les Kane was barked as his actual killer.

Retribution was swift. One of Crotty's supposed attackers, Alfred 'The Ferret' Nelson, disappeared from his Collingwood home three days before the election. There has been great speculation over the Ferret's final resting place, just as there has over the body of Teamster Jimmy Hoffa. At first The Ferret's body was thought to have been left in his car in the Yarra River off No. 21 South Wharf. Certainly the car was there but when it was pulled out there was no Ferret inside. Another suggestion was that he was buried under tons of concrete freshly poured as a ramp on the docks. A third on offer was that his body had been burned in an incinerator only 60 yards from the union's Lorimer Street offices. Other suggestions have included disposal in the bilge tank of a Hong Kong freighter or that he was dumped at sea. It is always possible his death was not concerned with the union dispute; he was thought to have fallen out with Joey Turner. Nelson was supposed to have been minding Turner's $60 000 share of the proceeds of the MSS robbery and it had gone missing. On the other hand his disappearance coincided with that of another Longley supporter, Alfred 'Darky' Brown.

On 10 December, the day of the ballot, Longley arrived early at the union offices where the dockers were lined up at the trestle tables to vote. He had his men outside the Williamstown docks helping their supporters vote inside—one story is that Bazley had a gun in one hand and, appropriately enough for a prospective vigilance officer, a foot on the ballot box. According to Longley's evidence at the Costigan Royal Commission a decade later, it was then that five cars arrived carrying the opposition Blue Ticket forces, including Charlie Wootton, Danny Corsetti (who later received seven years for his part in the MSS robbery), Bobby Dix (who had been fortunate enough to escape a conviction in a murder case at the army barracks at Camp Pell in 1947) and Doug Sproule. A gun battle broke out and Longley and his supporters were driven from the docks. And that was when the ballot boxes disappeared, only to reappear stuffed with Blue Ticket votes. The rest of the morning was punctuated by gunfire and concluded with the resignation, said to have been at gun point, of the protesting returning officer, Pat Cullen.

What was amazing was that the union members operated in a complete vacuum. There was no report of the battle in the next day's papers and it was not until 16 December that even a mention was made of the shootings. Much more space was devoted to a youth gang known as the Devil's Raiders from Williamstown, who had been creating havoc in North Altona. Longley may have lost but it was certainly not the end of things. The next day Doug Sproule's car was found burned out. Asked how this could have happened, he suggested it might have self-combusted. The vehicle was taken away by the police for forensic examination and found to be riddled with fifty bullet holes.

The day after the election another Longley supporter, Desmond Bernard Costello, who at the time was living in Preston under the name of Studd, was kidnapped. Again this may not have been strictly union rivalry. Ten years previously Costello had been acquitted of the murder of the crippled standover man Osmond 'Hoppy' Kelly in Fitzroy. He was also thought to have been yet another receiver of the proceeds of the Mayne Nickless raid, as well as being one of the abductors of Nelson. Costello's body was found on 14 December 1971 dumped in a ditch at Clifton Hill by the site of the new Eastern Freeway. One arm was shattered and part of a hand had been blown away, suggesting he had been trying to protect his face. The event elicited one of those statements that came to be thrown back in the face of the union by its critics. In a version of 'we catch and kill our own', Terrence Gordon, the federal secretary of the union, told the press, 'I know managing directors who have got shot, wharfies who have got shot. What is happening within the union is the union's own affair and will be settled inside the union.' There have also been suggestions that Costello was killed by members of Sydney's Toecutter Gang.

That month Ian Revell Carroll, who was known as Fingers and would later be part of Chuck Bennett's Great Bookie Robbery, was arrested on two charges of carrying an unlicensed pistol. Fined $150, he denied he had been a bodyguard for a union official.

Over the next fifteen months there were numerous incidents of gunfire between the rival groups and on 20 December 1971 Laurence Richard Chamings, whose brother had been killed the previous year in a quarrel over bail money, was wounded in the shoulder and survived for the time being. Jim Bazley also survived a shooting in May 1972 when he was hit in the thigh and shoulder as he stood outside his North Carlton home, and again in the September when he was hit in the head and hand while sitting in his car. Longley's second wife and daughter also survived when, on 25 January, the day after the results were published announcing the success of Shannon's team, a bomb was thrown at their home. After that Longley left for New South Wales to attend trial for his part in the Mayne Nickless receiving, leaving Linus 'The Pom' Driscoll behind to sit guard on his house and family.

On 13 March 1972 the car and home of docker and later brothel keeper Joey Hamilton in Longmore Street, St Kilda West, were shot-gunned by mistake for next-door neighbour Charlie Wootton's. The same day Hamilton survived after being shot in the groin outside his sister's home. In May, the shooters got the right target when Wootton's house and car were hit. Two years later he was shot in the shoulder. On 26 September that same year Francis Bayliss, suspected of stealing the ballot box, was found with four sticks of gelignite as well as a sawn-off shotgun. Questioned, he said he needed them for his own protection. 'You're not silly.

You know what's going on,' he told the police. Then, shortly after 4 a.m. on 15 December, Brian Sulley was shot twice in the head as he walked away from the union offices in Lorimer Street. He told the police that he heard two shots but didn't see who fired them.

There was great excitement when on 22 December 1972 a body was found in a field at Tarneit, near Werribee. At first it was thought it might be that of The Ferret, but on further inspection the body was far too big. In fact, it belonged to another painter and docker, the street fighter, standover man and extensively tattooed John Lewis Morrison, known as The Face because of scarring from adolescent pimples. His body was so badly decomposed that an accurate time of death could not be established, but he had disappeared some six months earlier. Again it may not have been union troubles that led to his death by shotgun. He had been having problems in Sydney following a moderately successful robbery there.

Then, in May 1972, it was Pat Shannon who, pointing out that dockers were not flower arrangers, tempted fate when he unfortunately added, 'Remember, no stray bullet or bomb has harmed a non-Union member.' It was less than a year before one did. A little after 6.30 p.m. on 21 April 1973, Yugoslav-born hospital cleaner Zlatko Kolovrat went to the Moonee Valley Hotel on the corner of Rose and Brunswick streets with his young sons, Nicholas and Peter. They were sitting with their father just inside the main bar when Laurence Chamings was shot dead as he tried to reach the safety of the outside lavatories. A stray shot fatally hit eleven-year-old Nicholas Kolovrat between his eyes.

Naturally, no one was able to identify the killer but now, with the death of a young boy, the police were able to lean more heavily on the underworld than was often the case, and eventually the name they came up with was that of Sydney standover man Barry 'The Bear' Kable. Kable had had an unfortunate childhood, seeing his father Roy axe his mother to death in the backyard of their Newtown home in April 1944. From then it was all downhill, and in March

1956 he was sentenced to three years for robbing a taxi driver. Judge Curlewis said he was sorry he could not have had him whipped.

One possibility for the murder was that Chamings had threatened to shoot Kable following an argument during a card game at a Melbourne Sunday beer party. There was also a suggestion that a Brendon McMahon had quarrelled with Chamings, who thought he had been cheated over the proceeds from a housebreaking. McMahon had escaped from Pentridge and was still on the run by the time Kable went on trial in October 1974. At least now Kable could provide the name of a man who might have attacked Chamings. The prosecution's evidence was not strong, much of it a so-called confession to a prison snitch, never a species liked by juries. Kable made an impassioned statement from the dock and called an alibi witness, Jill Frances Cayeux, who had known him for twenty years and was sure she had been drinking with him in Richmond that night. Kable was duly acquitted of the murders of both Nicholas and Chamings in less than fifty minutes. Cayeux was later sentenced to a minimum of three years for perjury. Kable returned to New South Wales where, at the end of February, he was attacked by three men (who were never identified), tied to a chair and beaten with axe handles. Although he suffered considerable brain damage, he survived. At the end of his life he was a 'derro' living on the streets of Darlinghurst.

Still to come was a killing that was even more important in the history of the dockers, and one that would directly lead to the disintegration of the union. It was a mild spring evening when Pat Shannon died in The Druids Hotel, on the corner of Park and Moray streets, South Melbourne, on 17 October 1973. The Druids was a hotel Shannon didn't visit often, but after drinking in the early evening with his offsider, John Patrick Joseph Loughnan, at O'Connell's Centenary Hotel, known as Murphy's, they moved three-quarters of a mile up the road to The Druids where at around 9.15 they met up with Noella Jansen, Loughnan's de facto, and Joan

Hoskings, whose husband was in hospital. According to Loughnan, at about 9.50, 'I heard crackers going off. All of a sudden Pat said, "You cunt," and fell off the chair. He died before the ambulance arrived.' In fact Shannon was shot three times and it was the first bullet through the heart that killed him.

Over the years there have been continuing suggestions that Shannon was set up. At first the police were convinced that he had been lured to his death by a mystery call and possibly shot by a hired interstate killer. One lawyer of the time supported part of that theory: 'Shannon was inveigled into a position sitting with people in a semi-circle. Whichever way he faced, he faced a door.' Within a matter of hours of Shannon's death, his long-time rival Billy Longley disappeared.

Unlike most cases involving dockers, this time the police had some help. Again, within hours of the killing, the father of docker wannabe and police dobber Gary Harding received an anonymous telephone call: 'The Dockies are out to shoot your son. Find him and hide him.' And he had left a note out for his boy warning him. Panic stricken, Gary Harding telephoned the CIB to say he wished to see his police contact, Detective Sergeant Murray Burgess urgently. It turned out Burgess had a little diamond mine in his hands. A terrified Harding spilled his version of the evening— that he had pointed out Shannon to a Kevin Taylor and that when Shannon was shot he and his mate Alfie Connell were in Park Street a hundred yards away. It was Billy Longley who had ordered the killing and Taylor who had done the shooting. All Harding had done was throw the gun away into the water at No. 2 South Wharf.

At first Taylor denied any knowledge of Shannon's death, saying he had been with his girlfriend Karen and Alfie Connell's wife, Diane. But shown the gun, now retrieved from the docks, he changed his story. He said Longley, who had been in Ararat prison with him, had told him Shannon had tried to rape his wife. He had offered $6000 for Taylor to shoot him.

On 26 March the next year Shannon's inquest took place and in a blaze of publicity and newsprint the coroner committed Taylor, Connell, Harding and the still absent Longley to stand trial. When the trial itself began on 5 August the prosecution hedged its bets as to motive. Longley had promised $6000 to Taylor either because Shannon was giving his wife a hard time or as a settling of old union scores. Unusually, all three defendants went into the box.

First was Kevin Taylor, who promptly changed his story. He hadn't killed Shannon as he had told the police. That night he had been at The Druids as a favour to Longley who had looked after him in Ararat gaol. He had thought he was simply to wave the gun about and eject a few cartridges as a warning to Shannon. But as they walked to the hotel together he chickened out. Longley took the gun from him, went in, came out a couple of minutes later and told him to get rid of the gun but to keep the silencer. He had heard some women screaming but no shots. Why had he changed his story? That was Longley again. He had threatened he would kill Taylor and his girlfriend if he went to the police. As a story it wasn't all that bad. And if he had got some support from Gary Harding he might have been all right. Unfortunately for him he didn't. Harding had his own agenda. There was no suggestion from him that Longley was the killer. Cut-throat defences only benefit the prosecution. Taylor and Harding received the death penalty duly commuted to life imprisonment. Connell was found guilty only of manslaughter and was sentenced to four years with a minimum of two to be served. Now, in a high-profile surrender with the press pre-warned, Billy Longley gave himself up. Thoughts of bail turned into pipedreams and it was into Pentridge, where Harding and Taylor were beginning their sentences, to await his trial.

Shortly after 2 p.m. on Saturday 13 September 1975, when he returned from the visitors' room, Gary Harding was stabbed to death in his cell in 'A' Division with a sharpened table knife. The knife was found in the lavatory in his cell. Suspicion fell immediately on Taylor, who had been with him moments before and after his killing. For his part Taylor immediately spoke to a warder to say he had found the unfortunate Harding and that he had nothing to do with his death. It was a position from which he never resiled.

Longley's trial began on 10 November, two months after Harding's death. Trials can be very boring things for both the jury and the spectators—an endless trawl through masses of documents—but when Taylor came to give evidence without Harding to contradict him, things picked up both for Longley and the public gallery. Now Taylor had a third and final version. And, best of all, it provided an out for Longley. It was he, Taylor, who had done the killing. Longley was in no way involved. Certainly $6000 had been on offer, but from Harding on behalf of a man known as Puttynose, rather than Longley. In fact, the villain of the whole piece was the dead Harding who had told him Longley was due to be knocked himself.

Longley did not give evidence but instead made a short statement, saying he knew who had planned to kill Pat Shannon but 'they would kill me if I named them'. That was the reason he could not 'give evidence from the witness box and be subject to cross-examination'. Any suggestion Pat Shannon had been having an affair with his wife was ridiculous. He had merely given Taylor a lift to The Druids and had then gone on to see a friend. He had not seen Harding at all that night. The gun that had been used was his but he said he had given it to Taylor a few weeks before to go rabbiting.

With Longley confident of an acquittal, on 19 November the jury retired for six and a half hours before returning a verdict of guilty. He was sentenced to imprisonment for his natural life. The publicity surrounding the inquest had no doubt gone against him, as had his absence. Would he have done better to have stood his ground from the start? From a trial point of view he might, but whether he would have survived is another matter. In February 1976, Longley appealed against his conviction, claiming there was no evidence on which he could be found guilty. He lost by a two to one majority. The Chief Justice and Justice Lush thought there was sufficient evidence but, in a dissenting verdict, Justice Anderson said he would have allowed the appeal.

The mid-1970s were relatively quiet years for the dockers but in December 1977 there was one attempted murder and the killing of June Thompson, closely associated with the union. First, Victor George Allard was wounded on 5 December 1977 at the Bayview Hotel in Cecil Street, South Melbourne, where he had been drinking with friends in the afternoon when a man walked in, fired one shot and left, shortly followed by Allard's friends who left him to be found by the police. The bullet lodged in Allard's bowel.

Then came the death on 13 December 1977 of thirty-four-year-old blonde June Thompson of Coogee Bay, Sydney, whose body was found under the Bass Strait ferry loading ramp in Melbourne by two men who had posed as Harbor Trust employees. She had been shot in the back of the head. A close friend of both Ferret Nelson and Dessie Costello said she had come to Melbourne ostensibly to see friends, but it may have been in connection with union business. It was the sixty-second murder in Victoria that year, equalling the 1961 record. Thompson was by no means a square-head. An accomplished thief, the previous October she had appeared in the Sydney Federal Court on a charge of imposition following unemployment benefit frauds in the suburbs said to total $1 million. She also had a number of aliases. She was possibly killed to keep quiet but another version is that her killing was part of a game that went sadly wrong. Whichever is correct, Les Kane was called in to clean up the mess of her death. A man known as Pudding was charged with her murder but the coroner refused to commit him for trial.

The drug-dealing Victor Allard did not last long after that. On the night of 9 February 1979 he was shot opposite a pizza shop in Fitzroy Street, St Kilda. Two men, one of whom was said to be extremely fat, ran off down the street while Allard died in the gutter.

Dennis Allen, the eldest child of brothel owner Kath Pettingill, and his girlfriend Sissy (formerly Heather Hill, whom he later married in 1981 while in Pentridge) were standing with Allard when he was shot. One way of not paying debts is to kill your creditor, and Allard, who had been supplying the local prostitutes, was owed a large sum of money. If, as many suspected, Allard's killer was Dennis Allen or someone acting on his behalf, it was a prototype of a killing by the bank robber Roy 'Red Rat' Pollitt. Five years later Pollitt shot Lindsay Simpson by mistake for Simpson's brother-in-law, the drug dealer Alan Williams, to whom Allen owed more than $15 000. Pollitt received a minimum of eighteen years. No one was charged with the Allard shooting.

Over the years there were stories that Longley would bid for a retrial. In March 1980 he gave *The Age* a seven-page pamphlet arguing his innocence. In February the next year his new solicitors were reported to be sifting through fresh evidence which Longley claimed would clear him, but nothing came of it. Principally it was Taylor saying Longley was not involved but the Court of Appeal had disposed of that evidence years earlier.

Why did Harding turn on Longley in the first place? As always, there are various theories on offer. Once Harding had received the threats he may have run scared and tried to cut himself a deal for immunity or at worst a shortish prison sentence for manslaughter. After all he was not the actual killer. Inexperience and possibly fear told on him. The unwritten general rule is that the first dobber gets the benefit, but not in his case. One unanswered question is how did the dockers know quite so soon that Harding was involved?

Did Longley organise the killing of Shannon? To this day he continues to deny any involvement. His friend, the former detective Skull Murphy, is by no means convinced that he did. 'I have certain reservations that the person who went to jail was the right bloke,' he said in a television program, 'but I didn't lose any sleep over it.'

Mark 'Chopper' Read, a great champion of Longley, does not believe he would have used inexperienced youths when Ray 'Chuck' Bennett, Toecutter Linus 'The Pom' Driscoll and, indeed, he himself were all on hand. All were known, tried and trusted hardmen. Why would Longley use two idiots such as Harding and Taylor on a spur-of-the-moment job? He has a point. A key platform of the Crown's case was indeed that it was Longley's own gun that was used by Taylor but his lawyer, John Walker, thought only a fool would have allowed their own gun to be used. If, however, Longley did use Harding and Taylor and his own gun, it was an amazing miscalculation for which he paid dearly.

Read has an interesting and by no means wholly impossible version of events. He claims that, three weeks before Shannon was shot, Jack Twist met Lou Wright, by now a leading light behind the scenes in the union, in a Port Melbourne hotel and said the war must stop; both Shannon and Longley must go. Others discount this, saying that by the 1970s Twist was a spent force and was banished from Melbourne, but in 1982 Frank Costigan thought that Twist was one of a triumvirate—Puttynose Nicholls and Sproule were the others—still in control of the union. Additionally Wright, known as The Godfather and described by journalist Tom Prior as 'particularly formidable', has been vastly underrated. There is also little doubt that people knew the killing of Shannon was coming: on the evening he was shot, Bobby Dix, one of his minders, did not appear. How on earth did Longley know Shannon was going to be drinking in what was not one of his regular hangouts? Not that speculation did Longley any good. For him, in April 1976, it was back off to Pentridge from where, in time, he would continue the chain of events that broke the union.

So, who had killed the unfortunate Harding? Taylor was dobbed in by two prison snitches, Peter Grant and Tibor Bariska, both doing life for murder. If the police thought the evidence they received from the grasses was sufficient for a conviction they were wrong. For one reason or another both backtracked in quick time. Taylor was not even committed for trial.

It was the dockers who ruled the other prisoners at Pentridge. At any one time there would be a number of them serving sentences and they banded together. Unsurprisingly, Longley was not popular with the majority of dockers then in Pentridge. Hardman he may have been but there was no way he was going to survive without help. And help came in the form of Chopper Read who, to get respite from H Division, had Kevin Taylor slice off a good part of his ears. He had been before the classification board to ask for a transfer into the mainstream of the jail and had been refused. He was not satisfied and asked Taylor to oblige him. This at least got him in the prison hospital for a period.

It was another docker, John 'Piggy' Palmer—later acquitted of the Car-O-Tel motel murder in St Kilda in 1984 and then serving a sentence for rape—who sparked a five-year struggle that became known as the Overcoat War because of the coats worn to conceal weapons, even in the height of summer. In it, Read headed a team against a crew led by a career criminal connected to the dockers. In theory it blew up over a question of who had eaten the sausages that were to be served as a Christmas treat in 1975.

All this was merely an excuse. The dockers wanted Longley. One night acid was poured on his blankets as he slept but Read was determined to protect him. What Longley really wanted was a new trial and it was after Read had been badly stabbed in the war that he began to talk to a British journalist, David Richards, who wrote for the *Bulletin* and who had cut his teeth as a crime reporter in Melbourne. Richards persuaded senior Victorian officers to allow him to go undercover with Skull Murphy to see what senior members of the union were up to. And he found all sorts of things, including standovers, ghosting, tax rorts and a brother and sister forced to allow an SP bookmaker to operate at the Station Hotel in Port Melbourne, which led to a shotgun attack when the pair did not cooperate.

Richards' findings, coupled with what Longley had to say, would be the catalyst that would ultimately bring about the deeply controversial and much criticised Royal Commission, which opened on 1 October 1980 headed by barrister Francis Xavier (Frank) Costigan. And the star of the Costigan Commission was undoubtedly Longley, as indeed he had always intended.

Apart from anything else he could say, Longley threw some light on what had happened to Charlie Wootton, the boy with the cartridges at the time of Freddie Harrison's murder. Things had gone well for Wootton. He had become a professional gambler, and a very successful one at that, because his bank accounts showed transactions of $250 000 in one year. In 1973, when Shannon was shot dead, Wootton was one of the union members who paid for a bereavement notice. He later served two months for consorting with sixteen reputed thieves. The next year, in December, he was acquitted of eighteen charges of consorting, but the following year he was convicted of a gaming offence, with yet another five years.

Longley described Wootton as 'one of the faceless men behind the docks'. He had big interests in trotting and nightclubs, including the Red Aces, the Hungarian and the Zorro—known throughout Melbourne as Charlie's Place—all in Acland Street, St Kilda. In 1980 he was warned off all trotting tracks in Victoria after a search of his home revealed a .22 silencer, five Buddha sticks and a substance used to pep racehorses. He was said to have close links with Sydney head honcho George Freeman, with the drug-dealing former New South Wales policeman Murray Riley and with John Doyle, Riley's Hong Kong–based partner.

Longley's enemy, Jack 'Puttynose' Nicholls, did not survive the Commission. On 16 June 1981, shortly before he was due to give evidence on subpoena, he was found shot through the head in his car on the Hume Highway some 270 kilometres from Melbourne. The day of his death he had been drinking heavily with friends in Albury. He left a note:

> To my members and executive, I tried very hard but the rotten
> Fraser government did not want me to survive. Do not think
> I have taken the easy way out but the rotten system has cut
> my life short. I had big ideas for advancement but these were
> chopped short. Farewell Comrades, Jack Nicholls XX.

The coronial inquest returned a verdict of suicide but many
observers, including Doug Meagher, counsel for the Commission,
thought Nicholls had been given either an ultimatum or some help.

Over the months the Costigan inquiry expanded to an extensive
examination of how often illiterate union members had been used
for drug dealing and tax evasion schemes that cost millions, as well
as money laundering and dealings with the Nugan Hand Bank.
In his report Costigan wrote:

> I became satisfied that the union, at least in Victoria, Newcastle,
> Queensland and South Australia (if not in Sydney as well), was
> an organised criminal group following criminal pursuits. At
> least in Victoria those in charge of the union recruit exclusively
> those who have serious criminal convictions. The union gives
> active assistance to those criminals, be it in the selection of
> criminal activity, or in harbouring and protecting the criminals
> from the consequences of their crimes.

It all led to the establishment of the National Crime Authority. It
did not lead to a new trial for Longley but it did get him out of
Pentridge to the less harsh conditions of Ararat Prison. In all, he
served thirteen years and on his release he joined with the now
retired Skull Murphy, setting up as business mediators.

As for the Painters and Dockers' Union, following the Costigan
Commission's report, dissatisfied members began to drift to other
unions. The Hawke government then passed legislation that unions
with fewer than 1000 members should be deregistered, and, as a
result, the registration of the Federated Ship Painters and Dockers'
Union was cancelled on 1 December 1993.

Shooting Stars

9

Some criminals have allure, some have talent, some pay great attention to detail. Ray 'Chuck' Bennett had and did all of those things. Like Bruce Reynolds, the leader of Britain's Great Train Robbery, he had the brains and charisma to organise and lead a team. He was regarded by Chopper Read, himself no slouch, as not only a top gang tactician but also 'one of the Australian underworld's foremost bank robbers'. Bennett, once a member of the so-called Kangaroo Gang—which was in fact a series of close-knit gangs that shoplifted in Europe almost with impunity in the 1960s and 70s—was serving a sentence in Parkhurst, a high-security prison on the Isle of Wight off the south coast of England, when he devised the Great Bookie Robbery.

Built in 1880, the Victoria Club at 141 Queen Street was where Victorian bookmakers would meet to settle up on the first day after a weekend's racing. In 1975, towards the end of his sentence, Bennett obtained a period of home leave and, amazing as it may seem, returned to Australia on a false passport to case the premises before returning to complete his sentence. Although security was incredibly lax for the amount of money floating around—some moonlighting detectives would look in to see things were all right and they invariably were—over the years a number of individuals and teams had considered the club as a target and decided it was too much like hard work. They included highly talented James 'The Jockey' Smith and the Chinese–Australian Leslie Woon, whose career in crime spanned twenty years. The *Victoria Police Gazette* described Woon as 'not afraid to dirty his hands when planning a job. He doesn't mix with the criminal element; using different names for his flat, car and telephone'. If Woon turned it down it certainly must have looked too much like hard work.

Now Bennett, another who had acted as a minder for Billy Longley in Melbourne's waterfront war of the early 1970s, put together a team and took them out of the city for a period of training away from their wives and girlfriends. His second in command was another nominal painter and docker, Ian Revell 'Fingers' Carroll. Other members included Norman Leung Lee, who ran a dim sim restaurant, Bennett's cousin Vinnie Mikkelsen, Anthony Paul McNamara and, while he denied it to his death, Dennis William 'Greedy' (sometimes 'Fatty') Smith, who was always thought to have been the driver. Although they had all worked together before, neither of the standover brothers Les or Brian Kane was part of Bennett's team; neither—and particularly Brian—was thought willing to accept the discipline required. They were both said not to have minded their omission but it must have grated. Another who missed out was Bennett's great mate Brian O'Callaghan, but that was because he was in Long Bay at the time. Bennett is said to have given him $100000 from the takings. When Bennett was satisfied the team was ready, and after a weekend dress rehearsal when the club was empty, he chose Wednesday, 21 April 1976 after the three-day Easter weekend's racing, when over a hundred bookmakers were to meet to settle up at the club.

The money was delivered by armoured car at midday and within minutes at least six men armed with machine guns burst into the settling room, tackled the armed guards and ordered the bookmakers to lie on the floor. The team cut open the metal cash boxes filled with more than one hundred calico bags with untraceable notes. Just how much money was taken has never been established—certainly not less that $1.5 million, possibly up to $15 million. The raid was over by

12.15 and most of the robbers were gone into the next-door office block and then into traffic in Queen Street. A reward of $70 000 was promptly offered. Curiously it was one day when the moonlighting detectives were not on their unofficial duty.

The immediate problem Bennett faced was disposing of the money. In 1998 Phillip Dunn QC, who had represented Norman Lee, said his client had told him that for a month the money never left the premises. The robbers had rented offices upstairs from the Victoria Club and it was removed at their leisure over the next four to five weeks. 'When you think about it, that's very smart, verging on genius almost,' he said.

What robbers must not do immediately after a touch is spend money like drunken sailors, and this requires group discipline. Laundering requires care, and on this occasion the racetrack, one of the traditional avenues, was hardly open to them. The Great Train Robbers in Britain had been caught because they splashed out on cars in an endeavour to launder the money instead of changing it through a trusted solicitor. When Peter Macari 'Mr Brown' took $500 000 from Qantas airlines he bought a flat and fast cars, which he could not possibly justify. Bennett was far too astute to allow something like that to happen. Some money went into property; some went to Manila with Greedy Smith, who opened the Aussie Bar, which was advertised on a hoarding at the North Melbourne footy ground in Arden Street. The profits from this vice den and money laundry went into the purchase of brothels and bars throughout Asia as well as racehorses and to pay off up to fifty corrupt police officers in Manila. Some more money went to Canada. But there was a nasty scare when, on a visit to a solicitor, Bennett's mother collapsed and the paramedics called to her aid found some $90 000 worth of cash in her clothes. Amazingly no questions seem to have been asked.

It was not until 1977 that Norman Leung Lee was arrested and charged with the robbery. He was one who had been spending and had bought $60 000 of dim sim equipment. He was also trying to launder money through a solicitor's trust account. On 19 August he took $60 000 in a plastic bag to a solicitor saying he wanted to invest it on behalf of a friend. But Lee remained as staunch as Bennett had expected. The magistrate ruled that there was no evidence to link the unmarked money to the robbery and refused to commit Lee for trial. He was the only one of the team ever charged and his acquittal really spelled the end of the investigating squad.

Just as there were few, if any, continuing success stories among Britain's Great Train Robbers, so, over the years, did the Great Bookie Robbers met more than their fair share of bad luck. Most of them, in fact, died early and often violent deaths. First, though, there was the danger of other gangs, including the Sydney-based Toecutters, wanting a share of the proceeds; and it spoke enormously well of the regard in which Bennett was held that they decided to leave him personally alone. Another story floating around after the robbery was that Les and Brian Kane might decide they wanted a slice of the takings. There was speculation that Bennett would therefore make a pre-emptive strike against them. He was seen as not averse to removing his enemies before they had the chance to remove him. But, when it came down to it, the problems seem to have been personal rather than business.

It was in the winter of 1978 that painter and docker and blagger Les Kane first thought he was going to be knocked, or at least that was when he told his second wife Judi his fears. Apart from the standover, he had a good income going on the Geelong docks, picking up several pay packets a week. Brother Brian, also a nominal docker, was a debt collector and enforcer. Few were brave enough to resist his invitations to settle a debt.

Just as standover man John 'Nano the Magician' Regan could make people disappear in Sydney, so could Chuck Bennett in Victoria. He would knock on people's doors and say, 'Come with me.' And one of those who went with him was a friend of the Kanes, a young man with a deformed arm known as Wingy, who had been going out with a girl fancied by a friend of Bennett. After Wingy's disappearance Brian Kane took up the matter with Bennett at a fundraiser at a pub in Richmond owned by the old Tigers player Francis Bourke, but for the moment things remained calm.

The next was another fight, thought to have been set up by Bennett, between Brian Kane and Bennett's cousin Vinnie Mikkelsen. Offered a drink by Kane in the Royal Oak in Church Street, Richmond, Mikkelsen replied somewhat unnecessarily, 'I don't drink with old men.' Kane had been a Golden Gloves fighter but now he was forty; Mikkelsen was the younger but with less ability. Out on the pavement the fight ran a good twenty minutes until Mikkelsen bit off part of Kane's ear. It could not be reattached and from then on Brian Kane grew his hair long.

In August that year Les Kane, Judi and their two children rented a unit at Mountain Highway, Wantirna. On 19 October three men were waiting in the house when the family returned around 9.15 p.m. from visiting relations. Kane was shot in the bathroom of the house and his body was dumped in the boot of his pink Ford Futura and driven off by the men. What was so odd was that the three men, two of whom Judi had known for years, did not attempt to mask up. One was Chuck Bennett, the second was Vinnie Mikkelsen and the third was Laurie Prendergast, the offsider of all-purpose hitman Chris 'Mr Rent-a-Kill' Flannery. Kane's body was never found and it was thought quite possible that he became dim sim in Norman Lee's restaurant. But there were sure to be reprisals and at the end of November Mikkelsen's house in Nathalia Street, Broadmeadows, was burned out. In the meantime Brian Kane went against all the known rules of gangland and decided Judi Kane should go to the police. His reasoning appears to have been that he would find Bennett and kill him. The others could wait.

On 1 December, Prendergast was arrested and in the evening Judi Kane picked him out on an ID parade. The other two were arrested later. The trial itself started on 3 September that year but by then Bennett had been charged with an armed robbery on 2 August 1979 and was in custody. Despite an incident when an attempt was made to force her car off the road, Judi Kane stuck to her guns, identifying all three men. But there were problems for the prosecution. 'What was obvious was that the Crown case had very serious issues,' says one lawyer who watched the trial, 'and the defence challenged every bit of it.' There was no doubt that Kane was a wife beater. Judi Kane had had plastic surgery on two occasions after his ministrations and it was suggested at the trial that she had either killed her husband herself or, more probably, had arranged for his disappearance.

Then there was the lack of forensic evidence. According to Judi, her husband had been machine-gunned, yet there was no chipped paint and no cracked mirror in the bathroom, let alone a bullet hole in the wall where he was shot. Surely not every bullet had hit Kane. The only evidence that her husband had been alive on the day he was meant to have been killed was from Judi. Many thought that, while Kane was certainly missing, it hadn't happened quite in the way the jury was being told. Some thought he might have been killed up to a week earlier. All the men called alibis and, something unusual in a major criminal trial, Bennett actually gave evidence. Norman Lee came to court to say Bennett had spent the evening with his family. Prendergast had a brother, Billy Lewis, who closely resembled him and there were suggestions that the man Judi Kane saw could have been Lewis instead.

In the pre-DNA 1970s, juries liked 'no body' cases even less than they do today. Some states still hadn't come round to prosecuting when no body could be found. Kane hadn't been gone all that long. Given his lifestyle, there was always the chance he could still be in smoke. Part of the defence case was that two people came to give evidence who said they had seen him after the alleged shooting and abduction. On 21 September, after a retirement of only two and a half hours, the jury returned a verdict of not guilty.

Brian Kane could never accept the death of his brother or the verdict. 'There wasn't going to be a life for Brian after Les's death, ever,' says a family friend. 'He just wanted Chuck's head on a platter.' Once, seeing lawyer Phil Dunn having coffee at a café in Lygon Street, he attacked him, calling him a dog and demanding to know how he could have acted for Mikkelsen. It was only the intervention of 'The Munster' Graham Kinniburgh, who was with him, saying 'he was only doing his job', that prevented a serious incident.

After the acquittals Prendergast went straight into hiding and Mikkelsen flew out of Melbourne the next day. The witness Lee went to Singapore. Bennett was in Pentridge at the time but declined to go into segregation. He knew reprisals were likely and was said to have taken out fresh life insurance. His thirteen-year-old son was sent out of the country.

There had been strict security throughout the Bennett trial but there was none on 12 November 1979 when he was taken to the first floor of the old Melbourne Magistrates' Court on Russell Street to answer the robbery charges in Court 10. Bennett was waiting without handcuffs and with an unarmed guard outside the courtroom. On the landing was a man wearing a dark suit and apparently carrying a small briefcase; he was sitting on a bench at the head of the stairs, making no effort to hide himself away. The man shot Bennett three times in the chest with a .38. Bennett staggered down the stairs and out of the courthouse into a courtyard where he collapsed. Taken to St Vincent's Hospital, he died within the hour. The gunman escaped after threatening Bennett's escorting officer and a federal policeman, possibly via the rear stairway leading to the court's car park. From there it was easy enough to go into any of Swanston, La Trobe or Franklin streets. Other accounts have him walking down the front stairs of the court building and into a waiting car.

Unsurprisingly, the underworld buzzed with rumours, one of which was that Brian Kane and his brother Raymond had imported an interstate hitman for a fee of $50000. The name of Toecutter Linus 'The Pom' Driscoll was the one on police lips. This was unlikely since he was also thought to have modified the machine guns Les Kane's killers used. Another rumour was that two police officers, one of them Sergeant Brian 'Skull' Murphy, had given the gunman the money to kill Bennett. Another theory was that the killer was Chris Flannery, possibly with an assist from a police officer. This was certainly suggested by the press; but, even given his tendency to go where the money was, it is unlikely since Flannery was aligned with Prendergast. At the inquest the coroner found there was no evidence whatsoever to suggest that Murphy and the other officer were implicated in the murder. Many years later Murphy was asked 'if a Brian had killed Bennett'. He replied, 'Yes, but it wasn't this one.'

Both Ray and Brian Kane made statements that they were not involved. Ray gave his lawyer Frank Galbally the names of the people he had been with, adding that he would make himself available for interview. Brian Kane's statement was shorter and more combative: 'I do not believe there can be any evidence whatsoever connecting me with this killing. Therefore I will say nothing further about this matter as there is no way in which I can assist the police.'

More than thirty years on, it is now generally accepted that the killer was Brian Kane. After Bennett's acquittal he had become more and more secretive, calling friends and family at odd hours, arriving in the dead of night, never giving his name over the telephone. In fact, Kane had been getting into the courthouse night after night around midnight, pacing out the distances. His likely escape route has also become clear: he was taken straight to Essendon Airport and put on a light plane to Adelaide, where he boarded a commercial flight to Perth. And there he stayed for the next three months. Eventually Kane was told he was no longer hot—at least as far as the police were concerned—and he returned from the west coast.

The day after Bennett's death, his old mate Brian O'Callaghan, then serving a thirteen-year sentence for armed robbery, escaped from a prison van taking him to work at the prison bakery in Long Bay, Sydney. With O'Callaghan temporarily on the loose and possibly making his way to Melbourne, the press and police predicted immediate trouble and possibly an all-out gang war; but, for the time, that did not materialise. Callaghan stayed out until he was dobbed in and caught in a house in Carlton two years later but he didn't seem to have busied himself on his former offsider's behalf.

Within the month, John Mervyn Kingdom, a friend of the Kanes, walked into St Vincent's Hospital in Melbourne with three bullets inside him, in the groin and stomach. He told the police he had been walking in North Fitzroy when he 'felt a pain' but that he had neither heard nor seen anything. One theory was that he had been kidnapped and shot as a reprisal for Bennett's death. Things quietened down for the next few months but then there were further reprisals—though not, at first, from the Bennett side. Early in the morning of 15 July 1981, Norman McLeod, Mikkelsen's brother-in-law, was shot three times through the window of his car outside his home in Coolaroo by two men armed with shotguns. The police thought he was possibly killed by mistake for Mikkelsen, whose car he was using. No charges were ever brought.

Brian Kane spent 26 November 1982 with an old friend, Sandra Walsh. In the evening, around 8.30 p.m., they went to the Quarry Hotel in Brunswick for a few drinks. About an hour later Sandra went to the lavatory and Kane was at the table when two men came in. One of them, tall and thin and wearing a black balaclava, walked over and shot him, knocking his teeth out. If the police hoped to get any help from Sandra they were wrong. 'He was shot and that's all

I'm saying.' Kane died the next day and later Sandra Walsh made a statement in which she said she had driven him in her Jaguar to the Quarry Hotel. But that was a mistake, she told the coroner eleven months later, she had been confused. Earlier in the day she had lent her car to a Trevor Russell who had dropped the Jaguar off there during the evening. In criminal circles, and who should know better, the names of Vinnie Mikkelsen and the appropriately named Russell 'Mad Dog' Cox were being barked. Neither man was ever charged. Much later, when the case was reopened in 2009, the name Greedy Smith came into the frame.

As for the others on the Bookie Robbery? Over the years those suspected of being on the Victoria Club team were arrested for other jobs, served long sentences and died young. Anthony McNamara died in Collingwood in 1990. He had become a drug addict and it was suspected that he had been given a hotshot. After Brian Kane's death, Norman Leung Lee moved quietly to Singapore but the lure of Victoria proved too much. On 28 July 1992 he failed to close the doors as the getaway van accelerated during a robbery at the Ansett Air Freight Terminal at Melbourne Airport. Lee was thrown from the van and, armed with a .357, ran after it. An inquest would hear that he appeared to bring up the gun before he was shot by a member of the Police Special Operations Group. A post-mortem showed that Lee had a 70 per cent blockage of his left coronary artery and the chase after the van might well have killed him anyway. It was thought he had returned to Melbourne some time earlier and had since been involved in a number of successful robberies. Another on the Ansett raid, Stephen Barci, who was also shot by police, received a ten-year minimum sentence, as did the driver, Steven Asling. At least Barci had some fleeting pleasure during his time in gaol. On 4 March 1998, six years into his sentence, he managed to have a twenty-nine-year-old woman smuggled into Dhurringile minimum security prison dressed in a prison uniform. She was there for over six hours before dogs searching for drugs found her under a blanket.

Another of the Bookie Robbers, Ian Carroll, following in the master's footsteps, also became one of the great planners of armed robberies, including an attack on a bullion van in Tooborac, an hour north of Melbourne, in spring 1981. He would leave nothing to chance, and team members were supplied with not only weapons but also a medical kit in case of injury. Carroll was killed on 3 March 1983 in an argument in his own backyard, in a supposedly safe house in Mount Martha on the Mornington Peninsula. His killer was the celebrated bank robber and escapee Russell 'Mad Dog' Cox, born Melville Peter Schnitzerling and the one-time lover of 'The Matriarch', Kath Pettingill. Searching the house, the police found what they described as a 'huge number' of weapons, including machine guns and uniforms from a security firm, some hidden in a false ceiling. The house had also been used as a hideaway by a number of criminals, including Cox and the former South Australian police officer Colin Creed. Cox was later tried for the Carroll murder and acquitted after the magistrate said he could not decide who had fired the first shot. He and Creed were identified as being part of a gang running through Victoria, New South Wales and South Australia that had pulled off nine armed robberies, netting them in excess of $1.3 million. Creed, a master of disguise, was captured in Perth in September 1983. He served twelve years of a twenty-one-year sentence for assorted robberies.

After the shooting, Cox fled with his green-eyed, dark-haired girlfriend, Helen Eva Deane, Chuck Bennett's sister-in-law. Cox had met her a year after his November 1977 escape from the supposedly escape-proof Katingal, the prison within a prison at Long Bay. For the next five years they led the police a merry dance, with the *Sydney Morning Herald* quoting a police spokesman saying of Deane, 'She's a crook, but obviously she's doing something right. Like Cox she's no fool. She hasn't even been sighted for five years.'

Cox was not caught until he was trapped, possibly by another escapee Raymond Denning, in a failed robbery in Doncaster in July 1988. Cox was finally released in December 2004 and went to Queensland.

If Greedy Smith was indeed in on the robbery, as distinct from merely laundering the proceeds, he partially survived the robbers' curse, living until August 2010 when he died following a heart attack aged sixty-five. In his later life he sold drugs from his Rolls-Royce. In February 2002 he received three years on a series of drug charges. He had suffered from diabetes and melanoma, and part of his leg was amputated. The remainder of his leg had the emblem of the North Melbourne Football Club, of which he was a keen follower, tattooed on it. In his career he had acquired over fifty convictions. He died still denying that he had been a driver in the Bookie Robbery and the getaway driver in the killing of Brian Kane. Chuck Bennett's offsider Brian O'Callaghan, regarded as one of the great robbers of his era, died in October 2010 at the age of sixty-two. He had been a cocaine addict for some years.

* * *

Another robbery in Victoria that was also meticulously rehearsed and planned—possibly for up to a year—and the takings from which dwarfed the lower estimate of the Bookie Robbery, was the theft from an Armaguard security vehicle in Richmond on the morning of 22 June 1994. It was a deceptively simple operation. The van was stopped as it turned from Punt Road towards the South Eastern Arterial—apparently by a council road gang.

The whole set-up was fake. The man with the stop sign halted the vehicle and another of the supposed workers had a key that fitted the van doors. Two of the crew were dragged into the rear compartment and handcuffed. One of the robbers then drove the vehicle into a dead-end street and the gang escaped with a haul of over $2.5 million. The team had been seen on a number of occasions rehearsing and carrying out their supposed roadworks and the operation was thought to have been financed by a series of smaller bank raids in and around Melbourne. Around $40 000 was recovered when what was probably a second team began to change notes in Melbourne banks some two months after the robbery. None of the robbers was ever charged and the fallout among the players seems to have been negligible. One man who had been questioned but not charged was found dying on the pavement in a Brunswick street in December 1997. He had been beaten with a wheel brace. Of course, the killing may not have been related in any way to the robbery.

That was a totally professional operation, but the same could not really be said for the behaviour of the Melbourne robber Alex Tsakmakis, a man who owned a company that made car ramps and who struck fear in the hearts of lawyers and judges alike. In early 1978, Tsakmakis trussed up an athlete, Bruce Walker, with chicken wire and pitched him into the bay after an argument over money. He was given bail and took the opportunity to rob the Hawthorn Tattslotto agency of a paltry $1500. As he left he ordered the owner and his wife to the floor and shot them both in the head. They survived. On 17 March that same year three jewellers were shot and killed in almost identical circumstances in a diamond robbery in the Manchester Unity Building in the city centre. Tsakmakis was convicted of the Tatts robbery and also the Walker killing and, while in prison, boasted that he was responsible not only for the diamond robbery and killings but also for the diverse deaths of Brian Finemore, the curator of Australian Art at the National Gallery of Victoria, murdered on 23 October 1975, and prostitute Margaret Clayton, shot twice in the head in a North Fitzroy massage parlour in June 1979. He also was thought to be responsible for the disappearance of Willie Koeppen, owner of The Cuckoo restaurant in Olinda, on 26 February 1976. Koeppen apparently owed him money.

While in Pentridge, Tsakmakis set fire to Barry Robert Quinn, who was serving life for the murder of two men during a robbery at the Car-O-Tel motel in St Kilda in 1974. Quinn had been taunting Tsakmakis over the rape of his girlfriend. The following day Tsakmakis threw industrial glue over his tormentor and then flicked matches on him until one ignited. The death notice from his fellow prisoners posted in the *Sun* read, 'Barry, We always stuck together.'

Tsakmakis lived for only a few more years. He had earlier made an enemy of Chopper Read, who stabbed him in the neck, so said Read, to teach him manners. In 1988 Tsakmakis wanted to try to take control of the prison and had been picking up $1000 weekly financing drug sales. Now he wanted Read to team up with him against the robber Craig Minogue, who in March 1986 had bombed Russell Street Police Headquarters, causing the death of a young police constable, Angela Taylor. In June 1988 Minogue made a pre-emptive and terminal strike by crushing Tsakmakis's head with a pillowcase stuffed with weights from the prison gym. Tsakmakis died in St Vincent's Hospital. Minogue received a sentence concurrent with the twenty-eight years he was serving for the Russell Street bombing. In prison he began to study politics and prisoners' rights. In June 1990 he told a reporter from the *Herald Sun*, 'It's not as though I have brutally struck down Mother Teresa in the yard.' Read reflected, 'God bless the name of Craig Minogue. Killing Tsakmakis should get him to heaven, all sins forgiven.'

* * *

In November 2004 the *Herald Sun* ran a poll asking its readers whether they thought Paul Steven Haigh, currently serving life in prison, should have early release. At the age of twenty-one he had killed six people—more or less anyone who stepped in his path during and after a series of botched robberies. In 1978, less than three months apart, he shot Evelyn Abrahams in the back in a raid on a bookmaker's in Chapel Street, Prahran, and pizzeria owner Bruno Cingolani in the stomach in South Caulfield. Cingolani had refused to hand over his takings and tried to grab a knife from a drawer. On 27 June the next year Haigh shot Wayne Smith, the boyfriend of a St Kilda woman he believed was claiming he was a police informer. The next month he killed Sheryle Ann Gardner and her nine-year-old son Danny. She died because she knew too much of the earlier killings, and later Haigh maintained he had not initially intended to kill the boy but, because Gardner had demanded that Danny go with them on a drive to Ripponlea, his death was inevitable. Gardner had been involved in one of Haigh's murders and had to be killed to eliminate any possible chance that she, too, might inform. Haigh went to their funerals and later commented that she had lived by the sword and died by it. The sixth victim was his girlfriend, Lisa Maude Brearley, stabbed 157 times. He said he had lost count and therefore had to begin again. Sentenced to life in prison, on 14 November 1991 he helped in the death of an inmate, Donald George Hatherley. He maintained he had simply held his legs, thus assisting the man to commit suicide, but he was convicted of murder. In 2009 his application for a minimum term to be set was refused by Justice Betty King. In April 2011, now representing himself, he appealed Justice King's decision claiming he was no longer a 'monster' and that he deserved 'to be let out of the cage'. The Court of Appeal reversed the decision and Haigh will now be able to apply for a minimum term to be set.

And the result of the poll? Out of a total of 1579 calls, amazingly 2.9 per cent had voted in Haigh's favour.

Chopper Read and Mr Death

10

Whether Mark Brandon 'Chopper' Read and Dennis 'Mr Death' Allen, the eldest and most deadly of 'The Matriarch' Kath Pettingill's brood, would like to be linked in the same chapter is doubtful. Indeed, Read says that he beat up Allen in the lavatories in H Block at Pentridge. What is not in question is that they were both seminal figures in the Melbourne underworld in the 1980s and early 1990s.

Read, born in 1954 and the child of a former soldier and a mother who was a devout Seventh Day Adventist, was brought up in the then blue-collar suburbs of Fitzroy and Collingwood. Bullied at school as a teenager, he was placed in mental hospitals by his mother, who thought he was not only dyslexic but autistic as well, and was given shock treatment. Still in his teens and already the leader of the Surrey Road gang, he began his criminal career proper by standing over drug dealers. Later he emulated the Sydney Toecutters, who took money from their victims by using bolt cutters or blow torches on their victims' feet. From then on, he went on a decade-long spree of extortion, robbery, beatings and killings.

Read has claimed to have killed nineteen people but his detractors suggest this may well be an exaggeration. They suggest that it is a case of 'if the truth gets in the way of the legend, print the legend'. One man who certainly went down was the drug dealer Siam 'Sammy' Ozerkam, whom he shot to death in the car park of the St Kilda nightclub Bojangles on 12 June 1987. Claiming self-defence, he was acquitted. Read had been wearing a bullet-proof vest he claimed had been supplied to him by the police.

By the 1970s Read was in the feared H Block at Pentridge and it was there that he had Kevin Taylor, convicted of the murder of docker Pat Shannon, cut off his ears. One suggestion is that this is the basis of his nickname Chopper; another is that it comes from the size of his member, but Read claims it derives from a cartoon character. In prison he led the so-called Overcoat Boys in a war with a team of painters and dockers over the imprisoned Billy Longley.

Perhaps his highest-profile exploit was his attempted kidnap on 26 January 1978 of County Court Judge Bill Martin in an abortive attempt to obtain the release from J Ward at Ararat of his close friend Jimmy Loughnan, serving a sentence following a botched robbery at Box Hill, Melbourne. Read took the lift to the sixth floor where Martin was in court, walked over to the bench and threatened him with a firearm. He was promptly disarmed by the tipstaff. Despite the ingenuous plea by his barrister that Read was 'a comic character Charlie Chaplin would have portrayed sympathetically', he received thirteen years. Later, during the Overcoat War, he fell out with Loughnan who stabbed him in the back. Charitably and unusually, Read, who lost a sizeable length of intestine as a result of the attack, took no reprisal against his former friend, who died in the fire in the Jika Jika unit at Pentridge on 29 October 1987.

In the spring of 1992 Read was sentenced to six years in Tasmania for shooting biker Sid Collins, a member of the Black Uhlans, and was declared a Dangerous Criminal under s. 392 of the Tasmanian Penal Code. He had bitterly contested the case. He married a taxation office employee in prison but the marriage was dissolved and in January 2003 he married his long-time friend Margaret Cassar. After his release in 1998 he turned his undoubted talents to writing and in 2005 joined a club circuit lecture tour with the Rules footballer Mark 'Jacko' Jackson and disgraced New South

Wales detective Roger Rogerson. When Collins, then involved in a Russian mail-order bride business, disappeared in Queensland in August 2002, Read was briefly questioned. He denied any involvement, although in his most recent version of his life, *One Thing Led to Another*, he admits he did shoot the biker in 1992.

Over the past decade Read has become a celebrity ex-criminal, with a board game named after him, as well as a beer ('Chopper Heavy'). He has continued to write books, which have sold over half a million copies. *Chopper*, the film of his life, was highly acclaimed. More recently he is said to have been suffering from hepatitis C, contracted from using a blood-stained razor in prison, but has declined a liver transplant, saying he considers himself well down the list of worthy recipients.

* * *

Of the Pettingill family, Read seems to have really had time only for Dennis Allen's brother Peter, a rapist, drug dealer and the second-eldest son of Kath, although it was Dennis who, before his death in 1986, was an undoubted king of Melbourne crime.

The Pettingill family was one to be reckoned with. Perhaps in terms of international crime they were small fry, but in terms of the carnage that they in general, and Dennis in particular, inflicted, they were leaders of the field.

The eldest of the former brothel keeper's seven children, Dennis Allen was born on 7 November 1951 and grew up in West Heidelberg in what was the old Olympic Village. He built a substantial drug trafficking empire, at the same time working as an enforcer, robber, murderer and police informer. As a juvenile he recorded a string of minor convictions and then at the age of nineteen he was charged with rape. He was acquitted and convicted of unlawful carnal knowledge and put on a $200 bond to be of good behaviour.

His career took off when, on 17 October 1973, with his younger brother Peter and two others, he went to a girl's flat in Sandringham after being paid $500 to shoot her boss. The girl said she did not know where he was and, for her pains, was raped by Peter Allen. Her young sister was indecently assaulted. A shot was fired through a wall and Peter Allen clubbed the girl's boyfriend with a pistol. It was a pattern of violence that Peter Allen would exhibit for the rest of his life. On this occasion Dennis received ten years and was ordered to serve a minimum of five. Dennis and his brother had separated after the assaults and Peter, who had gone on a shooting spree around Melbourne, received fourteen years. In August 1985, Peter Allen was released after serving twelve years. In 1988 he received a maximum of thirteen years for dealing in heroin and conspiracy to commit armed robbery. In 1994 he received another seven for drug trafficking while in prison. In 2007 it was announced that he was to be given a sentence audit.

Meanwhile Dennis Allen served only four years and was immediately in trouble on his release in 1978. First, he had his young half-brother Jamie Pettingill to stay for four nights. Unfortunately Jamie was on the run from a young offenders' institute at the time and Allen was charged with harbouring. He was charged separately with possessing a pistol and a rifle and quickly added another gun charge and another of theft. Convicted on the gun charges, he was allowed to remain on bail while he appealed, but he failed to appear at his trial.

Despite the fact that he was supplying guns to Jamie, who was now undertaking a series of betting shop robberies, he stayed at large until May 1979, when he was attacked in a hotel in Frankston. He had been called by a girl who said she was in danger. She was right. Shots were fired and Allen was hit over the head with a rifle. He had thoughtfully armed himself with a piece of pipe before he went into the hotel, and as he staggered out he was arrested. He was successful in pleading self-defence but the earlier gun conviction stood and he was returned to prison for breach of parole.

Released on 2 July 1982, Dennis Allen moved into the drug business in Stephenson Street, Richmond, where his one-eyed mother—whose right eye had been shot out by another woman in a fight—ran a brothel. Kath Pettingill lived in number 106, which she rented, and owned 108, for which she had paid $28000 and which she used as a massage parlour. Allen lived with his mother, his wife (whom he had married in prison) and their two children. Late in 1982 he was arrested for possession of heroin. Property prices in the neighbourhood were going up. He was obliged to pay $35000 cash when he bought a house in Chestnut Street just before Christmas. He also started to grow cannabis plants and was arrested for that enterprise in February 1983.

There had been a temporary setback for the family on 16 February 1982 when Jamie took the rap for Dennis over the shooting of a barman two years earlier. Jamie received a remarkably lenient four years for that and two other armed robberies. When he was released his brother employed him as a standover man.

Throughout his life Dennis Allen acquired 'brothers'. Greg Pasche was one of them. At the age of thirteen Pasche had met Lex Peirce, one of Kath Pettingill's sons by Billy Peirce, when they were in Turana Boys' Home and used to spend weekend leave with Kath. When she was visiting Peter Allen in Long Bay Jail in Sydney she heard that Pasche needed $500 for bail, so she paid it and he returned to live with her in Stephenson Street. Two weeks later, on 27 May 1983, Pasche vanished and did not reappear until the late summer when his decomposing body was found on Mount Dandenong. He had been stabbed so fiercely in the head that the blow had fractured his skull. There was a variety of reasons why he might have been killed. He was drug dealing and debt collecting on behalf of Dennis Allen and also working as a male prostitute.

Shortly after that, another Dennis Allen associate, drug addict Victor Gouroff, disappeared. He was last seen on 20 November and his body was never found. Allen was considered to be a prime suspect in his death as well as that of a woman shot in the same year. Gouroff had convictions for armed robbery, theft and possession of firearms and had also met Allen in prison.

At least Allen was not wasting the money he was earning. Before the end of the year he bought another three houses, including 35 and 37 Stephenson Street, from where he would run his drug dealing and do his killings. Once, sent out by his mother to buy dog food, he returned hours later. He had forgotten to buy the meat but had bought another house instead. Accompanied by a minder who was paid $2000 and who paid cash for all purchases in shops, Allen would still try to steal nails from boxes on the hardware store counter.

Building work took place at 106 and 108 Stephenson Street so that clients could go into the massage parlour at 108 and order their drugs, which would be passed through from 106. If the brothel was raided in a drug bust, there would be little evidence on the premises. Allen was also acting as an armourer and it was about this time that he became a police informer. On 11 August 1984 in a drugged and drunken fit, he shot and killed another dobber, Wayne Stanhope, whose van was found dumped 70 kilometres out of the city the next afternoon. There was no trace of the body although clothing identified as the victim's was found in a national park. The body may well have been eaten by wild pigs. The reason for the killing was never clear but it is thought Stanhope had been fiddling with Allen's stereo equipment, which enraged him.

Allen had now become involved with drug dealer Alan Williams, as well as bent Sydney cop Roger Rogerson and hitman Chris Flannery. At Allen's instigation Roy 'Red Rat' Pollitt killed the wholly innocent council worker Lindsay Simpson, having mistaken him for his brother-in-law Alan Williams, who was owed between $15 000 and $20 000 by Allen for drugs. On 18 September 1984, Simpson was shot outside his home in Cheverton Road, Lower Plenty, as he was about to take the baby stroller from his car. His wife, still in the car, heard someone shouting 'Get down, sucker' and heard her husband say 'You've got the wrong man' before he was shot. In August 1989, Pollitt and a Gary Jones were charged with conspiring with Allen to murder Williams. Pollitt was sentenced to a term of twenty-four years reduced by the Court of Appeal to eighteen for Simpson's murder. 'I had to shoot the guy because he saw my face,' he said. In Kath Pettingill's revealing but not altogether unbiased memoir *The Matriarch*, she maintains that Dennis Allen killed Simpson himself and confessed to her that he had done so. Indeed she gives a different account of a number of other killings that have been attributed to her son. In prison Pollitt developed a talent for painting and after his release he married the owner of the art gallery where he exhibited.

Business was going well. Dennis Allen now owned a property company to manage his house purchases. Then, in November 1984, a prostitute named Helga Wagnegg, who had been given a hotshot by Allen, died. She had only recently been released from a sentence for an attempted robbery at another brothel. In his role of informer, Allen told the police that her body could be found in the Yarra River. Police observation and pressure were paying off and, by November 1984, Jamie Pettingill had joined his brother Trevor in facing drug dealing charges. Six months later, on the eve of the inquest of the unfortunate Wagnegg, Jamie, again acting on his brother's behalf, bombed the coroner's court in Flinders Street. Fortunately, he panicked and threw the bomb too early, causing only minor damage. Five days later, on 14 May, he died of a heroin overdose. He was then twenty-one and, like so many others, had been introduced to the drug in prison. There was speculation, with nothing to back it up, that Dennis had given him the fatal overdose.

Those who knew Jamie claimed he was frightened of injections and would never inject himself.

Dennis Allen must have been passing high-quality information to the police because this career criminal was repeatedly given bail and, on conviction, was being bailed pending appeal. At the time of his death three years later, he was awaiting trial on no less than sixty charges. He had suffered one minor inconvenience on the way. On 21 January 1986 he appeared at the County Court in respect of charges of possessing heroin relating back to 1983. Two days later there was a police raid on his home; seven pistols, two shotguns and a silencer were found. Two days after that Allen was shot in the leg. He hoped that this ruse would abort the trial but the judge merely adjourned it until Allen was fit. It resumed on 3 June and this time he swallowed a small dose of rat poison. Again the judge retained the jury but Allen had his way when the jury was shown books of photographs, one of which contained a picture of some gelignite, the charge in respect of which had been dropped. A retrial never took place although the case was relisted for the September.

It was after this that Allen committed the murder for which he is best known—that of Anthony John Kenny, who was a member of the Nomads, a sister chapter of the Hells Angels Outlaw Motorcycle Gang (OMCG). Kenny, as befitting any self-respecting renegade biker, had convictions for theft, assault and rape. On his release he was involved in the supply of amphetamines to prostitutes. He was arrested at the home of Roger Biddlestone, a key member of the amphetamine supply group. Then this vice-president of the Nomads committed a mortal sin: he cooperated with the police and was expelled from the chapter. He drifted on the fringes of crime and drugs and was introduced to Dennis Allen, with whom he became friendly.

On 7 November 1985 after an afternoon's drinking at the Allen house with his friend Peter Robertson and some others,

Kenny was shot. An essential for any killer is to have the ability to dispose of the body quickly and cleanly or else to walk away. Allen lacked talent in this field. 'Dennis was good as a killer but not as a disposalist,' said Jason Ryan, son of Vickie Brooks, Kath Pettingill's third child, so adding a new word to the English language. After Allen had killed Helga Wagnegg it was left to his brother Victor Peirce to dispose of the body. Again it was Peirce who was the disposer. He took a chainsaw and, when that became jammed full of skin and blood, used a chopper on the legs so the body would fit in an oil drum. Filled with cement and Kenny, it was rolled into the Yarra River at Kew. Peter Robertson was charged and acquitted when Kath Pettingill told the court that Dennis had confessed to her that it had been his finger on the trigger. By this time, Allen was dead and so the jury was deprived of his testimony. Allen had a heart condition and when his health deteriorated in January 1987 he entered hospital, staying nearly two months. His drug intake was by then totally out of control; he would keep himself awake on drugs for up to a fortnight. He was, recalls Adrian Tame, former *Truth* journalist and Kath Pettingill's biographer, 'a truly frightening human'. As Allen left hospital on 11 March he was arrested and charged with the murder of Wayne Stanhope. He could no longer walk and had to be moved in a wheelchair. His luck both in and out of the courts had run out. He was remanded in custody and returned to St Vincent's Hospital, where he died on 13 April.

By 1995 three of the family—Peter, Victor and Trevor—were serving sentences. Jason Ryan was surviving tenuously on the outside after being discharged from the witness protection scheme. In 2002, Peter Allen, by now regarded as one of the best jailhouse lawyers in the state, was released from his sentence for armed robbery. He was subsequently convicted of yet another robbery, which took place in January that year, and sentenced to a total of nine months' imprisonment. The conviction was quashed on 6 February 2006. The next year, serving fifteen months for burglary, he claimed his sentences had been miscalculated and sought a writ of *habeus corpus*.

After her last release from prison following a drugs conviction, Kath Pettingill moved to Venus Bay, a small town some three hours outside Melbourne, where, perhaps surprisingly, she has become a pillar of the community, receiving a Community Service Certificate. An innately well-mannered woman, 'She has a magnetism, you can't ignore her,' says Tame.

But all was still not straightforward for the Pettingill clan. On 1 May 2002, Victor Peirce was shot dead as he sat in his car in Bay Street, Port Melbourne. Apart from a shoplifting charge, described by his solicitor as 'shitty little', he had not been in court for some years. Nevertheless it was thought he was still heavily involved in the cocaine industry and that his execution was over a $29 000 debt. Either that or he was killed because he had accepted a contract and failed to deliver. His death drew a number of notices, including an oblique one from Chopper Read: 'Don't worry Vic, Kath will keep an eye on things.' In 2007 the police claimed it was Benji Veniamin, a member of Melbourne's New Boys, who had killed Peirce on the basis that if he had not shot first, Peirce would have killed him. Wendy Peirce, Victor's wife, was controversially awarded $153 000 by the Victims of Crime Assistance Tribunal in 2007. In 2009 the man who drove Veniamin to Bay Street that day was found guilty of being an accessory to the murder.

There was more trouble for the family in September 2008 when Wendy Peirce was sentenced to six months for threatening and stalking her former husband's lovers. There was worse to come in March the following year when she and her twenty-four-year-old daughter Katie were charged with attempted murder after allegedly arranging for twenty-two-year-old heroin addict Tong Yang to launch a meat cleaver attack at the Clare Castle Hotel, Port Melbourne, which left its victim, Mark Lohse, with a slashed face. Unfortunately, Lohse was the wrong target. Tong Yang seems to have been paid only half his $200 fee when it was discovered he had attacked the wrong man. A Robert Sales said he thought he had been the intended victim; his daughter had begun a relationship with a former lover of Katie Peirce. In October 2009, Tong Yang, who pleaded guilty, was jailed for six years and six months.

Then, on 15 December 2009, Katie, mother of two-year-old Zoe, was found dead in a house in Greensborough. She had been staying there with a Wayne Evorall. Her underwear, clothes and handbag were reported to be missing. Initially the police noted no obvious injuries but the coroner's report said that there were mysterious bruises to her body and bruising under her right eye. The Pettingill family believed she had been given a hotshot, although there was apparently no heroin in her body. The death certificate lists the cause of death as pneumonia 'in the setting of mixed drug toxicity'.

In May 2010, twenty-one-year-old Jamie Pettingill, the son of Trevor, pleaded guilty to an attack on a man outside a nightclub in Russell Street in April 2009. It was his first appearance for a crime of violence, the court was told. He was jailed for thirty months, wholly suspended. A co-accused, Jay Young, who was on a suspended sentence at the time of the incident, drew a three-year sentence with a minimum of twelve months to be served.

In January 2011, Wendy Peirce was arrested for allegedly trying to steal a trolley full of groceries from a St Kilda supermarket. The charges relating to the Port Melbourne attack had already been dropped. By then she was almost completely estranged from the family.

Victoria's Finest

11

For many years politicians and high-ranking officers in the Victorian police force believed that, while corruption thrived in New South Wales, when it came to the Murray River it drowned. They were deluding themselves and others with them. From the foundation of the force there were troubles at all levels.

In 1851, after Victoria separated from New South Wales, a fine-sharing policy was introduced in an effort to recruit constables. Naturally, this had disastrous consequences. The police were keen to weed out sly-groggers, whose convictions produced fines, while serious assaults, which did not, went undetected. It was after the April 1852 robbery of the barque *Nelson*, when some 232 kilograms of gold was stolen, that arrangements were made to recruit police from England and the first of the many commissions and committees was appointed to examine policing in Victoria.

After the subsequent inquiry the first chief commissioner, William Henry Mitchell, was appointed, but, unfortunately for the force, he lasted little more than a year before he resigned due to his deteriorating health. *The Argus*, never a supporter of the early police, paid tribute:

> Nothing could be worse than its condition when he took the reins ... corruption, perjury, ruffianism of every description were rife throughout the force, till it had become a public nuisance, not a safe-guard. In a few short months, with the aid of a strong will, a sense of duty and a competent intelligence,

all this has been so far reformed, that to calm observers like ourselves, it appears little short of miraculous.

The first long-lasting commissioner, the gambler, drinker and womaniser Captain Frederick Charles Standish, was not such a success. Born in England on 20 April 1824, he was one of the most popular men on the racecourse until, in 1852, he was forced to sell his mortgaged properties to pay his gaming debts and set sail for the colonies. He was appointed assistant commissioner of the goldfields, and in September 1858 he became chief commissioner of police in Victoria at a salary of £1200. In 1853 he had already been rejected for an appointment when he applied under an assumed name.

He was not a good choice. Standish certainly undertook some reforms, including the use of the telegraph and the railway for communication and transport, but his control was lax and he did not believe in any formal training for officers. There was preferment for Irish Catholics, who made up 82 per cent of the force. From 1860 to 1863 there were no fewer than three select committees looking into Standish's administration; the third suggested he be replaced. He survived. Standish also had a close interest in the leading brothels in the city and it was he who took the Duke of Edinburgh on a tour during his visit to Melbourne. Clearly Standish had an artistic eye. One of his preferences was for naked white women placed on black chairs.

Standish did not, however, survive the Ned Kelly outbreak. Legend has it that the hunt for Kelly was suspended while the weights for the Melbourne Cup were declared. After his resignation he continued his rackety ways. In 1882 he was nearly thrown through the window of the Melbourne Club by Colonel Craigie Helkett, whom he had called by a 'provocative name'. He died in the club on 19 March 1883 of cirrhosis of the liver. His appropriate legacy is the Standish Handicap, run at Flemington on New Year's Day.

After Kelly's capture there were serious concerns about the inefficiency of the country police and, more importantly, the corruption among those in Melbourne. In particular, one superintendent, Fred Winch, who had conducted a system of organised corruption, had allowed sly-grog shops, prostitution and gambling to flourish over a twenty-year period. He had also blocked honest Melbourne police trying to stamp out these pursuits. He was allowed to retire without charges, his pension intact. The Detective Branch was seen by the Longmore Commission of 1881 as a 'standing menace to the community'. It was institutionally corrupt and there were also complaints about the uncontrolled use of informers. The commission recommended that the Detective Branch be disbanded. Nevertheless, the force was still the place to be; in 1888, 500 young men applied for the fifty positions available.

Even the great successes of the Melbourne police were not above suspicion. The well-known thief John Christie was thought to have lived with the wife of Levi Walker while the skeleton key maker and bank robber was in Pentridge. Worse, he had 'dressed her like a lady'. Christie, who resigned in dubious circumstances, was not a fan of the efforts of the force. However, it may have been a bit of sour grapes when he wrote: 'One does not expect the genius of a Sherlock Holmes for comparatively small wages but the pretensions of the Victorian force are such as to warrant the public in expecting a high average of successes.'

Chief Commissioner Thomas O'Callaghan led a chequered life. He joined the police aged twenty-two in November 1867 and, after becoming a detective, he was reduced to the ranks in 1871 for supplying liquor to a prisoner. Eleven years later he was accused of exhibiting disrespectful behaviour towards the 1882 Longmore Commission which declared him 'not trustworthy'. Despite this he was promoted to inspector in 1892, superintendent three years later and chief commissioner in July 1902. The 1905 Cameron Royal Commission found 'many blemishes' in his administration and that he had an improper interest in licensed premises in Carlton. However, he remained in office until he retired on 31 March 1913. He is the prototype of the corrupt commissioner Thomas Callinan in Frank Hardy's novel *Power without Glory*.

In November 1923 the dreadfully underpaid Melbourne police staged a three-day strike. It followed a long struggle led by Constable William Brooks to obtain better conditions, more pay, a reduction in hours and longer meal breaks. The officers had no confidence in their then commissioner, Alexander Nicholson, who until recently had been stationed in Ballarat and consequently had no idea of the problems confronting a city force. To add to their complaints he introduced a system of secretly monitoring beat officers with special supervisors known as Spooks. Beat officers found indulging in unacceptable behaviour, such as taking free meals or sleeping on their shift, would be reported and fined or more severely disciplined. When two officers were found drinking tea and fined, the night shift refused to go out. Nicholson did have the sense to declare that the supervisory system would be amended but the premier, Harry Lawson, totally misjudged the force's mood and announced that in effect they could like it or lump it, and they chose the latter. This meant the city was now in the hands of criminals who mugged and robbed; store windows were smashed and the stores looted, trams were set on fire. A thousand 'specials' were brought in to quell the rioters and, after four hours of fighting, the streets were once again under control. By the end one ex-soldier had been killed and 237 civilians were in hospital. In the wash-up two officers were dismissed and 634 were discharged, which effectively meant the end of their police careers. Only two were employed by other forces. Brooks was not even called to give evidence at the subsequent Royal Commission.

The distinguished army officer Thomas Blamey began and ended his police career as chief commissioner in scandal. His appointment on 1 September 1925 when he was forty-one was generally well received by property owners and police alike. It also averted the possibility of an inquiry into allegations of corruption in the force, particularly the Licensing Branch. Now that Blamey, with his fine war record, had been appointed, the 'right man' was in the post and things would soon be cleaned up.

Indeed Blamey had many suitable qualities. As a military man he looked on the force as a similar operation and was innovative in matters such as training, man management and organisation. He also increased wages. Unfortunately he held the view that liquor was an adult version of mother's milk and should be available to all with as little let or hindrance as possible. He could be found in smart hotels drinking after hours on a regular basis, something that provided, for the right people, a cast-iron guarantee against police raids.

Worse, on 21 October 1925, within weeks of his appointment, someone who carried the commissioner's police badge Number 80 was found in a brothel in Bell Street, Fitzroy, run by Mabel Tracey, who masqueraded as a teacher of elocution. When the place was raided by three constables from the Licensing Branch, the holder had an explanation: 'It's all right boys, I'm a plainclothes constable. Here is my badge.' All the constables agreed that it was not Blamey who held the badge, although it was definitely his.

Blamey maintained that the badge must have been removed from his key ring the day before the raid and that he found it three days later in his locker at his club. However, his next-in-command, Superintendent Daniel Lineham, said quite specifically that he had seen the badge on Blamey's desk only seven hours before the raid. A public inquiry was refused and instead Lineham was accused of disloyalty. Now Blamey produced a witness, an old army friend, who said he had been with Blamey and his family from 9 p.m. until just before midnight on the night of the raid. The best and most likely explanation is that Blamey lied to protect a married friend who had met him after dinner at the club and asked him if he had any grog in his locker. Blamey had handed over his key ring with his badge on it telling the man to drop it back later. He was rather admired for his refusal to betray his friend but it was hardly a good example to the lower ranks. Indeed it is a classic example of how corruption spreads in a police force.

While Blamey restored morale among his officers, he lacked judgment, and importantly he dismissed a series of allegations of corruption and brutality—thirty in 1933 alone—against officers.

His career ended with another fudged cover-up. On Saturday 23 May 1936 the head of CIB, Superintendent John O'Connell Brophy, was in St Vincent's Hospital suffering from a gunshot wound. Brophy was highly regarded by the underworld and celebrated in the couplet, 'Ashes to ashes and dust to dust; if Brophy don't get you then Piggott [his colleague] must.' He had accidentally shot himself in the right arm while handling a pistol. Unfortunately those who visited him in hospital could see that he had also been shot in the face and the chest. 'Injuries [that], even for the most persistent pistol cleaner, it would have been difficult to receive,' said LEB Stretton, counsel at the subsequent inquiry. It was time for a revision of the facts. Now the heroic officer had been shot while chasing car bandits near the zoo. The press did not give up and on 5 June the county court judge Hugh Macindoe was appointed as royal commissioner to investigate the shooting of Brophy and the subsequent press statements made by Blamey. What was quite clear was that Brophy had been with a chauffeur and two women that night. All sorts of lame explanations—such as meeting in the dead of night with an informer—were offered as to how he came to be chasing dangerous bandits with innocent spectators at risk.

Forty-four witnesses, including both Blamey and Brophy, were called and much of the time was spent trying to refute 'scandalous' allegations that Brophy had been shot by an 'enraged' husband. Later there were allegations that Brophy was half naked and practising cunnilingus on his companion when the gunman approached. There were other, unproved, stories that it was Blamey who was having sex and O'Connell was sacrificed to protect him.

On 2 July, Macindoe submitted his report, which many saw as a whitewash. Unfortunately for Blamey, he said of the commissioner: 'I cannot accept his evidence that he believed it was an accident... [he] gave replies which were not in accordance with the truth, with the sole purpose of secreting from the press the fact that women were in the company of Superintendent Brophy.'

Blamey was finished. On 9 July he was required to submit his resignation. At first he tried to bluster his way out but he was told that if he resigned he could have a pension of £260 per annum but not otherwise. He resigned. The official police history whitewashes him: 'his only crime being a desire to preserve the reputation of his Force'. Blamey returned to the army where he served with great credit in World War II, becoming Australia's first field marshal, although General Douglas MacArthur, the allies' supreme commander in the Pacific, described him as 'sensual, slothful' and a 'doubtful character'.

When it came to it, the Brophy incident had not been the only cause of Blamey's fall. Apart from the fact that he routinely dismissed any complaints against his force, there had been allegations in 1930, 1933 and again in 1936 that officers were using the 'third degree' to get confessions. The first two had been brushed aside but on the third occasion Chief Justice Sir Frederick Mann commented publicly on police brutality, saying it was a 'growing evil', before he began to sum up in a rape case in which a sixty-year-old man claimed he had been beaten into making a confession.

Brutality allegations against Victorian police continued over the following decades and in 1971 one talented officer, Detective Brian 'Skull' Murphy, fell from grace following the death of Neil Collingburn, a painter and docker and skilled safebreaker. He was asked to go to Russell Street Police Headquarters to explain the ownership of a set of golf clubs. A fight broke out in the station and Collingburn died as a result of injuries he sustained. Murphy and a colleague were charged with his manslaughter and acquitted, but not before waterside workers stopped work on the day of Collingburn's funeral and they and students marched to put a mock coffin on the steps of the Russell Street headquarters. It turned out that Collingburn did indeed own the clubs.

* * *

One of the easier targets for corrupt police officers to stand over was the abortion racket. Throughout the latter half of 1969 the abortion reform advocate Dr Bertram Wainer, who had a practice in St Kilda, made allegations claiming that police officers were taking money from abortionists. On 9 December 1969 he handed in affidavits to *Truth*, which forwarded them to the Solicitor-General. They contained allegations that payments ranged from $600 to a lump sum of $1200, which would include cover for the 'possible fatality' of a patient. The chief commissioner was directed to investigate the complaints but five out of six officers refused to see him. The government then appointed an independent one-man board of inquiry in the form of William Kaye QC. The principal allegation was that, since 1953, some members of the elite Homicide Squad had been paid $150 a week each to look after the interests of abortionists.

The next year the formerly highly regarded Superintendent Jack Matthews, Jack Ford and two other officers were in the dock. One was Fred 'Bluey' Adam, there on the allegations of Peggy Berman who was claiming he had stood over doctors at the abortion clinic where she worked in return for warning them of police raids. Berman, who was godmother to a child of standover man Norman Bradshaw, claimed the doctors has been the victim of what she called a somersault. They had, she claimed, been paying Adam, who had passed them on to Ford, Matthews and the fourth officer,

Marty Jacobson, who demanded even more money. In particular, Berman had been giving Ford (her lover and then head of the Homicide Squad) a $600 monthly retainer from her employers as well as $200 a month of her own money for two or three years to pay his gaming debts.

In the trial Ford heaped abuse on his former mistress, claiming he thought she had tried to kill him. She had, he said, injected poison into a bottle of whisky through the cork with a hypodermic needle. It did none of them any good. Matthews and Ford were jailed for five years and released in rather under half that. Jacobson served thirteen months. Matthews was later given a job writing on consumer affairs at *Truth*, the magazine whose campaign had led to his destruction. He was assigned the chair of Evan Whitton, the journalist who had exposed him, but he took these humiliations in good part—perhaps he had no alternative. Adam was acquitted and died of stomach cancer on 14 April the next year. Also suffering from cancer, Berman unexpectedly survived after being told in the 1960s that she had only eighteen months to live. In 1973 she wrote her autobiography. She died aged seventy-nine after a heart attack in December 2002.

In 1975, following more allegations by Dr Wainer, Barry Beach QC held a fifteen-month-long inquiry, at the end of which he made adverse findings against fifty-five officers. It was an inquiry at which some of the cream of Melbourne's crime world gave evidence. Thirty-two officers were charged, but, following threats of strike action from the Police Union, none came to trial. The celebrity criminal Chopper Read has claimed that Wainer, who died in 1987, was not all he might have been and would patch up shot criminals with no questions asked.

Eight years later came another scandal. Following an internal investigation, *Operation Cobra*, the prosecution alleged that, from 1978 to 1982, Paul William Higgins, a former wrestler and twenty-year veteran of the Victoria Police, led a ring of corrupt officers working for the wealthy Geoffrey Lamb, Melbourne's brothel king of the day. Lamb, whose empire included an estimated twenty-five illegal massage parlours and who owned two luxury homes in Hawthorn and Kew as well as a Lamborghini, had extremely expensive personal habits. His lavish informal parties involved recreational use of drugs as well as women. When Lamb came to the conclusion in 1977 that he could use a little police protection, he contacted someone he knew in the New South Wales police who, for a fee of $10000, put him in contact with Higgins. He and other police officers were invited into Lamb's circle and girls were on the house, a facility of which Higgins regularly availed himself.

Lamb would regularly carry up to $10000 in cash, which came in handy because he was soon paying thousands of dollars to police each month as protection money. In exchange, his sex empire flourished as the police on his payroll would warn him about any raids planned for his various parlours on the city fringes. Money was handed over on the first of the month in the back room in the office of Higgins's squad. In return Higgins and others were able to stop investigations in their tracks, fabricate evidence if necessary and even lean on the working girls if they were thought to be taking it too easy.

Higgins would instruct junior officers in his squad to make false entries on running sheets when Lamb was visited. On one occasion an officer was taken by Higgins to one of Lamb's establishments at Rathdowne Street, Carlton, and sent in to pick up a gun from Lamb. Higgins then allegedly told him to record that the .32 revolver had been received from a Drummond Street dobber. Lamb himself alleged that he had been told by Higgins that, if questioned by police internal investigators, he was to say he was an informant. On his behalf Higgins and another detective helpfully planted a number of bombs in rival concerns. They also planted a tin of detonators in a child's toy box at the home of rival

James Robert Slater on 9 August 1978 at the height of one of the periodic brothel wars which broke out in the city.

Another significant soldier in Geoffrey Lamb's army was the armed robber and killer Alistair Farquhar 'Sandy' MacRae, said to be Lamb's second in command and believed to be involved in up to twenty suspicious deaths or disappearances. Higgins and Lamb finally fell out over an affair the detective had with Lamb's wife, Lorraine Goyne, who later died from a drug overdose. Lamb's empire began to crumble when he fell for a gorgeous ex-model turned prostitute who had also succumbed to heroin. He tried to help her break her addiction but instead ended up using himself. In 1991 at Higgins's preliminary hearing, Lamb meekly told the court he had blown $20000 a week on heroin and had used up all his brothel profits. Once, MacRae, in one of the kinder acts of an untidy life, had chained him to a bungalow wall on his Mildura property in an effort to wean him off the drug.

On 6 April 1993, Higgins received a seven-year jail sentence with a five-year minimum when convicted of conspiracy to pervert the course of justice after pleading not guilty. To his great chagrin, much of the evidence against him was supplied by MacRae. The cost to the taxpayer of the investigation and trial was more than $30 million. In 2004, Lamb died, aged sixty-one, in an armchair in his modest West Heidelberg home.

* * *

From the middle of the 1980s the Melbourne police and the underworld were at each other's throats, often with fatal and sometimes tragic results. On 7 October 1985 gelignite and detonators were stolen from the Tryconnel Mine at Blackwood. On 17 March the next year a Holden Commodore was stolen and on 25 March, packed with the explosives, it was parked in a no-standing zone in front of Russell Street Police Headquarters. Shortly after 1 p.m.

the vehicle was detonated by remote control, killing Constable Angela Taylor and injuring twenty others, including magistrate Iain West and Constable Carl Donadio, who were leaving the Melbourne Magistrates' Court across the road at the time. Damage to the headquarters building was estimated at more than $1 million. After a painstaking reconstruction of the car and the bombs, Craig William Minogue and career criminal, robber and one-time actor Stanley Taylor were convicted and sentenced to life for the murder of Constable Taylor. Minogue's brother Rodney had his murder conviction quashed by the Victoria Court of Appeal. Peter Michael Reed—who was alleged to have shot at the police when he was arrested but, in an unsworn statement in court, claimed they had opened fire first—was acquitted of the murder but sentenced to thirteen years for possessing explosives and resisting arrest. He later married Nicola, daughter of the drug dealers Terrence and Christine Hodson. The motive for the bombing seems to have been revenge against the police over previous convictions and sentences.

In the two-year period from 1987 eleven suspects were shot dead by the police. And the underworld ultimately retaliated in cowardly fashion. Victims of the police included Mark Militano, who was a member of a group of criminals from the Flemington–Ascot Vale area specialising in armed robberies. On 25 March 1987 he was shot six times by members of the Armed Robbery Squad outside his Kensington flat when they went to question him. One bullet lodged in the back of his neck as he was running away. The coroner found that he had been pointing a gun over his shoulder before he was shot. One member of Militano's team who survived, only to die in prison, was Santo Mercuri, convicted of an armed robbery on 11 July 1988 when $33000 was stolen and a security guard, Dominik Hefti, was shot.

In the most celebrated case, Graeme Jensen left a hardware store in Narre Warren in Melbourne's outer east on 11 October 1988 and climbed into his Commodore sedan. He was approached by members of the Armed Robbery Squad who told him not to move. Instead he accelerated. Officers opened fire and Jensen was shot in the back of the head. By the time the car crashed into a power pole Jensen was already dead. At the inquest the evidence was that the police saw him pick up a weapon and they shot to protect themselves. A sawn-off bolt-action shotgun was produced which they said had been found in the car. Jensen's friends and relations would not accept the evidence.

There is no doubt that Jensen, then aged thirty-three and described as something of a lady killer, was an armed robber by profession. He had convictions from the age of fifteen, when he had robbed a bank and been sent to a detention centre. This had been followed by imprisonment for housebreaking and, at the age of twenty-three, three more charges of armed robbery. He had escaped from custody and robbed yet another bank. Released in 1987 he had, said the police, resumed his profession. At the time of his death he was suspected of being part of the team that specialised in bank robberies in the inner western suburbs. It was over the Hefti killing that the police wished to question Jensen.

Around 4 a.m. on the day after Jensen's death a newsagent, going to open his shop, saw a Commodore parked in Walsh Street, South Yarra. It was empty but the lights were on, the doors open, the windows smashed. He telephoned the police and Constables Steven Tynan and Damian Eyre were sent to investigate. While they were looking at the damage they were attacked. Tynan was shot in the head at almost point-blank range and Eyre, who had an instant's notice of the attack and tried to struggle with the gunman, was shot three times. It was the first multiple killing of police officers since Ned Kelly's gang shot three officers near Mansfield, northeast of Melbourne in 1878.

The police hunt that followed the double shooting was, not unexpectedly, massive, and the Victorian Government posted a $200 000 reward. With a hundred police drafted to comb the underworld, the crime rate dropped. One of the men whose name came into the frame was Jedd Houghton, a known friend of Jensen. He was traced to Bendigo, where he was staying in a caravan park with his girlfriend. A listening device was planted and discovered by Houghton. The police, listening before he dismantled it, realised their cover was blown and moved to arrest him. He was still in the caravan park when the police opened fire and he was hit with two shotgun blasts. He died instantly and his friends believed that he had been shot as a reprisal for Walsh Street.

Seventeen-year-old Jason Ryan, an accomplished little thief, named Gary Abdallah as being involved in the Walsh Street shooting. Ryan, a member of the extended Pettingill family, had been convicted of a drug-dealing offence and, deciding cooperation was the best way towards daylight, became an informant.

On 22 February, Abdallah went to see the police with his solicitor and was told that it was only rumour against him. Six weeks later, on 9 April, he was killed when police not connected with the Walsh Street inquiry shot him. They said he had threatened them with a firearm. It turned out to be an imitation one and again friends of the victim refused to accept the official version. Abdallah died after forty days in a coma.

Jason Ryan, it appeared, had been trying to deflect interest from himself but on 31 October the police arrested him over the Walsh Street attack, along with two Pettingill sons, Victor Peirce and Trevor Pettingill, as well as Ryan's best friend, Anthony Leigh Farrell, and Peter David McEvoy, who lodged with Ryan's mother. The police named Jedd Houghton as the sixth man involved in the Walsh Street attack.

Ryan, who became a witness for the Crown, gave the following self-exculpatory version of the killings. The other four had stolen the Commodore, left it in Walsh Street and waited for the police to come. Ryan had not wanted to be involved and had stayed behind. When they returned Farrell told Ryan that he was the one who had done the shooting. There was some backup to the story from Peirce's de facto Wendy, who temporarily disappeared into the witness protection program. At first she had stood staunch and given Victor Peirce a false alibi but in July 1989 she made a thirty-page witness statement and asked to go into the scheme, claiming her husband had a pathological hatred of the police.

At the committal proceedings Wendy Peirce gave evidence that on the night of the police murders her husband had left her and the children at a motel saying, 'Don't worry I won't be late. I'm going to kill the jacks that knocked Graeme [Jensen].' The next morning he had told her they were dead. At a pre-trial hearing in January 1991, Wendy Peirce walked out of the witness protection program and declined to give evidence. Found guilty of perjury in December 1992, she was sentenced to eighteen months' imprisonment with a minimum of nine to be served. In her absence the case now effectively depended on the evidence of Ryan, whose story became less and less credible as he was questioned and who finally admitted to a string of lies. By the time he came to give evidence he was on his fifth version of events. There were no eyewitnesses and no forensic or fingerprint evidence of the men to assist the prosecution. On 26 March 1991, after a retirement of six days, to no one's great surprise the jury returned a verdict of not guilty on all the men. *The Age* reporter Peter Gregory thought that the Crown evidence left the jury with 'no other option'. The trial was another estimated to have cost around $30 million.

It was only after Peirce's death on 1 May 2002 that Wendy Peirce admitted that he had in fact told her he killed the Walsh Street policemen. Her apparent move to the prosecution and away from the family had been a ruse to weaken the case against him. More recently she has blamed the police for provoking the Walsh Street killings by shooting Jensen, with whom she had had an affair. In January 2011 she said she would refuse to answer questions if a new inquest was convened.

Later, when a man from a different team was arrested, it became clear that Jensen and his firm had not been involved in the murder of security guard Domenic Hefti, which had begun the trail of events. The actual robbers are now alleged to have included Jason Moran, his father Lewis and Russell 'Mad Dog' Cox.

Into the New Century

12

In recent years, with the profits to be made from drugs, particularly amphetamines, things in the crime scene have changed radically. One of the reasons for the rise of gang violence in Melbourne stems at least in part from the high-risk policy, adopted by the police in Victoria during the 1990s, of using their own purchases of pseudoephedrine in an attempt to break into the city's network of dealers.

Amphetamines, which are relatively easy to produce, were being cooked in small illegal laboratories. The profits were many and the dangers few. There were even instances of people cooking amphetamines in the back of their car while they slept in the front. A conviction for a major trafficking in heroin could earn twenty years and upwards; for a similar amphetamine conviction the penalty was a quarter or a third of that. By 1990 Melbourne had become the amphetamine capital of Australia. Two years later, producers, rather than distributors, were to be the main target of the police.

There were other changes to policing practice around this time. The Victorian Drug Squad, far from being enlarged to try to stem the tide of heroin flooding the markets in 1992, was divided into three units. The first was to investigate the Asian heroin syndicates, the second the Romanian drugs gangs and the third the local amphetamine market. By the middle of the decade a system had been devised whereby the police would buy chemicals from wholesalers and, under a system of controlled deliveries, officers or their trusted informers—if that is not an oxymoron—would sell the chemicals on to the producers, providing evidence for prosecutions.

All well and good in theory. In the three years from 1998 nearly sixty clandestine laboratories were discovered. In 1999, a man regarded as Australia's biggest amphetamines manufacturer was arrested and sentenced to four years and a Melbourne identity was charged with conspiracy involving a shipping container of chemicals. But then the wheels began to fall off. There were allegations that chemicals were being stockpiled by the police; a secret bank account was opened and sometimes chemicals went missing. In December 2001 the Drug Squad was disbanded and replaced with a major drug investigation division. But the damage had been done.

Opinion over the cause of the violent troubles in the city varies, but everyone agrees that drugs have been the catalyst. The violence stems from either the amphetamine manufacturer's arrest or the murder of Melbourne gang figure Alphonse John Gangitano in Templestowe in 1998, or possibly both. Whichever is correct, a long-running turf war resulted, with the Sunshine Crew, sometimes known as the New Boys, from the inner western suburbs, co-led by Carl Williams and a henchman who did much of the dirty work of killing people, Andrew 'Benji' Veniamin, struggling for power against the more established, if loose-knit, Carlton Crew, whose members included Gangitano, Jason and Mark Moran, and Graham 'The Munster' Kinniburgh. Since 1998 there have been more than thirty gangland killings in Melbourne, many of which can be linked to the power struggle between the rival bosses. Had he still been alive, the contract killer Chris Flannery would have been a rich man.

At first everyone seemed to get on well together, drinking and dancing in the city's clubs—Monday night would be Billboard night, Tuesday at Chasers and a third night at Sheiks—but then the drug trade, pride and that often fatal notion of respect reared their ugly heads.

Williams had left school at the age of eleven and was soon selling amphetamines, moving steadily up the criminal hierarchy. His father George, who was thought by some to be the real brains behind the operation, pleaded guilty in 2005 to dealing in a commercial amount of amphetamines and was sentenced to four and a half years with a minimum of twenty months to be served.

Gangitano was known as the Robert De Niro of Lygon Street. He had no visible means of support and in his will gave his occupation as 'Gentleman'. The leader of the Carlton Crew was regarded as unstable. 'One minute he'd be charming, polite and the next he'd go psycho on you. He'd drive along the pavement knocking over dustbins,' recalls one former friend. In 1991 Gangitano believed that a contract had been taken out for his execution by Chopper Read; he retreated with his family to Italy. He only returned when Read was jailed in October 1992 following his conviction for the attempted murder of biker and drug dealer Sid Collins in Tasmania.

Gangitano was said to be involved in horserace fixing and to have connections with west coast identities. At the time of his death he was awaiting trial on a charge of affray but he had previously faced far more serious legal challenges. He was confidently suspected of killing popular gangland figure Gregory John Workman. The two went to a wake together and had then gone on to a party to raise bail for an alleged robber. Gangitano became abusive and he and Workman went outside. Two sisters saw the shooting and made detailed statements of seeing Gangitano almost literally with a smoking gun in his hand. The women went into a form of protective custody, living in a caravan, dining on takeaway food and collecting changes of clothes at a roadside stop. Unfortunately, thanks to the authorities, it was not all that protective. The sisters were contacted by Carlton Crew stalwart Jason Moran, who told them that if they gave evidence they and their families would certainly be killed. They were taken to see a lawyer and made statements withdrawing their evidence after which they absented themselves from Victoria, spending a year in Europe on a trip paid for by Gangitano. Inevitably the charges were dismissed and Gangitano's lawyer, George Defteros, put in a bill to the police for $69 975.35. At the time it was thought highly probable that East St Kilda criminals would exact revenge for Workman's death, but none came immediately.

Three years later Gangitano had other problems. He had fallen out with the Moran brothers, who now controlled a large part of the drug dealing organised from Lygon Street in Carlton. On 16 January 1998 he was killed in his home, almost certainly by Jason Moran, who, despite limited earning capacity in the outside world, was able to send his children to private schools. Moran, in a link with history, was married to one of Leslie Kane's daughters.

Gangitano's solicitors thought of him as 'a respected business-man, devoted family man and loyal friend'. They inserted a death notice in the *Herald Sun* which read: 'In loving memory of a loyal friend that we now entrust to God. Together now with your dear parents. Partners and Staff, Pryles & Defteros.' Other lawyers were not so sure. One remembers him as a man who 'never ran anything, never was involved in the big money networks ... he had everyone conned but he was really a gambler, never paid his debts and bills.'

Chopper Read may have had little time for Gangitano but his admirers included the bail justice Rowena Allsop, who knew both him and his great friend Dominic 'Mick' Gatto, regarding the fallen leader as a man of parts unknown to those not close to him. In turn Allsop came under some criticism for being as close to Gangitano as she had been. Only a few hours before his death they had been drinking together before his curfew came into effect for the night. Prevailed upon to speak at his funeral—held at the underworld's favourite church, St Mary's Star of the Sea, West Melbourne— dressed in turquoise and her voice trembling with emotion, she spoke of the departed's wit, his love of Oscar Wilde and his passion for Dolce & Gabbana aftershave lotion.

Another tribute placed in the *Herald Sun* was more ambiguous: 'The impression you left on me will stay eternally in my heart.' It was purportedly placed by Jim Pinakos, whose headless and dismembered body—with a steel arrow through the heart—had been found buried in packages on Rye beach in July 1989.

The police believed that the scenario of the killing ran more or less as follows. Jason Moran was involved in an argument with Gangitano and shot him. Although he denied it, also present when 'the Lord of Lygon Street' was killed was Graham Kinniburgh, who saw what was happening and ran out through a security mesh on the front door, cutting himself. Later he went upstairs to see what the security video had recorded. On the sound principle that lies should be as close to the truth as possible he told the police he had indeed been to see Gangitano, who was on the telephone actually speaking to his west coast friend John Kizon, who was having dinner with a barrister in Perth. Gangitano had asked Kinniburgh to leave as he was due to have a meeting with an unnamed man. Kinniburgh went to buy some cigarettes and returned half an hour later only to find his host dead. The coroner had no doubt that both Kinniburgh and Moran were implicated. Moran also posted a touching eulogy in the *Herald Sun*: 'Words can't express how I feel. There will never be a man such as yourself. Whatever I asked of you was done 110 per cent. I will love you always. Your little mate Jase.'

Gangitano's death was followed by other killings in rapid succession—beginning, on 23 November 1998, with that of 'Mad' Charlie Hegyalji in Bambra Road, Caulfield South. A one-time standover man turned amphetamine dealer, the Hungarian-born Hegyalji was either extremely careful or paranoid. He filled notebooks with the numberplates of cars he thought might be following him. His house was surrounded by thick hedges and a security camera covered the front door. His precautions did him no good. His CCTV was not recording when he was shot four times in the head as he walked down his garden path shortly before 1 a.m. The list of people who might have wished to see him dead was endless and an open verdict was returned, with the coroner saying, 'No suspects have been identified.' Two days after Hegyalji was killed, Raymond Mansour, who had convictions for a gamut of offences—including burglary, theft and assault as well as possessing heroin—survived an attempt on his life when, around 2 p.m., he went to a meeting near his Brunswick home and was shot five times with a small-calibre weapon. Mansour staggered to a milk bar in Albion Street and was taken to Royal Melbourne Hospital.

The following year Victor Peirce's one-time employee Vince Mannella died shortly before midnight on 9 January when he was shot and killed outside his home in Alister Street, North Fitzroy. Mannella, regarded as a most personable man, had interests in nightclubs and coffee shops and convictions going back to 1971 when he was found carrying a dagger. On 20 February 1981 he shot the owner of a café in Nicholson Street, North Fitzroy, hitting him seven times. For this he received a minimum sentence of seven years. Almost immediately after his release he was found in one of Gangitano's casinos in Fitzroy along with a speed merchant, and he was under scrutiny by *Operation Phalanx*, the Drug Squad's investigation into Higgs.

In late 1998, Mannella was the receiver for a group that stole wholesale quantities of foodstuffs and it is possible his death stems from problems with that involvement. The preferred and more likely version is that his death was ordered by the same cartel that disposed of Gangitano. Another suggestion is that he was taken out as a pre-emptive strike prior to the killing of his brother Gerardo on 20 October 1999.

* * *

On 13 October 1999, Jason Moran shot Carl Williams in the stomach in a public park in Gladstone Park, Broadmeadows, over a failed amphetamine deal. Williams had been undercutting them and had also supplied them with substandard amphetamines. Mark Moran, who was with his half-brother, urged him to finish Williams off but, unfortunately for the pair and many others, he did not. Gallantly, the wounded man made no complaint and claimed in the teeth of the evidence that he did not know the identity of the shooter. But it took Williams less than a year to exact partial revenge.

On 15 June 2000, Mark Moran, pastry chef, designer drug dealer and standover man, was shot dead as he was getting into his car outside his luxury home in Aberfeldie. Two blasts from a shotgun were followed by one in the head from a revolver. Moran's actual killers were thought to have been Dino Dibra and Benji Veniamin but really there were no prizes for guessing the contractor.

Between the deaths of Gangitano and Mark Moran, eight other identities were killed in Melbourne. Not all of them were necessarily involved in the drugs war. A year after Gangitano's death the fraudster Jim Belios was killed in an underground car park in St Kilda Road during the evening of 9 September 1999. He had been shot in the back of the head. In the days before his death he had been trying to pass fake diamonds as real and he was known to be heavily in debt. The fake diamonds are a more likely reason for his death. Recalcitrant debtors usually receive a beating; debt, in the underworld, tends to die with the debtor.

Frank Benvenuto, shot on 8 May 2000, may have died as part of a long-running struggle for control of the Footscray Wholesale Fruit and Vegetable Market. It is true, however, that shortly before his death he had quarrelled with the Moran brothers. His killer was probably Dino Dibra, highly placed in the Sunshine Crew, whose activities ranged from growing hydroponic marijuana, car rebirthing, kidnap and extortion to the drug dealing that brought the gang into conflict with the Carlton Crew.

The year 2000 was definitely not a good one for the uncommitted and unprotected. First, Richard Mladenich—who liked to be known as King Richard but who was often known as Spade Brain because of injuries he received in a never fully explained incident in Pentridge—was killed in room 18 of the Esquire Motel in Acland Street, St Kilda, at 3.30 a.m. on 16 May. The distinctly odd Mladenich, who allegedly had once been walked off the pier at St Kilda by an infuriated detective, dealt in drugs but had also been the minder for Mark Moran, which may have sealed his fate. A long line of identities might have wished him harm, but his killer was again thought to be Dino Dibra, possibly with an assist from Rocco Arico.

Dibra did not last the year. He was shot outside a house in Krambruk Street, Sunshine, on 14 October. His trio of killers was thought to include Benji Veniamin and another drug dealer, Paul Kallipolitis. However, ex-lawyer Andrew Fraser claims that Lewis Moran told him he had killed Dino Dibra because it was Dibra, rather than Williams, who had had Mark killed.

The next year only saw the end of George Germanos, shot in a park. Germanos, a bad-tempered power lifter, had worked both as a nightclub bouncer and in the drug trade. Shortly before his death he had beaten a well-connected boy who was admitted to hospital. As a result, his death was almost inevitable. On 22 March 2001 he was shot and killed when he went to a meeting in a park in Armadale. Four months later, on 1 May 2002, Victor Peirce went down in Port Melbourne and later that year, on 15 October, Paul Kallipolitis was shot dead at his home in Sunshine. Benji Veniamin was again a suspect in his death.

In late 2002 the Melbourne drug wars appear to have escalated after what was intended to be a peace meeting in the La Porcella restaurant on the corner of Faraday and Rathdowne streets in the Little Italy district of Carlton. Present were representatives of the Carlton Crew and the New Boys as well as west coast biker Troy Mercante and a major independent amphetamine dealer,

Antonios "Tony" Mokbel. The meeting quickly degenerated into violence. The dealer upset Carlton Crew member Nikolai 'The Russian' (sometimes 'The Bulgarian') Radev and, after his bodyguards had been taken out, Mokbel was beaten within an inch of his life. Carl Williams was ordered to take him to a doctor to be patched up and it was then that Williams changed sides. None of the Carlton Crew had intervened to prevent the beating and he felt vulnerable.

Once more the body count began to mount. Sometimes it was personal, but more often it was business. The veteran crime reporter John Silvester, who thought there were simply too many people in Melbourne trying to deal in drugs, saw it as a dangerous game of musical chairs in which the loser was usually shot. An arsonist, extortionist and drug dealer, Radev died in the afternoon of 15 April 2003, shot after he met with what has been described as 'a group of criminal identities' at the Brighton Baths Café. They then drove to Queen Street, Coburg, where Radev was shot. Two men who were with him ran away and so could not identify his killer, believed to be Veniamin allegedly acting on orders from Williams. Nor has the contractor been identified, although it has been alleged Mokbel paid for the hit. Regarded, even in the circles in which he moved, as a violent and dangerous competitor, Radev was thought to have killed a man and taken his identity until his own naturalisation papers came through. His funeral was not well attended.

In May 2003, *Operation Purana*, a team of some sixty detectives, was set up to solve the Melbourne underworld murders and possibly to make pre-emptive strikes towards stopping the feuding. Almost immediately, however, on 21 June 2003, Jason Moran, who had lasted for some years longer than his half-brother, was shot dead in front of his and other children in the car park of the Cross Keys Hotel in Essendon after they had been to an Auskick football clinic.

Moran had already survived one threat to his life when the robber Mark Anthony Smith, who had been convicted and jailed for a minimum of thirteen years for the murder of a man on a Craigieburn building site in 1987, failed to carry out the contract. As a reprisal Smith was shot in the neck on 28 December 2002. He survived and went interstate.

Down with Jason Moran went Pasquale Barbaro, his bodyguard. The killing had been slated for the previous week to coincide with the anniversary of the death of Mark Moran, but the prosecution alleged at the committal of three men accused of the murder that one of them had then failed to spot Jason. Because the killing had been in front of children, it was regarded by some of the underworld as particularly shameful, but over the years it rather set a trend.

Barbaro's death had some unlikely postscripts. Mark and Cheryl McEachran, frustrated by their inability to conceive a sixth child, snatched a three-week-old baby in a shopping centre. Their choice could not have been much more unfortunate. The baby Montana Barbaro was that of Barbaro's cousin Giuseppe, known as Joe, a drug dealer with links to the upper echelons of the crime scene. The child snatchers were jailed for a total of nineteen years and ordered to pay $20 000 to the child's mother. In turn the kidnapping served Joe Barbaro well. He told the court the kidnapping had changed his life, and now thought, 'How could I have put another parent through that sort of agony?' He received a modest five-year minimum for drug dealing.

With the second of the Moran brothers gone, it was probably only a matter of time before a move was made on Graham Kinniburgh. Over the decades, the modest, influential and shadowy Kinniburgh, once a member of the dying breed of safebreakers, rose to become a kingpin of the city's crime scene. With a career spanning three decades, he was one of the relatively few mobsters who have bridged the gap between the underworld and respectability and was well known for his discreet connections to Melbourne's establishment. Born in a slum in Richmond, he was regarded in his early days as having a razor-sharp temper and the ability to back it up with his fists. He began his career as a fringe member of the shoplifting Kangaroo Gang and was then a member of the so-called Magnetic Drill Gang, which was responsible for stealing $1.7 million from a New South Wales bank, a jewellery haul from a Lonsdale Street office, and a raid on safety deposit boxes in Melbourne. He was also thought to have been the organiser of a bullion snatch in Queensland.

Early in his career he was charged with receiving stolen property from a burglary at the home of magnate Lindsay Fox. When the police raided Kinniburgh, he was found to have a unique pendant owned by Mrs Fox in a coat pocket as well as $4500 in cash in a drawer. He offered the police the cash if they did not charge him but they declined. He was charged with both the burglary and the bribery but he had an identical pendant made in Hong Kong, so casting doubt in the minds of the jury that the pendant was, in fact, unique.

Over the years the lantern-jawed Kinniburgh, known as The Munster because of his facial resemblance to the television character Herman Munster, refined his public image. He was seen with barristers and solicitors around the law courts and with owners and jockeys at Caulfield and other Melbourne tracks, where he was a genial and successful tipster as well as being privately regarded as a race fixer. He was said to have been kind enough to help a jockey pay an $80 000 tax bill. Although he claimed to be a simple rigger, he lived in the well-heeled suburb of Kew, could be seen in fashionable restaurants such as The Flower Drum, and was well able to mix socially with the fraternity, the police and straight people alike. He was, said one Melbourne barrister who knew and socialised with him, 'one of the top three crims I ever met'.

In 1994, when Kinniburgh's son married into one of the city's established families, the wedding was held at St Peter's Anglican Church, East Melbourne, and the reception was at the oldest of the Melbourne establishments, the Windsor Hotel. In a scene that could have been taken from *The Godfather*, intelligence police snapped not the bride and groom but the guests, so updating their files. Many of the guests wore Ray-Bans throughout the evening and Kinniburgh's speech was said to have resembled one by Marlon Brando. A few months before his death, his barrister daughter Suzie married the son of a former attorney-general.

In the month before Kinniburgh died he took to carrying a gun, something he had not done since his early days. Shortly before midnight on 13 December 2003, he was shot in the chest as he left his car outside his home and walked to his drive carrying a bag of groceries. It is thought he managed to get one shot off from his own gun. It was said that no gangland killing could be regarded as such until Carlton Crew member Mick Gatto, the semi-official newspaper epitaph writer and tribute payer to so many of the city's underworld figures, had inserted a flowery death notice in the *Herald Sun*. His tribute to The Munster is a fair example of his work:

> You were a true Chameleon, you could adapt to any situation,
> rubbing shoulders with the best of them and being able to talk
> at any level about any topic. I was so proud to be part of your
> life. This has left a void in my heart that can't be replaced. I love
> you 'Pa' and I will never forget you.

Unkind people thought that Kinniburgh's ability to talk to the police on many topics may have helped to keep him out of prison in the years before his death. The week before he died Kinniburgh held a series of meetings in Carlton restaurants with the cream of the local villains. Indeed, the day before he was shot he had been seen having coffee in Lygon Street with a detective from Carlton CIB. Others would have none of it, believing Kinniburgh of all people to be staunch.

* * *

Earlier in the year, two relatively minor figures had left the game. First, Willy Thompson, nightclubber, kickboxer and dealer, was shot and killed in Waverley Road, Chadstone on 21 July as he sat at the wheel of his expensive Honda S-2000 convertible. He had also appeared in films such as the low-budget *The Nightclubber* filmed at the Tunnel nightclub and the Men's Gallery. He had been followed from a martial arts class at the Extreme Jujitsu and Grappling Gym. He may have been a relatively small player but it had been worthwhile for Radev to firebomb his car eighteen months earlier. On 25 October, Thompson's friend Michael Ronald Marshall, who trained at the same gym and who sold lollipops and drugs, was gunned down in front of his son outside the family home in South Yarra as he returned from buying hot dog buns. It was a planned killing and a stolen Ford, believed to have been used by at least one gunman, was found burnt out in Port Melbourne.

The killings climaxed early in 2004 when, on 23 March, Williams' bodyguard Veniamin, now regarded as dangerously erratic, was shot in the head at lunchtime in a back room of La Porcella. He had gone there for a meeting with Mick Gatto. The heavily tattooed Veniamin, a small man who was said to have lively soft brown eyes and was believed to receive $100000 a hit, arrived at the restaurant at 2 p.m. in a borrowed silver Mercedes; which he had double parked. At the time he was disqualified from driving and in the months before his death had racked up some forty speeding and parking tickets.

Gatto was at his usual table. A former heavyweight professional boxer who was regarded as a great fixer, Gatto demanded a fee of $5000 from anyone wishing to sit with him. The Royal Commission into the Building Industry had described him as a standover man; he preferred 'industrial consultant'. Gatto and Veniamin went into a back room and within minutes Veniamin was dead. Later it would be said that Veniamin was on the verge of giving up his criminal enterprises but was reluctant to do so in case it was thought he was a quitter. Quitter or not, at the time of his death the police had him in their sights over five murders, including those of Frank Benvenuto, Dino Dibra, Paul Kallipolitis and Nic Radev. Veniamin died after what has been described as 'an altercation'. As Gatto waited for the police he apologised to the restaurant owner for the undoubted inconvenience caused by the shooting. His good manners could not turn back the clock and the restaurant closed down shortly afterwards. It was said the price on Gatto was now $400000. The word on the street was that Veniamin's close friend and employer Carl Williams would be killed before he arrived at the church to bury his friend. On this occasion, as indeed on so many others, the word was wrong. Over the years there were a number of attacks on Williams and his demise was confidently and regularly, if prematurely, predicted.

Now the deaths and attempted hits came faster. The next to go was Lewis Moran, on 31 March. The decision to kill Jason's father and Mark's stepfather, a man with strong ties to the Painters and Dockers' Union, was said to have been taken at the wake for Veniamin. Lewis Moran had been in the crosshairs, if only because he had offered a mere $50000 for the killing of Williams. It was just thirty hours after Veniamin was buried that Moran was shot in the Brunswick Club on Sydney Road. Two men, one with a hand gun, the other armed with a shotgun, came into the main room of the club, shot and injured Herb Wrout, the man with whom he was drinking, and killed Moran at close range as he was running in a panicked circle. The contract was said to have been worth $140000, not all of which was paid.

In February 2007, Noel Faure, the grandson of the 1920s stand-over man Norman Bruhn, suddenly and unexpectedly pleaded guilty to Moran's murder. Although the gunmen who shot Moran and his offsider were masked, Noel Faure had been caught on CCTV and recognised by a tattoo of a bird on his hand. Said to be in poor health, he was jailed for life with a twenty-three-year minimum after a hearing conducted via video link from prison. On 29 May 2008, Evangelos Goussis, already convicted of the murder of standover man Lewis Caine, was found guilty of the Moran murder and Wrout wounding. On 9 February 2009 he received life imprisonment with a minimum non-parole period of thirty years.

Lewis Caine—also known as Sean Vincent—was shot and killed in a cul-de-sac in Brunswick on 8 May 2004. He must have had some good qualities, even if they were not immediately apparent to the world in general. After all, he charmed the beautiful and otherwise intelligent lawyer Zarah Garde-Wilson off her perch. At the time it was thought he had accepted a contract to take out Carlton Crew member and former lawyer Mario Condello as a reprisal for the death of Benji Veniamin. After his release following the killing of David Templeton in a nightclub fight on 18 September 1988, he took up with Garde-Wilson, then with the firm Pryles and Defteros, in a relationship a court was later told was 'one of integrity and love'. They both began to study reiki with a view to becoming qualified healers. When Caine was killed Garde-Wilson applied unsuccessfully to have his sperm taken and frozen. Of him, a senior underworld figure spoke appreciatively, 'I thought he was trying to go lead a normal life, I don't think he was a gangster or a big timer.'

It was established that the trio of Lewis Caine and his two killers had been drinking in The Plough and Harrow Hotel— once The Canada—in Carlton for some hours before Caine's death. Apparently he became moody and began to question their allegiance. He was shot in his car and, although at first the gunmen claimed they had alibis, later Goussis somehow came to maintain that it was a question of self-defence. Given that Caine's body was found with his seatbelt on, it was, said the prosecution, an unlikely story. There was also the question of what had happened to the gun with which Caine was said to have threatened him.

* * *

As the French gangster Raymond Zemour discovered to his cost years earlier in Paris, walking one's dogs has often been a dangerous time for the gangster. In spring 2004 police foiled an attack on Mario Condello as he walked his Jack Russell terriers close to his home near Brighton cemetery. Perhaps foolishly he then went into print on the subject of the gang wars and within a matter of weeks, along with his own solicitor George Defteros, was arrested for conspiracy to murder Carl Williams. Condello was said to have offered $150 000 a head to kill Williams, his father George and a bodyguard. There was to be a bonus of $50 000 on completion.

Again Condello went into print saying that the enquiries he was making into the value of contracts, and so on, was simply to find out how endangered a species he was himself. Defteros, who adamantly denied any involvement, voluntarily gave up his practising certificate until things were sorted out. Although he was committed for trial, the magistrate indicated that she thought the evidence was slender at best and later a no bill was entered. In March 2005, Condello was given bail on the grounds that he was going 'stir crazy'. He was offered round-the-clock police protection but declined. Defteros now said he would apply for the restoration of his practising certificate and in 2007 he returned to the law and resumed his highly successful career.

On 9 June 2004, Carl Williams himself was arrested and charged with conspiracy to murder Jason Moran and Pasquale Barbaro as well as Michael Ronald Marshall, along with existing charges of conspiracy to murder a police detective and drug trafficking. What did the apparently generous man do for a living? He thought himself to be a commissioner. That is, he bought and sold jewellery on commission. He was remanded in custody and that spring collected a seven-year sentence, with a minimum of five to be served, for a $450 000 drug trafficking operation.

Defended by Robert Richter QC, Mick Gatto went on trial in May 2005 for the murder of Andrew Veniamin at La Porcella the previous year. Gatto maintained that it was Veniamin who had attacked him, and not vice versa, and that while they struggled five shots were fired from Veniamin's gun, which Gatto had managed to turn on him. An expert witness, pathologist Dr Malcolm Dodd, agreed that it was difficult to determine individual reactions to particular injuries and that even people shot in the brain could remain active for a brief time. This produced the unkind comment in *Melbourne Underworld News* on 17 May that, since 'Ol' Benji was brain dead from birth', this was a difficult call to make. Gatto was triumphantly acquitted and after the trial his wife Cheryl told journalists, 'An innocent man has been vindicated and we couldn't be happier.'

By then there had been no *Purana*-related murders for over a year—the last had been that of Caine in May 2004—and as the months wore on, the police became more confident that the Melbourne underworld war on the streets was over. (It may, of course, have transferred to the prisons, where a number of the former participants were now lodged.) The police were wrong and the newly re-appointed police commissioner, Christine Nixon, became a hostage to fortune when on 7 February 2006 she told reporters that the 'gangland issue' was under control. It was certainly not under control so far as Mario Condello was concerned. His trial for inciting murder, in which Condello had expected to give evidence relating to allegations of police corruption, was due to start the following day. But now he was a seriously endangered species.

Instead of Condello making the allegations, his barrister Robert Richter QC told the court: 'Unfortunately, I announce my client won't be answering bail. He was murdered last night,' adding, 'He died confident of his acquittal.' Around ten o'clock the night before his trial, Condello was shot at his Brighton East home as he was talking on the telephone.

Shortly afterwards came the suggestion that there had been another underworld killing. Career criminal Lee Patrick Torney, who had killed Sidney James Graham in a dispute over the proceeds of a bank robbery in Hawthorn, vanished. In March 1999, Torney had been found in possession of twelve rifles and a shotgun. Later he turned informer and became a Crown witness. He was last heard of in April 2005 and fears for his safety increased when he did not appear at his brother's funeral later in the year. One suggestion was that he had been entrusted with a large amount of money to pay a solicitor and somehow was unable to account properly. For some weeks searches in Golden Point near Castlemaine, an area with a large number of abandoned mines, failed to produce his body but it was eventually found badly decomposed at the bottom of a mineshaft. In 2007 his one-time offsider Graham Holden, who had beaten him to death with a shovel, received a minimum sentence of four years. Torney had been standing over him after their cannabis-growing enterprise failed when Holden moved the plants without approval and most of them had died. Unfortunately the coroner's office forgot to return Torney's head with the body, which his family had already cremated before the omission was discovered. His son generously took the mistake in good part, saying his father would have 'laughed his head off'.

Faced with the possibility of life without parole, a number of men whom the underworld had thought might be staunch began to roll over into the arms of the Director of Public Prosecutions; in the hope that they might see the light of day before they were wearing incontinence pads. And most prominent among them was Carl Williams. On 7 May 2007 after a series of plea bargains, Williams pleaded guilty to the murders of the Morans and Nic Radev's offsider Mark Mallia, whose charred body was found in a drain in West Sunshine on 18 August 2003, and conspiracy to murder Mario Condello. Williams had previously been found guilty of the murder of Michael Marshall. Justice Betty King sentenced him to life imprisonment with a minimum of thirty-five years, meaning his earliest release date would be in 2042. He was less than pleased, hurling abuse at the judge and labelling her 'a puppet of *Purana*'.

Outside court Jason Moran's mother Judy was, for once in her life, too upset to comment. Williams' mother Betty thought the sentence unfair because Jason Moran had shot first and then tried to shoot her son another three or four times. She told the press that Carl had originally wanted to be a policeman. Williams' estranged wife Roberta, who served a short sentence in 2004 for drug dealing, was reportedly thinking of converting to Islam but ultimately apparently rejected the faith. She said that she and her daughter would be standing by Williams even though it was reported there was potentially another Mrs Williams on the scene. Since Williams' imprisonment she has become something of a B-list celebrity, modelling for *Zoo Weekly* and making after-dinner speeches.

* * *

There was plenty of activity going on outside the overall Melbourne gang wars, and the full disaster of the 1990s drugs policy of the Victoria Police became brutally clear on 18 October 2006 when, after three years on remand, a former senior Drug Squad member, the high-flying Detective Senior Sergeant Wayne Strawhorn, was convicted of trafficking two kilograms of pseudoephedrine to the late Mark Moran. It was Strawhorn who had helped introduce the chemical diversion program. He was acquitted on three of four other charges, including trafficking the chemical to members of the Bandidos outlaw motorcycle gang. He was sentenced to a maximum seven years' imprisonment. In June 2008 his appeals against conviction and sentence were dismissed.

Strawhorn had not been the first Drug Squad officer to be arrested in recent times. In October 2003 Malcolm Rosenes was jailed for a minimum of three and a half years for drug trafficking and his offsider Stephen Andrew Payton received a similar sentence. After Strawhorn's conviction it soon emerged that, in previous months, Drug Squad officer Ian Ferguson had received a minimum of eight years for conspiracy to traffic heroin and money laundering. Detective Senior Constable David Miechel, who had been the handler for the drug dealer and informant Terence Hodson, went down for a minimum of fifteen years reduced on appeal to twelve after convictions for burglary, theft and trafficking a commercial quantity of drugs. The charge of burglary followed the theft of drugs from another dealer's house in East Oakleigh on AFL Grand Final day, 27 September 2003. Unfortunately for Miechel and Hodson, they had been seen throwing bags over the back fence and were promptly arrested.

Hodson had been expected to give evidence against senior police officers when, on 16 May 2004, he and his wife Christine were found shot dead at their home in Kew. Within hours of the East Oakleigh burglary Hodson's police file was stolen and released in the underworld, showing he was an informer. After their deaths, charges were dropped against Detective Sergeant Paul 'Killer' Dale from the Drug Squad, who it was suggested had masterminded the burglary. He had denied any dishonest involvement.

In November 2006 two other officers, Stephen Cox and Glenn Sadler, received seven and ten years respectively for conspiracy to traffic in a drug of dependence in a commercial quality with Ian Ferguson. They were alleged to have leaned on a drug trafficker to traffic on their behalf, giving them about 30 per cent of his takings, and also to give up other dealers. In return they would give him a portion of drugs seized. In 2009 their appeals against conviction and sentence were dismissed.

After this spate of sentences, Sergeant Bill Patten, an original member of the Ceja anti-corruption task force, claimed that up to two dozen officers had escaped corruption charges and that the only proper investigation would have been a Royal Commission. Other officers in difficulty at the time included Matthew Bunning — a former member of the Drug Squad—who was sentenced to a minimum of three years for providing information about intercepts, and former Victorian officer James McCabe, on secondment to the National Crime Authority, who failed to appear in Sydney to answer charges of robbery and drug dealing. He fled to Cambodia. He was later expelled by the Cambodian authorities and on his return to Australia in 2008 pleaded guilty to stealing 1 kilogram of drugs.

In February 2007 the Office of Police Integrity told Commissioner Nixon that it had evidence against dozens of officers who had been involved in drug dealing, theft and associating with criminals. The OPI maintained that another Royal Commission was not necessary and that its office was best placed to deal with corruption. Another officer who fell by the wayside that year was a one-time detective senior constable, Paul Hatzakortzian, who was jailed for a year after pleading guilty to dealing in drugs. At the time he had been working at the Sexpo adult lifestyle exhibition while moonlighting from the Sexual Offences and Child Abuse Unit.

In February 2010 charges of perjury against Deputy Police Commissioner Noel Ashby were dropped. He had been accused of lying, saying when questioned at an OPI hearing that he had not received information of a serving detective who was being investigated for murder. Justice Robert Osborn ruled that the charges could not be sustained because the hearing at which he was alleged to have lied was not conducted within the law. The deputy commissioner who had heard the case had not been formally authorised to do so. As a result the Director of Public Prosecutions, Jeremy Rapke, withdrew the charges.

They had arisen out of the death of Shane Chartres-Abbott, a twenty-eight-year-old bisexual prostitute who specialised in rough sex, shot in Howard Street, Reservoir, in July 2003 on his way to court to stand trial for the rape–murder of a thirty-year-old Thai woman in a St Kilda motel. Her tongue had been bitten in half and Chartres-Abbott, who claimed to be a 200-year-old vampire, was running the defence that he had been lured into a snuff movie in which he himself would be killed. As he left his home with his pregnant girlfriend and her father, he was shot in the neck, in what was believed to be a contract killing in revenge for the woman's death or possibly to prevent him naming his other clients in court. *Operation Briars* was later set up to establish whether police officers were connected with the killing. It was suggested that one had given the hitman Chartres-Abbott's address. On 27 March a career criminal identified only as JP pleaded guilty to Chartres-Abbott's murder and was sentenced to life imprisonment with a fifteen-year minimum. He had apparently confessed while not even a suspect. He had also agreed to give evidence against senior officers allegedly linked to the case.

In 2009 former police media director Stephen Linnell was sentenced to eight months' imprisonment wholly suspended and fined $5000 on perjury charges. He had agreed to testify against Noel Ashby, admitting he leaked to him information on *Operation Briars*. In June 2010, after the Ashby decision, Linnell's convictions were quashed. The OPI alleged that Ashby passed on the information to former police union boss Paul Mullett and that, as a result, one of the targets of the investigation, a detective sergeant, was tipped off. Charges against Mullett were also dropped. Linnell later wrote a book, *Don't Tell the Chief: The Untold Story of Police, Politics and Power*.

In November 2010 the OPI admitted it was incapable of dealing with an allegedly corrupt officer, Officer X, who was said to have links to Carl Williams' father George and the Moran family and also to have been the victim of a robbery while guarding $4 million worth of cigarettes in the 1990s. It appears that files on Officer X have vanished.

* * *

On 9 February 2006, Nicholas Ibrahim was shocked to be convicted of the murder of the standover man Sam Zayat—a close friend of Nic Radev—with whom he had quarrelled over the purchase of his share in the Khokolat nightclub for $200 000 with $20 000 down. The pair had been friends and in the week prior to his death Ibrahim had arranged $50 000 bail for Zayat. On 10 September 2003, the night of his death, Zayat went with his pit bull terrier and a former solicitor's clerk, Ali Aydin, to meet Ibrahim out in the country near Tarneit, west of Melbourne. Aydin told the magistrates' court at the committal proceedings that, when Zayat conducted negotiations, 'It was not your average settlements in the security chamber of the Commonwealth Bank.' The allegation was that Ibrahim had a pump-action shotgun and after words were exchanged he chased the unfortunate Zayat over a barbed-wire fence before shooting him. Aydin ran some 12 kilometres to the Sunshine Police Station. Both Zayat and Ibrahim had drug-related convictions. In 1994 Zayat had been charged with the murder of his lover and the attempted murder of her sixteen-year-old son. He was convicted of the latter. In 1998 Zayat and Radev had been charged with a home invasion in which an old man was beaten and his five-year-old granddaughter threatened with a handgun.

Ibrahim was right to be shocked by the murder verdict. The foreperson had made a mistake and had intended to say 'Not guilty but guilty of manslaughter'. The error was corrected and Ibrahim was duly convicted of manslaughter. There had been all sorts of evidential problems in the case, with Aydin at one stage refusing to give evidence. Ibrahim appeared to be relatively happy when he received a fifteen-year sentence.

* * *

It may be that, with the death or imprisonment of most of the warring Melbourne parties, Christine Nixon was only one out when she said before Condello's death that the gang wars had been halted. But, to mix a metaphor, pendulums continue swinging and where one door shuts another opens.

Would the Carlton Crew and the New Boys survive these deaths, arrests and imprisonments? In November 2004 reporter John Silvester thought, 'The survival of the Carlton Crew will depend on the acquittals of some of their senior members.' And as for the New Boys? 'There'll be the new New Boys.' And even if they did not survive, the *Melbourne Underworld News* was quite sure. 'The vacuum we've been talking about is growing day by day and rest assured folks—the current crews are in strife but let us say this right fucking now lest there be any confusion: This is not the fucking end.' And, of course, it wasn't.

* * *

This sense that the Melbourne drug scene had job vacancies caught the attention of OMCGs from further afield. To add to Victoria's appeal, Western Australia, Queensland and New South Wales had introduced laws to make it easier for police to monitor and curtail the illegal activities of biker gangs. The 2009 Sydney airport biker fracas between Hells Angels members up from Victoria and the local Comancheros, which resulted in the death of Angel Peter Zervas, prompted anti-association laws. So the pastures down south sure looked greener.

Bikers have had a presence in Victoria since as early as 1973, when the Hells Angels chapter was inaugurated. In 1976, one of the most savage biker gang feuds in the Australian history of OMCGs was between the Coffin Cheaters and the Morwell-based Resurrected. So brutal were the attacks that the sentencing judge dished out generous jail terms, commenting that biker gangs:

…dehumanise their members and those with whom they associate, they enshrine … a code of conduct that is at its best puerile and at its worst bestial, degrading and depraved in the extreme.

The judge's comments were condemned by some as gross generalisations, and Melbourne-based God's Squad leader Dr John Smith explained that many of the organised crime allegations were myths and that club members simply liked the macho culture and medieval pageantry of membership.

Although various biker clubs undertook public relations activities to improve their image, such as toy and teddy runs for underprivileged children, in 2003 it was estimated that, Australia-wide, biker gangs controlled 75 per cent of the methamphetamine trade. And these were not dumb, hairy, unsophisticated petrol heads. When premises connected with the Brothers Motorcycle Club in Melbourne's western and northern suburbs were raided in 2003, Organised Crime Squad detectives found drugs, a stolen Harley-Davidson and a stash of classy weapons which included a mobile phone pistol loaded by splitting the phone and inserting ammunition under the screen. The Rebels also had a presence, led by president Geoffrey 'Nuts' Armour, who was not averse to heavy-handed debt collecting for other non-biker crime gangs. In an interesting glimpse of underworld interaction, Amour shacked up with Suzanne Kane, daughter of the long-dead painter and docker standover man Leslie Kane.

By 2006, the Melbourne Hells Angels numbers were thought to be dwindling. Police relaxed into the view that bikie gangs were not such a high priority in Victoria. This all changed dramatically in 2010. Early in the year Victorian police acknowledged that OMCGs were flourishing and, in particular, the Comancheros, Bandidos and Finks were muscling in on tabletop dancing venues, brothels, security businesses and the club scene. Furthermore, they were recruiting local heavyweights such as kickboxers and convicted offenders.

The Comancheros established Melbourne headquarters in 2009 and appointed Amad 'Jay' Malkoun, a former kickboxer and convicted heroin trafficker, as president. They were said to be standing over nightclubs to the tune of thousands a week. In March 2010, three Bandidos members were believed responsible for luring a nightclub manager, Robert Bottazzi, to a meeting in Port Melbourne and bashing him repeatedly with baseball bats over a debt. Soon after, police investigated the Finks over a huge brawl on the King Street strip club area.

Further investigations, one led by the Australian Crime Commission, uncovered links in Victoria between prominent Italian criminals, Chinese triads, western-suburbs Lebanese identities, corrupt Melbourne port workers and OMCG members. Deputy Commissioner (Crime) Sir Ken Jones, himself a former Harley rider, stated reassuringly in August that criminal bikie gangs were being closely monitored and that he would talk to government about outlawing the fortification of gang clubhouses. By October, he acknowledged that the number of fully patched biker gang members had jumped from 3000 to 4000 in three years, and that smashing biker involvement in organised crime was now a high priority for state police. Sir Ken confirmed that biker gangs were active in Victorian clubs, security firms and brothels as 'a gateway for dealing in drugs, often ecstasy and amphetamines'. He had also heard that one gang had offered to buy a hotel in Mildura for $1.7 million.

The spate of underworld killings up to 2006, and the feeling that most of the bad guys were dead or in prison, may well have been the invitation interstate bikers needed to beef up their presence in Victoria; however, there was certainly one man from the old crime families still standing.

Opinions vary as to whether the last surviving member of the Moran clan, Desmond Moran, known as Tuppence, was the accountant and moneyman or whether he was a kangaroo short in the top paddock and never as involved in the underworld as his brother Lewis and nephews 'Handsome Harry' Mark and the out-of-control Jason. Chopper Read believes the former and that Lewis, the titular head, was merely an old drunk. It is likely that after the deaths of Lewis, Mark and Jason, Desmond had access to the millions made over the years by the family in the abortion racket, thefts, standovers, SP bookmaking and, more recently, drugs, which was cleverly invested by lawyers and accountants. Certainly, Desmond should never have told the press he was the last Moran standing; he paid dearly for that display of hubris.

At 8.50 p.m. on Tuesday 17 March 2009, Desmond was shot at in his driveway at Langs Road, Ascot Vale. He had been driven home in his Mercedes by a friend and the shot was aimed at the driver. The bullet hit the steering wheel. Moran described the shooter (who wore a loose balaclava helmet which allowed more than a glimpse of his face) as 'an inbred albino'. Some weeks earlier Moran had been involved in a fight with a racing identity and at the time this was thought to be the likely cause of the shooting, rather than a rekindling of the underworld ashes. There was, however, worse to come.

Around midday on 15 June, Desmond was shot twice by masked gunmen at Ascot Pasta and Deli, a regular haunt of his. His sister-in-law, Judy Moran, arrived shortly afterwards screaming his name. She was arrested and charged with his murder, something she denied. Read claimed that before she was taken to the police station Judy Moran went to talk to the ashes of her late husband, saying, 'I'm sorry Lew.' The cognoscenti thought the Moran fortune was behind the killing. Also arrested and charged with his murder was Les Kane's daughter Suzanne, along with her boyfriend Geoffrey 'Nuts' Armour and Michael Farrugia. They all denied the charge. In April 2010 all four were committed for trial. Then came a turnaround. On 26 November, Farrugia pleaded guilty to manslaughter. The plea was accepted on the condition that he would give evidence against his three co-defendants. In December he was sentenced to a minimum of two years, which, with time served, meant he would be eligible for parole in August 2011.

When the murder trial began in February 2011 Judy Moran was in the dock on her own and it became clear that the prosecution thought it had been all about money. Tuppence had access to funds which Judy Moran thought were hers. Trouble had broken out at a benefit for Wrout in the Union Hotel, Ascot Vale, when Kane told Tuppence, 'You'll never be half the man your brother was.' The first shooting had been by Armour, as had the second and fatal one. Michael Farrugia said he had been recruited for what he thought was a debt-collecting expedition but despite being told to wait in the car he followed Armour and saw him shoot Tuppence with a Glock. When Armour returned to the car Judy Moran asked Armour if he had got him.

In her defence, Judy Moran claimed that at the time of Tuppence's shooting she was at the cemetery giving the two angels on Mark's grave a wash and polish. It was the ninth anniversary of his death. Other problems seemed to have been reasonably deflected. Some wicked person had dumped the gun and car used in the shooting at her home and in a panic she had tried to get rid of them. All right, a call had been made on her mobile when she was meant to have been at the cemetery, but that must have been done by someone else. Nor had she said 'Murder on' to Armour. She had actually said 'Murderer', referring to the fact that Armour shot kangaroos for dog meat. In this she had some support from an expert witness on speech patterns.

By the time the jury reached the seventh day of its deliberations, Judy Moran and inexperienced jury watchers must have thought that, at the very least, there would be a hung jury. But the trouble was that, while one can explain away an individual point—say the remark to Armour or the disposal of the gun—the cumulative effect became overwhelming. The cognoscenti also knew that

Melbourne juries like to take their time, and they duly convicted her. Trial observers had watched Moran under cross-examination and whenever the going got rough—which it did on a regular basis—her cheek began to twitch. Later it emerged that Suzanne Kane had pleaded guilty to being an accessory after the fact and had effectively been sentenced to time served. Nuts Armour had also pleaded guilty. Given that Dessie must have known who had it in for him but did nothing to change things around, it may well be that he was a kangaroo short.

After the verdict there were stories that, when drink had been taken, Judy Moran would boast that Lewis, her second de facto, had arranged the offing of his predecessor Les Cole in Sydney as a mark of love for her.

* * *

Carl Williams hadn't been concentrating properly either. At 12.50 p.m. on Monday 19 April 2010 he was attacked from behind by a fellow prisoner with part of an exercise bicycle in the maximum-security Acacia unit of Barwon Prison. He staggered to his cell where he died, apparently after suffering a heart attack. Later it was claimed and denied that corrections officers had been playing indoor cricket instead of umpiring their charges.

It was not difficult to identify the suspected killer because the attack had been filmed by security cameras. Less easy to identify was the motive. Williams' companions in the secure unit were men known to have been generally friendly towards him and had been sharing the accommodation for at least nine months. One suggestion has been that it was simply a jailhouse quarrel. A more sinister alternative is that the attack was a contract hit paid for by interested parties outside the jail, possibly to prevent him giving evidence in forthcoming high-profile cases. There have also been suggestions that Williams was taken to a nearby Corio motel to have sex with two Tasmanian prostitutes and that he and his father had been allowed to go for a 2008–09 New Year holiday. Rather ambiguously a Corrections spokesperson said, 'Corrections Victoria has never approved prostitutes to visit Carl Williams in jail,' which is not quite what was being alleged.

At first the man charged with Williams' murder could not be named for legal reasons. The other man in the unit was Thomas Ivanovic, also known as Little Tommy. The sometime drug dealer and one-time trusted member of the Williams Crew during the gangland wars had been jailed for eighteen years in 2003 for the shooting murder of a motorcyclist in a road-rage incident the previous year. Williams had asked him to be godfather to his daughter Dhakota, but Ivanovic was jailed before the christening.

Police sources said they had been told that Ivanovic was on the phone at the time of the attack and told the person he was speaking to what was occurring in front of him. Eventually, after several months of speculation, the suppression order was lifted and in October 2010 the accused was named as thirty-seven-year-old Matthew Charles Johnson.

The death of Carl Williams started a chain of repercussions. In June 2010 the case against a convicted murderer and Sergeant Paul Dale over the murders of the Hodsons collapsed and, because of insufficient evidence—notably the absence of Williams—the case was dismissed. In August, *Taskforce Petra,* the team that had been investigating the killings of the Hodsons, was wound down and its work taken over by *Taskforce Driver*, which was investigating who would benefit from the death of Williams. The allegation had been that Dale had paid Williams $150 000 to organise the hit on the Hodsons. Dale, who remained 'a person of interest' but who has always denied any involvement, has left the force and now owns a service station.

In February 2011, Dale gave an interview to Mark Buttler of the *Herald Sun* saying he had not even been interviewed over the Carl

Williams killing and it was laughable to consider him a possible suspect. He complained that a witness in the Hodson killing had been offered financial and other inducements to give evidence against him. He also denied that it was he who, within hours of the AFL Grand Final day burglary, had stolen and distributed a secret police file showing Hodson was a grass.

In November 2010, Roberta Williams, heavily pregnant by her fiancé Rob Carpenter, somewhat nauseatingly announced that the baby had been conceived the night before Williams died. The implication was that it had been his final gift to her. She later made what many would see as a self-serving video, *Kill or Be Killed,* to be released after the birth of the child, in which she repented her life and apologised to what was left of the Moran family. Whether she will receive the hoped-for profits from the video or whether the Attorney-General will step in remains to be seen. Roberta Williams' fifth child, Giuseppe, was born in January 2011 and a three-page photo spread in a women's magazine indeed confirmed her view that 'my baby is Carl's gift'.

* * *

Of course, it is still not THE END. The last few years have seen a resurgence in Asian gangs with a mainly Vietnamese membership. In May 2010 a leaked police report named Yellow Klique, based in Richmond, which had set up drug dealing networks in the Housing Commission flats in Elizabeth Street. Members, some said to be as young as fifteen, had been shopping around for guns. Other gangs currently include Central Crew, based in the city; Brothers 4 Life; Young St Albans and Kings Park, from the western suburbs; and Young Spring Boys from Springvale. There were also signs that Yellow Klique had formed an alliance with Central Crew and were said to be in conflict with Brothers 4 Life. In the last two years the gangs were said to have been linked to nearly a dozen attacks, stabbings and affrays, including the firebombing of a home in Toorak. The city's Asian Gang Squad had been disbanded in 2006 but in June 2010 there were reports that *Taskforce Echo* had been formed to deal with the gangs.

On 22 November 2009, outside the city nightclub Bubble, a haunt of the gangs, twenty-one-year-old bouncer Ahmad Chokr saw a man in the queue drop a knife. He challenged him and a brawl ensued involving, depending on reports, up to twenty Asian men. It was all captured on CCTV. Chokr was attacked with a machete and had an arm and a leg almost severed. In September 2010 Chyong Nguyen received two and a half years' jail for his role in the assault. Five more young men faced court in late December 2010, when bail was denied.

After the police report was leaked, long-time youth worker Les Twentyman conceded, 'We've got a problem with quite a few ethnic gangs—Polynesian gangs, African gangs and Asian—but they've become more prominent in recent times.' The violence has spread to other suburbs. Just before Christmas 2010 a group of skateboarders were enjoying a warm evening near the crowded St Kilda foreshore when they were attacked by a gang of about ten Asian males. Weapons wielded by the gang included a meat cleaver, and one boarder had to have surgery on his badly slashed arm.

Because the general public is much more interested in old-fashioned blue-collar gang warfare than alleged bad behaviour among the ethnic community, an almost unnoticed war has been going on in the western suburbs between Lebanese families, the Chaouks and their rivals the Haddaras. It may not have reached the levels of the Assyrian war in Detroit, Michigan, in the 1990s but the death toll has been mounting.

Until the last five years the Chaouk family were largely unsung, but already one of their members, Mohamed Ali Chaouk, had been strong enough to see off the prince of Lygon Street Alphonse Gangitano when he went to stand over Bunnies nightclub in

Footscray, where Chaouk was on the door. He and another bouncer worked Gangitano over and told him to stay away from Footscray. Gangitano then tried to save face by saying it was police officers who had given him the beating, but he stayed out of Footscray from then on.

The family first crept into the notice of the general public in 2005 when twenty-eight-year-old Mohamed Chaouk was shot and killed by police during a raid on the family's property on Geelong Road in Brooklyn. He is alleged to have attacked an officer with a samurai sword. After that, threats were made to blow up St Kilda Police Station, allegedly by members of his family.

In June 2009, twenty-eight-year-old Mohammed Haddara was killed in a drive-by shooting in the driveway of his parents' Altona North home. In June 2010 a member of the Chaouks' extended family, Ahmed Hablas, was charged with his murder. According to the prosecution Haddara had been shot four times in the back, once when he was on the ground. Hablas claimed he had been kidnapped by Haddara and another man but had managed to get out of the car in which he was being driven at high speed. Haddara then chased after Hablas and the two became involved in a struggle. 'I found the gun in my hand,' said Hablas, adding that he did not have time to think before he fired. 'I suddenly realised I was alone and not about to die,' he told the police.

However, by then there was a machine gun attack on two men in a parked car outside the McDonald's franchise in Millers Road, Altona North. Things escalated when Mohammed Haddara's cousin Sam was shot in the face while in his car, also in Altona North. He survived but required extensive plastic surgery. The shooting was followed by police raids on Chaouk-owned properties where the police allegedly found weapons and thirty-six blank Australian passports hidden in a wall cavity. The youngest of the Chaouks, Omar, was charged with their possession. At a bail hearing, when Omar Chaouk's lawyer told the court his client should be released to protect the family, he received a dusty reply from magistrate Fiona Stewart, who said that was the very reason he should stay in custody.

But another brother, Matwali, claimed the passports and weapons were his and in August 2010, Omar was released on bail. The family patriarch, Macchour, and another son, Walid, were arrested but released without charge. Around the same time electrified knuckle dusters and an extendable baton were said to have been found during a raid on a Brooklyn car wash that had links to the Chaouks.

Then, mid-morning on 13 August, Macchour Chaouk was shot dead through a fence at the back of his home, often referred to as Fort Alamo, at the corner of Cypress Avenue and Geelong Road, Brooklyn. Born in Tripoli, Macchour came to Australia in 1969. He returned to Lebanon to marry Fatma and they had five sons and a daughter. At first an unsuccessful businessman—his fruit shop failed and his house was sold—in 1975 he was charged with assaulting a man with a metal bar in a dispute in a factory. But then the seriousness of his crimes escalated. There were charges of burglary in New South Wales in 1984, assault on the police, reckless driving causing serious injury, as well as a five-year sentence in 2000 for trafficking in heroin when he was caught by a police undercover operation. There had previously been a two-year sentence for a like offence. In 1985 Chaouk was involved in two serious road accidents, ending his working life. In 2010 bullets ended his life, full stop. The family regarded the killing as particularly serious since it had taken place during Ramadan. 'His blood does not come cheap, especially in Ramadan,' read a family statement obtained by *The Age*.

Dozens of Hells Angels members attended Macchour Chaouk's funeral on 16 August 2010 and made a very visible show of support. This prompted a warning from Sir Ken Jones, Deputy

Police Commissioner, that police were interested in the interaction between members of different organised crime groups and were keeping a close eye on gang activity.

On 17 September 2010, Steve Toveski was shot dead on Techno Park Drive, an industrial estate in western Melbourne. Two men, one in his sixties and the other in his mid-twenties, were arrested shortly afterwards but no charges were brought in relation to the death. Initially there were suggestions that it was a payback for the shooting of Chaouk but these were soon discounted.

In October 2010, twenty-six-year-old Matwali Chaouk pleaded guilty to possessing a .22 pistol and ammunition at a house in Burgess Street, Brooklyn, on 8 June 2010. He was remanded for sentencing but not before his mother, said to have cancer, appealed for an end to the feud. On 11 November he was sentenced to thirty months' imprisonment, with a minimum of eighteen months, much of which will be spent in solitary confinement for his own protection.

* * *

Will Mrs Chaouk's wishes be respected? Will the Haddaras and the Chaouks find enough common interests to end their feud? There may be evidence that a new kind of crime gang is emerging, which puts cultural and familial differences aside in the interests of profit. Bikies in their early days may have had a white supremacist attitude, but a new Bandidos offshoot on the Gold Coast is the Sons of Islam, made up of young Muslim men, some of whom have photos of Osama bin Laden displayed in their homes. Recent investigations into organised crime have unearthed multimillion-dollar drug syndicates with links between members of Chinese triads, bikie gangs, Italian and Lebanese crime families and rogue maritime workers.

In April 2011 some of the dust from the gang wars started to clear. Suppression orders, which prohibited the name of amphetamine dealer and racehorse owner Tony Mokbel being so much as breathed, were lifted, with Mokbel pleading guilty to dealing in a large commercial quantity of methylamine between July 2006 and June 2007. He also admitted to trafficking a large commercial quantity of ecstasy between February and August 2005. Now the public could learn what had been whispered behind hands over the past three years. First, in 2009 Mokbel had been acquitted of the 2004 murder of Lewis Moran. It had been alleged he had promised $140 000 to contracted hitmen and turned them over for $10 000 of the money. Secondly, in May the same year, the Crown had dropped the murder charge over the death of hot dog salesman Michael Marshall, killed in South Yarra in 2003. It was also immediately suggested—and denied by his lawyers—that Mokbel had cut a deal and would agree to give evidence both against senior police officers and over the killings of drug dealers Terence and Christine Hodson.

A man regarded by the lawyers who knew him as 'a good bloke, talkative, affable, who paid his bills' and who sent them work, had convictions stretching over decades for assault, threats to kill and resisting arrest. In 1992 he received six months for attempting to bribe a County Court judge. In 1998 a conviction on charges of conspiracy to traffic in amphetamines was overturned and the next year he was also cleared of a perjury charge. He had been building fashion and property enterprises when, on 24 August 2001, he was arrested and charged with the importation of pure cocaine worth $2 billion hidden in candles and statues from Mexico. When the court was told the case might take two years to come to trial, and this might cause Mokbel's business interests to collapse, his application for bail was granted.

Mokbel had, according to the stories in the underworld, set up a seven-figure fighting fund to deal with witnesses and a potentially vulnerable co-accused. In October 2001 his bail was revoked by the Supreme Court.

Mokbel's trial proceedings were seriously delayed by the arrests of two Drug Squad officers involved in the case, Stephen Andrew Paton and Malcolm Rosenes, who were not dealt with for a further two years. Then Mokbel's committal proceedings were adjourned in June 2002, a charge of threatening to kill a prison officer was dropped the following month and in September that year he was once more granted bail. There were also problems with prosecution witnesses. In 2003 a supergrass witness was jailed for eighteen months after a plea bargain. In February 2004 the supergrass was allowed to travel overseas on parole on his promise to return to give evidence against Mokbel. Three months later the man decided he wanted $500 000 to return to Australia. Despite his refusal to reappear, the case went ahead and Mokbel was committed for trial over the importation of cocaine.

In October 2005 he was charged with inciting others to import drugs and the court was told that the police believed he had been having an affair with his solicitor, Zarah Garde-Wilson, something she denied. He was bailed the next month with his sister-in-law Renate Mokbel standing surety and in February 2006 his trial for importing cocaine finally began.

He had already agreed to plead guilty to trafficking in ecstasy, speed and cocaine. Indeed, for some time it seemed as though Mokbel was well on his way to an acquittal on the importing charge. Despite prosecution objections his bail was continued and, after reporting to the South Melbourne Police Station on Sunday 21 March, Mokbel disappeared.

Immediately there were suggestions in the underworld that he had become another body in the gang wars. He had certainly been suspected of financing the deaths of Radev and Lewis Moran and his death might have been a reprisal. Not so, said the police; he had definitely flown. But to where? It was possible he was still lying low in Australia but the heavier money was placed on a return to his birthplace of Lebanon.

On 29 March 2006 Mokbel was found guilty in his absence in the drugs case and sentenced to a relatively modest twelve years. Meanwhile, there were skirmishes over the forfeiture of his $1 million bail money put up by Renate. In April 2006, Justice Bill Gillard ordered her to pay the surety or face two years in jail. In September 2006 jewellery and cash totalling around $1 million, which the police claimed was part of the Mokbel treasure, were dug up at a house in Alma Road, Parkdale. Mokbel was also said to have laundered money through the Tracksuit Gang—a group who attended races placing huge cash bets and, if the horse won, demanding clean notes.

On 5 June 2005, Mokbel was found in an ill-fitting toupee, sunning himself in Piraeus, a suburb of Athens, but it was not until May 2008 that he was retrieved. Preparations were made for the murder and drug trials, and down came the curtain on reporting anything about him.

Meanwhile, Mokbel's one time de facto Danielle McGuire, who had a daughter by him and joined him while on the run, was reported to be the companion of a biker. It is something that has not pleased the one-time multi-millionaire.

Even with Mokbel's final conviction, there is little suggestion that organised crime in Victoria has come to an end, with police Chief Commissioner Simon Overland stating in April 2011 that there is still 'more than enough work' for *Operation Purana* to be doing.

Will it be a family or a multicultural mixed gang that next tries to seize power in Melbourne's underworld? Watch this space.

Notes

Abbreviations used in Notes

A Crim R	Australian Criminal Reports
CDPP	Commonwealth Director of Public Prosecutions
HCA	High Court of Australia
MEPO	Metropolitan Police Office Records, National Archives (UK)
NAA	National Archives of Australia
NSWCA	New South Wales Court of Appeal
NSWCCA	New South Wales Court of Criminal Appeal
SLV	State Library of Victoria
VLR	Victorian Law Reports
VPRS	Victorian Public Record Service
VR	Victorian Reports
VSC	Supreme Court of Victoria
VSCA	Victorian Supreme Court of Appeal

1 Not So Marvelous Melbourne

Page 1, It was this raid: VPRS 1189 Files; *Victorian Historical Magazine*, vol. 73, no. 2, September 2002; *SMH*, 10 April 1852. **Page 2, Flanigan, who gave evidence:** For an account of the life and death of John Price, see Barry, *The Life and Death of John Price*. **Page 2, On 22 January:** *The Argus*, 27 March, 2 April 1869; *SMH*, 19 April 1869. **Page 2, She later opened:** VPRS 937/183/6 SLV1515 Mss 114; Lahey, *Damn You John Christie*, pp. 70–77; *The Argus*, 20 May 1872. **Page 2, In July 1870:** *Maitland Mercury*, p. 22, 26 July 1870. **Page 3, He was still operating:** Davidson et al. (eds), *Australians, 1888*, p. 373; *The Argus*, p. 17, 29 May 1888, 19 April 1893; *SMH*, 20 November 1902. **Page 3, When the police:** *Brisbane Courier*, 7 February 1881. **Page 4, Despite his long record:** *Maitland Mercury*, 27 November 1880; *The Argus*, 18 December 1880, 19 September 1881. **Page 4, He wasn't quick enough:** *The Argus*, 24 October 1904. **Page 5, By then, however:** *The Argus*, 22 February 1890. **Page 5, Nellie was bound over:** *Advertiser*, 9, 11 July 1910; *West Australian*, 9 July 1910. **Page 5, In August 1899:** *The Argus*, 28 August 1899. **Page 5, At the turn of the century:** 'The Push', *Timaru Herald*, 25 November 1899; *The Argus*, 19 March 1910. **Page 6, Additionally, Smith was:** *The Argus*, 7 November 1919; *West Australian*,

19 December 1919. Page 6, He and Ronald Pearce: 'Melbourne Pushes',
Ohinemuri Gazette (NZ), 18 April 1910; *The Age*, 31 October 1927. **Page 7, He
received ten years:** *The Age*, 19 August 1901; 21 September 1946. **Page 7, A
man working:** *The Argus*, 5 September 1893. **Page 7, Her hanging, along with
that:** Fitzgerald, *Studies in Australian Crime*, Second Series, pp. 272–91. **Page 8,
Ranged against that:** *Australian Dictionary of Biography*; *The Argus*, 12 January
1894. **Page 8, In turn the police:** Beale, A Compilation of Evidence from World
Sources, p. 122. **Page 8, The team of four:** In 1900 Cartwright was sentenced to
thirty months for breaking into the counting house of the Duke of Cornwall mine
at Fryerstown. *Ashburton Guardian*, 9 February 1898; *Mercury*, 10 February 1898;
Marlborough Express, 5 March 1898; *The Argus*, 13 July 1900. **Page 9, He was
apparently:** *R v Meredith and ors*. VPRS 521/41/23036; *The Argus*, 27 July 1935.
Page 10, In turn, Cornelius Crowe: Crowe subsequently had a curious career.
In 1906 he was acquitted of demanding money with menaces but was thrown
out of the force. In 1916 he was sentenced to three years for criminal libel but
the conviction was quashed and he was acquitted on a retrial. *The Argus*, 25
March 1916. **Page 10, O'Donnell, regarded as a man:** *The Age*, 8 January 1906.
No relation, Sgt E O'Donnell, a man described as having a peppery nature, was
known as Little O'Donnell. He was shot in the neck when searching for a burglar
in Carlton Gardens in July 1900 and was retired from the force. Curiously all
four previous Melbourne bombings had taken place in Fitzroy, three of them
in Nicholson Street. **Page 11, The *Australian Dictionary*:** Frank Hardy, *Power
without Glory, The Hard Way*.

2 Squizzy Taylor and Friends

Page 14, Bravely, Trotter swung: 'The Trotter Tragedy', *Truth* (Melbourne), 11
January 1913; 'Murder Mystery Still Unsolved', *Truth* (Melbourne), 18 January
1913. **Page 14, He jumped bail:** 'The Fitzroy Murder', *Advertiser*, 17 January
1913. **Page 15, Conlon was bound over:** *Truth*, 14 June 1914. **Page 16, There
were good descriptions:** *Victoria Police Gazette*, 2, 9 March 1916. **Page 17, You
are not fit:** *West Australian*, 18 March 1911. **Page 18, On 6 August 1918:** A
year later, in August 1919, Daley's luck held. The evidence of Detective O. Bruce
was that Daley loafed around Bourke Street 'from morning till night' and that
most of the time he was in the company of 'the most active and desperate
criminals'. Charged with being an idle person with insufficient lawful means
of support, Daley claimed he had trained boxers for the past ten years, earning
between £7 and £9 a week. He was discharged. *Western Argus*, 19 August 1919.
Page 19, What the quarrel: *Camperdown Chronicle*, 13 June 1912. **Page 20,
Unfortunately, they were arrested:** *Mercury* (Hobart), 3 March 1919. **Page 20,
They thought the shooting:** *The Argus*, 7 May 1919. **Page 20, Interviewed by
the police:** Truth (Sydney), 8 April 1929. **Page 21, Slater had been trying:** In
1922, along with Frederick Carmody, Slater stood trial for the murder of Thomas
Peter Monaghan, shot during a raid in 1919 on his father's home in Lower
Campbell Street. He ran an alibi defence saying he had been drinking at a sly-
grog shop. The first two juries disagreed and, after the third trial in May 1922, in

which the jury again disagreed, Slater was acquitted. Carmody was convicted at the first trial. Sentenced to life imprisonment, he was released in 1940. **Page 22, In June 1920:** *SMH,* 3 June 1920. **Page 22, They both received:** 'Conman and Gunman', *Truth* (Sydney), 21 September 1924. **Page 23, In November that year:** Cotter's luck held more or less throughout his career. In 1929 he was acquitted of discharging a shotgun after a blue outside the Oyster Cafe in Richmond and in 1936 he was again fined for possessing a firearm after shooting nine bullets at the windows of a neighbour who had annoyed him. *The Argus, 8 January 1936.* **Page 23, Now she asked:** *Truth* (Melbourne), 9 February 1924. **Page 24, When he finally decided:** *Sun,* 22 September 1922. **Page 25, The jury recommended:** *The Argus,* 22 February 1922. **Page 25, She worked rather downmarket:** *The Argus,* 26 April 1923. **Page26, He was also polite:** Conversation with SL and JM, 21 February 2006 **Page 26, I think it was:** Conversation with SL and JM, 21 February 2006. **Page 26, As he scaled it:** *Victoria Police Gazette,* 30 August 1923. **Page 27, The driver was to be:** Dower, *Deadline,* p. 9. **Page 28, The weekly newspaper:** 'Is Buckley Dead or Alive?', *Truth* (Melbourne), 12 January 1924. **Page 29, Now the wings:** *Truth* (Melbourne), 1, 23 March 1924. **Page 29, On 3 March:** Victorian State Archives, *R v Murray and Taylor,* Case No. 29 1924 30/P/0000. **Page 29, He had given:** *Truth* (Melbourne), 7 June 1924. **Page 29, When he broke:** *Truth* (Melbourne), 31 July 1948. **Page 30, His co-accused:** *The Argus,* 10 July 1928. In 1930 Dowdle was given a month for loitering as a pickpocket. An active criminal from the turn of the century, by 1913 he had racked up eleven prior convictions. More recently he had been working for Henry Stokes managing one of his baccarat clubs. He continued his career until 1944 when he was found not guilty of store-breaking. **Page 30, He surrendered:** *Truth* (Melbourne), 15, 23 March 1924. **Page 30, Another version:** The hangman, who had served in the First AIF and now worked as an engineer, was apparently paid £10. It was a good day for him. He received an extra seven shillings for a flogging he carried out at 1 p.m. His regular job paid £2/9s a week. Blaikie, *Remember Smith's Weekly,* p. 147. **Page 31, Now it thought he had:** *Truth* (Melbourne), 5, 19 April 1924. **Page 31, There had already been:** 'Is Buckley Dead or Alive?' *Truth* (Melbourne), 5 January 1924. **Page 31, A coat of arms:** *Victoria Police Gazette,* 18 October 1923. **Page 31, At first *Truth* had him dead:** *Truth* (Sydney), 27 February 1926 **Page 32, He died aged eighty-nine:** Kelly, *The Charge is Murder,* Chapter 12. **Page 32, On 15 June he:** Bookmaker and thief Allsop also had convictions in South Australia. In February 1954 Mr Justice Barry refused to accept an verdict by a jury awarding Allsop £80 for being called a 'welsher', 'robber' and thief'. Barrier Miner, 24 February 1954; *Western Argus,* 17 March 1925. **Page 32, The error was repeated:** Caylock, *As Game as Ned Kelly; Evening Sun,* 25 June, 12 August 1924. **Page 33, Nothing came:** For an account of the struggle and bombings of scab labourers, see Morton & Robinson, *Shotgun and Standover,* pp. 20–33. **Page 33, On 26 October the pair met:** Hugh Buggy, 'How "Squizzy" Taylor Died by the Gun', *The Argus,* 3 December 1949. **Page 34, Describing the scene:** *Truth* (Melbourne), 5 November 1927. **Page 35, Taylor's gun was found:** Anderson, *Larrikin Crook; The Age,* 28, 29, 31 October 1927. **Page 36, The convictions and sentences:** *SMH,* 13 April 1929. **Page 37,**

Notes

The *Weekly* also claimed: *Truth* (Melbourne), 18 January 1930. **Page 37, He was then fifty-three:** *The Argus:* 14 September 1935. **Page 37, His first gaming house:** *Camperdown Chronicle*, 14 October 1919. **Page 38, Instead of waging war:** Dower, *Deadline*, pp. 13–15. **Page 38, As for the long-dead:** *Smith's Weekly*, 3 November 1927. **Page 38, Later she met:** McCalman, *Struggletown*, p. 113.

3 Sex in the City

Page 39, The better-class: Davidson et al. (eds), *The Outcasts of Melbourne*, p. 51. **Page 39, Then, as now, brothels and drugs:** *Truth* (Sydney), 20 March 1926. **Page 40, There were assignation:** Evidence of J Dalton to Royal Commission on the Police 1881. **Page 40, He felt it did not:** Justin McCarthy, *The Commonwealth Block, Melbourne; Archaeological Investigation Report, Volume 1; Historical and Archaeological Report*, pp. 57 & 95; Australian Construction Services prepared for The Department of Administrative Services and Telecom Australia, 1989, p. 95; Evidence of Rev. John Good to the Royal Commission on Housing, 1919. **Page 40, When Standish ushered in:** Lahey, *Damn You John Christie*, p. 21. The visit is described in Standish's private diary in the State Library of Victoria. **Page 41, She maintained her occupation:** Pearl, *Wild Men of Sydney*, pp. 202–3. **Page 41, In 1878:** Victorian Parliamentary Papers 1878. **Page 43, The Supreme Court:** The previous year Maud Miller was fined £5 and costs for negligently driving a dogcart and colliding with a tramcar on St Kilda Road, injuring a passenger and damaging the tramcar. VPRS 937:306; *Barrier Miner*, 12 November 1898; *The Argus*, 3 July 1897, 12 November 1898. **Page 43, In March 1906:** VPRS 937:306; 'Madame Brussels' Notorious Bawdy House: Her Junketing Jezebels', *Truth* (Melbourne), 10 March 1906. **Page 43, He said he had been:** *Advertiser*, 9 April 1907. **Page 43, She was buried:** Davison et al. (eds), *Outcasts of Melbourne;* Robinson, *Madame Brussels.* **Page 44, As Madame Brussels' biographer:** Robinson, *Madame Brussels*, pp. 97–8; John Norton, 'Lechery and Lucre', *Truth* (Melbourne), 29 November 1906. In 1912, stricken with cancer, the forty-three year old William Judkins died, leaving a wife and thirteen-year-old daughter. Wren was a substantial donor to funds set up for the reformer's family. Judkins' brother George Alfred lived until 1958. Gillott died after a fall down a flight of stairs in Sheffield, England, on 29 June 1913. His body was brought back to Australia for burial. He left an estate of nearly £300 000, much of it to charity. *Truth* editor and Napoleon worshiper John Norton, increasingly alcoholic, died in 1916, leaving his fortune to his 'niece'. His wife negotiated a settlement with the girl. For an account of the era, see Pearl, *Wild Men of Sydney*. **Page 44, Two shillings and sixpence:** Perkins, *Sex and Sex Workers in Australia*, p. 38. **Page 45, She had been:** *The Argus*, 24 September 1904. **Page 45, In June 1908:** *The Argus*, 17 June 1908. **Page 46, The coroner thought:** *The Argus*, *Mercury* (Hobart), *SMH*, 6 December 1912. **Page 46, He admitted that over:** *Canberra Times*, 18 April 1934; 'Blonde Underworld Queen dodged gaol', *Truth* (Melbourne), 4 April 1941. **Page 46, She was also acquitted:** *Auld v Purdy*; *SMH*, 30 September 1933. **Page 46, In April 1935:** *Courier Mail*, 2 May 1935. **Page 46, The law was changed:** *The Argus*, 21 December 1937. **Page 47, He was acquitted:** *Courier*

Mail, 9, 30 January 1941; *SMH*, 2 February 1932, 11 May 1932, 30 September 1933, 18 April 1935, 29 July 1936, 15 November 1939, 3 May 1940; *The Argus*, 21 December 1937; *Truth* (Melbourne), 4 January 1941; *Toowoomba Chronicle and Darling Downs Gazette*, 9 January 1941. **Page 48, She died on 31 January 1958:** *Truth* (Melbourne), 1 February 1958. **Page 48, The war had set:** Allen, *Sex and Secrets*, p. 182. **Page 50, Outside the jail:** Dower, *Deadline;* Hickie, *Chow Hayes.* **Page 51, Known to have operated:** *Truth* (Melbourne), 1 February 1958. **Page 51, Other suburbs where sex:** Attorney-General's Street Prostitution Advisory Group, Interim Report, September 2001. **Page 51, The 1997 Dixon Report:** Advisory Committee Final Report 1997, *The Age*, 11 February 2000, *The Sunday Age*, 12 March 2000. **Page 51, In 2003 it was estimated:** *The Age*, 11 February 2000; Andrew Rule, 'He's Mr Goldfingers', *The Sunday Age*, 12 March 2000. In September 2010 Bartlett was alleged to have threatened his wife with a gun, something he denies. **Page 51, By the end of the:** *The Age*, 28 February 1999; Melissa Marino, 'Sex in our city? Plenty apparently', *The Age*, 8 June 2003. **Page 52, The women had to:** *The Age*, 9 May 1999. **Page 52, These incidents are likely:** Sullivan & Jeffries, *Legalising Prostitution Is Not the Answer.* **Page 53, Lelah was sentenced:** *Regina v Lelah* [2002] VSCA 96, 23 May 2001; *R v Hickey*, [2001] VSCA 75; Tom Noble, *Untold Violence; The Age*, 24 August 2000. **Page 53, Once repaid:** Padraic Murphy, 'Lured by wealth, sex slaves go home with little savings', *SMH*, 14 July 2003. **Page 53, In 2009 the High Court:** *The Queen v Tang* [2008] HCA Trans 181; *R v Wei Tang*, [2009] VSCA 182; Maris Beck, 'Inside Melbourne's sex trade', *Brisbane Times*, 12 March 2009. **Page 54, Two of the men:** Kate Hagan, 'Man found guilty in sex slave case', *The Age*, 18 October 2009. **Page 54, Estimates of unlicensed brothels:** Jeffreys, 'Prostitution Culture'. **Page 54, A 2006 study:** Chen, 'Estimating the number of unlicensed brothels in Melbourne'. **Page 54, In 2009:** Pickering et al., 'Working in Victoria Brothels'.

4 Unhappy Families

Page 55, The ugliest and nastiest: NAA. A.471.21795. **Page 56, Bruhn was very fond:** *The Argus*, 10 June 1921. **Page 57, But, unsurprisingly:** 'Five bullets—and death—for Razor Slasher Bruhn,' *Truth* (Melbourne), 2 July 1927. **Page 57, However, this may have been:** *Courier-Mail*, 30 September 1933. **Page 57, She was taken:** *Advertiser (The)*, 22 January 1929. **Page 58, Mona's brother forfeited:** *The Argus*, 17 June 1930. **Page 61, Apparently he would place:** *SMH*, 14 November 1949. **Page 62, A criminal's criminal:** John Silvester, 'The Criminal Dynasty That Began In The 1920s', *The Age*, 20 May 2004. **Page 62, In June 1984:** *The Age*, 15 June, 14 December 1977. **Page 63, At least Johnson:** G Walker, 'Temptress set free. But now she faces hell on the outside', *Sun*, 17 August 1989. **Page 63, He was convicted:** *R v Faure* [2000] VSC 208. **Page 64, In 2005 he received:** *DPP v Noel William Faure* [2005] NSWCA 91. **Page 64, She received a minimum:** *R v Vodopic* [2003] VSCA 172. **Page 65, Convicted and sentenced:** *Victoria Police Gazette*, July 1939; *SMH*, 21 December 1939; *SMH*, 12 March, 8 April 1940. **Page 66, In 1944, Kenneth Roy Cartledge:** VPG 306/1944. **Page 66, On his acquittal:** Flach, The Bearded Negro. **Page 67, In February**

1943: *The Argus*, 6 March 1943. **Page 67, The next year:** *The Argus*, 8 March 1946. **Page 67, He still had to serve:** *The Argus*, 7 June 1946. **Page 68, In May 1952 he was sentenced:** *Truth* (Melbourne), 16 June, 11 August 1951; *The Argus*, 20 December 1951; *The Age*, 28, 29 May 1952; *The Argus*, 31 May 1952. **Page 68, In addition to the beating:** *The Argus*, 3 October 1951. **Page 68, Six months of his sentence:** *The Argus*, 9 November 1951. **Page 69, Since Margaret had only:** *Victoria Police Gazette*, 26 September 1940; *The Argus*, 21 January 1942. **Page 70, He died in 1960:** R v Burles [1947] VLR 392; *The Argus*, 2 February 1934; 25, 27 March, 23 May, 1 August, 16 September 1947; He died in 1960: 'Death of a Thug', *Truth* (Melbourne), 6 August 1960. **Page 70, Nicholls was sent:** 'Shades of Mona Ryan', *The Argus*, 11 March 1938. **Page 70, In July 1941:** 'Maloney kids reverse routine', *Truth* (Melbourne), 15 July 1940.

5 World War II

Page 73, Many years later: Michael Duffy, 'Alive and kicking, a quiet achiever of the underworld', *SMH*, 16 April 2010. **Page 73, For the moment:** *The Argus*, 15 August 1940. **Page 73, Tiffen, who had sixteen:** *The Argus*, 3 August 1939. **Page 74, It was the spectators:** VSPR Inquests 1940/1030; *Truth* (Melbourne), 3 August 1940. **Page 75, Possibly those he had robbed:** *The Argus*, 11 July 1941. **Page 75, Albert Bayley was duly found:** *SMH*, 8 July 1942; *Canberra Times*, 3 September 1942. **Page 75, At the time:** *Mercury* (Hobart), 22 August 1945. **Page 79, This time he received:** *Canberra Times*, 23 October 1944; *The Argus*, 8 November 1944. **Page 79, No charges were brought:** *The Argus*, 10 March 1943. **Page 79, For this crime:** *Herald*, 21 April 1948; *The Argus*, 4 June 1948. **Page 79, During World War II:** *The Argus*, 23 February 1944, 27 May 1944. **Page 79, In December 1946:** *The Argus*, 11 December 1946. **Page 80, Ration coupons:** *The Argus*, 2 March 1945. **Page 80, His offsider:** *The Argus*, 7 March 1945. **Page 80, Those sheltering:** 'Clean up for crooks and dodgers', *Truth* (Melbourne), 7 April 1945. **Page 81, In the November:** *The Argus*, 12 June 1935; *The Argus*, 13 November 1935. **Page 81, The old-time confidence man:** Dower, *Deadline*. **Page 82, Described as a 'monitoress':** VSPR, Inquest 1945/182; *SMH*, 12 January 1946.

6 The Combine

Page 84, It was Turner: Hansen, *The Awful Truth*. **Page 85, Perhaps sensibly:** Dower, *Deadline*, p. 78. **Page 85, His first case of armed robbery:** *The Argus*, 13 August 1946. **Page 86, The battle for control:** *Advertiser (Adelaide)*, 1 April 1927; *SMH*, 1 April 1927. **Page 86, The judge, handing Newman:** *The Argus*, 1 August 1947. **Page 87, Coates's burial:** *Canberra Times*, 2 August 1947. For a detailed account of Coates's death and the events leading to it, see Morton & Robinson, *Shotgun and Standover*. For an account of his career as a conman in Europe, see Nat. Arch. (UK) MEPO 8/41. **Page 88, In September the next year:** *The Age*, 8, 21 February, 29 April 1950; *West Australian*, 13 February, 1950. **Page

89, He had been seen: For an account of the Allard case see Morton & Lobez, *Dangerous to Know*. **Page 91, Bradshaw was said:** Dower, *Deadline*. **Page 90, By the spring of that year:** *The Argus*, 4 September 1951. **Page 91, Obligingly the stipendiary:** *The Argus*, 15 August 1952. **Page 91, With the help:** Dower, *Deadline*; *The Argus*, 4 August 1934; *The Argus*, 9 November 1954. **Page 93, He had a diamond:** Prior, *The Sinners' Club*. **Page 93, Another regarded him:** Conversation with SL and JM, 22 February 2006. For the record, the others were Graham 'The Munster' Kinniburgh and the Sydneysider Bertie Kidd. **Page 93, Self-defence, said the coroner:** *Mercury (Hobart)*, 20 December 1947. **Page 94, Charged with murder:** *The Argus*, 7 February 1949; *SMH*, 18 February 1950. **Page 94, Now Turner was warned:** *The Argus*, 19 July 1952. **Page 94, 'Someone put the Chinese:** Mike Ryan & Don Greenlees, 'Joey stays one jump ahead', *Sunday Press*, 5 September 1982. **Page 95, Frank Galbally used him:** Galbally, *Galbally for the Defence*. **Page 96, Can you imagine me leaving:** For a fuller account of Turner's criminal and social life, see Morton & Robinson, *Shotgun and Standover*; Prior, *The Sinner's Club*; Ryan & Greenlees, 'Joey stays one jump ahead', *Sunday Press*, 5 September 1982; Paul Danilos, 'Saying Goodbye to a Colourful Criminal', *Herald Sun*, 7 January 1995. **Page 96, Keeping up with his offsider:** *The Argus*, 15 September 1951. **Page 98, After a six-hour retirement:** Violet Harkins was a friend of the Maloney family, particularly James Maloney's girlfriend Phyllis West. In 1942 they had been charged with robbery in company, but the charges were dropped. Their alleged victim, an American serviceman, received two days for contempt when he refused to give evidence, saying he had been drunk. *The Argus*, 8 April 1942. **Page 98, In June that same year:** *The Argus*, 19 June 1952. **Page 98, He was aged:** *Truth* (Melbourne), 2 June 1951. **Page 100, The cognoscenti thought:** VPRS 24/I/0000; 1958/1735; Dower, *Deadline*, p. 160. **Page 102, Bradshaw clearly had no intention:** For a full account of the Harrison shooting see Morton & Robinson, *Shotgun and Standover*. **Page 102, In the wash-up:** *Truth* (Melbourne), 6 August 1960. **Page 102, Yes, but his share:** 'Grave Combine Charges', *Truth* (Melbourne) 23 September 1961. **Page 103, It was thought to be:** *Cairns Post*, 4 February 1952; *Cairns Post*, 23 July 1954; *Courier-Mail*, 22 July 1954. **Page 106, The game is forfeit:** It was the effective end of MSS as it was. Its managing director, Devon Minchin, later wrote a factional novel, *The Money Movers*, about the raid. **Page 106, He was killed when his car:** Mike Ryan & Don Greenlees, 'Joey stays one jump ahead', *Sunday Press*, 5 September 1982. **Page 106, He died from cancer:** For an account of the MSS trial and Turner generally, see Morton & Robinson, *Shotgun and Standover*. **Page 107, Given a retrial:** R v Jones and Waghorn (1991) 55 A Crim. R. 159; Read, *Chopper from the Inside*.

7 Melbourne Market Matters

Page 109, Despite the evidence: *Truth* (Melbourne), 3 November, 1 December 1945. **Page 109, The same year Giovanni:** *The Argus*, 28 November, 1 December 1950, 22 September 1951; *Canberra Times*, 22 September 1950. **Page 109, *Truth***

took a close interest: *Truth* (Melbourne), 7 April 1951. **Page 113, 'I am a man:** Nick McKenzie & Richard Baker, 'Crime and Banishment', *SMH*, 23 February 2009. **Page 114, He was disappointed:** *R v Alistair Farquhar MacRae* [1995] VSC 108. **Page 115, It was thought his killing:** *Herald Sun*, 22 February 1999. **Page 115, In 2010:** *Mannella v The Queen* [2010] VSCA 357; *Herald Sun*, 4 September 2007. **Page 115, His sister, saying the family:** *Herald Sun*, 11 May 2000. **Page 115, Some time later:** John Silvester, 'Coming Clean', *The Age*, 1 October 2005. **Page 115, In 2002 he had served:** *The Age*, 25 September 2002. **Page 116, Italiano's funeral:** *R v Domenic Michael Italiano* [2005] VSCA 160; *Herald Sun*, 29 June 2005.

8 Some Painters and Dockers

Page 124, One year he had under-declared: *SMH*, 8 May 1981. **Page 125, One of its secretaries:** The New South Wales branch was just as keen on name-changing. On 3 February 1975 it was recorded at a meeting of the branch executive committee that forty-three members, of whom twenty-two adopted Italian-style aliases, changed their names. *National Times*, 29 September 1982. **Page 129, What is happening:** Richard Gill, *Herald*, 19 January 1972. **Page 129, There have also been suggestions:** Tony Reeves, *Getting away with Murder*, Part 3. **Page 129, Fined $150:** *The Age*, 14 December 1972. **Page 130, You know what's going on:** *The Age*, 14 December 1972. **Page 130, He told the police:** *The Age*, 16 December 1972. **Page 130, He had been having problems:** His widow Gladys later married a top-class criminal, the English-born Stuart Perry. Some years later Perry was believed to have been thrown out of a plane in Asia after $1 million belonging to a drug syndicate went missing. 'Bookie Robbery mobster finally runs out of lives', *The Age*, 1 September 2010. **Page 131, Judge Curlewis said he:** *SMH*, 1 June 1944; *Truth* (Sydney), 4 March 1956. **Page 131, Kable was duly:** *The Age*, 18 October 1974. **Page 131, Cayeux was later sentenced:** *The Age*, 18 October 1974. **Page 132, According to Loughnan:** Inquisition into the death of Pat Shannon, VPRS File 1804–1979. **Page 132, Whichever way he faced:** Conversation with JM, 13 March 2009. **Page 135, A man known as Pudding:** VPRS Inquest 1979/1599. **Page 136, No one was charged:** VPRS Inquest 1980/66; Tame, *The Matriarch*. For a full account of the trials of Harding, Taylor and Longley and the subsequent death of Harding, see Morton & Robinson, *Shotgun and Standover*. **Page 136, I have certain reservations:** Jackson, In Your Face, p. 146. **Page 139, He left a note:** Inquest upon the body of John Salisbury Nicholls, VPRS 24/1, File 1982/890. **Page 140, In his report:** Costigan Royal Commission. **Page 140, The Hawke government:** For a full account of the troubles of the Victoria branch of the Painters and Dockers' Union, see Morton & Robinson, *Shotgun and Standover*.

9 Shooting Stars

Page 142, If Woon turned it down: For an account of Woon's activities, see Morton & Robinson, *Shotgun and Standover*. **Page 143, 'When you think**

about it: *Daily Telegraph*, 9 June 1998. **Page 143, The profits from this vice den:** 'Bookie Robbery mobster finally runs out of lives', *The Age*, 1 September 2010. **Page 146, 'What was obvious:** Conversation with JM, 13 March 2009. **Page 146, Prendergast had a brother:** VPRS Inquest 1979/1955. **Page 147, On 21 September:** VPRS Inquest 1979/1955. **Page 150, Much later, when the case:** VPRS Inquest 1983/1635. For a full account of the Bookie Robbery and the Bennett–Kane quarrel and killings, see Morton & Robinson, *Shotgun and Standover*. **Page 150, Another on the Ansett raid:** *R v Barci & Asling* (1994) 76 A Crim R 103; *Barci v Heffey* [1995] VSC 13. **Page 152, Chuck Bennett's offsider:** Mark Buttler & Anthony Dowsley, 'Melbourne gangland figure dies', *Herald Sun*, 12 October 2010. **Page 154, Killing Tsakmakis:** Read, *Chopper from the Inside*. **Page 155, In 2009 his application:** *R v Haigh* [2009] VSC 185.

10 Chopper Read and Mr Death

Page 156, What is not in question: Read, *Chopper from the Inside*; Tame, *The Matriarch*. **Page 157, Read had been wearing:** Read, *Chopper From the Inside, Chopper 2 Hits and Memories, Chopper 3 How to Shoot Friends and Influence People*; Khazar, 'Chopper's Whoppers'. **Page 162, Pollitt was sentenced:** *R v. Pollitt* [1991] 1 VR 299. **Page 164, 'Dennis was good:** Anderson, *Shotgun City*, p. 167. **Page 164, The next year:** *R v Allen* [2006] VSCA 3. **Page 165, There was more trouble:** AAP Newswire, 15 September 2008. **Page 165, In October 2009:** Daniel Fogarty, 'Man jailed for meat cleaver attack', *The Age*, 9 October 2009. **Page 166, The death certificate:** Adam Shand, 'Underworld twist on daughter of slain underworld hitman Victor Peirce', *Herald Sun*, 26 October 2010. **Page 166, A co-accused:** *Herald Sun*, 29 May 2010.

11 Victoria's Finest

Page 167, *The Argus*, never a supporter: Haldane, *The People's Force*, p. 39. **Page 169, 'One does not expect:** Private Papers of John Christie Undated entry, probably 1897, State Library of Victoria. **Page 170, Brooks was not even called:** Brown & Haldane, *Days of Violence* p. v; Haldane, *The People's Force*. **Page 173, There were other:** Morgan, *Gun Alley*. **Page 173, The official police history:** Royal Commission on the Alleged Shooting and Wounding of John O'Connell Brophy, Report, VPRS 3992 and VPRS 2570; Hardiman, 'Police Accountability in Victoria'. **Page 173, The first two had been brushed:** VPRS 3992, Unit 2590, File 29916; Haldane, *The People's Force*; 'Police Treatment of Suspects', *The Argus*, 19 June 1936. **Page 174, It turned out that Collingburn:** For a full account of the case and the trial, see Morton & Robinson, *Shotgun and Standover*, pp. 96–9. **Page 175, She died aged seventy-nine:** Berman & Childs, *Why Isn't She Dead?*; Geoff Wilkinson, 'The Power of Peg', *Herald Sun*, 21 December 2002. **Page 175, The celebrity criminal:** Read, *Chopper From the Inside*, pp. 166–7. **Page 177, In 2004, Lamb died:** *The Queen v Alistair Farquhar MacRae* [1995] VSC 108; *The Age*, 7 April 1993; *Sunday Herald Sun*, 18 November 2001; *Sunday Herald Sun*, 24 April 2004. **Page 178, Minogue's brother Rodney:** *Minogue v R* (VSC)

Notes

(unreported) 22 June 1989. In October 1987 Craig Minogue survived the fire at Jika Jika. In 1988 he killed a fellow prisoner, the violent robber Alex Tsakmakis, beating him to death with gym weights. He effectively received three months for the murder—a life sentence to run concurrently with his sentence for the Russell Street bombing. In more recent years he has campaigned vigorously for prisoners' rights. **Page 181, In January 2011 she said:** Anthony Dowsley, 'Hatred drives gangland widow Wendy Peirce', *Herald Sun*, 8 January 2011. **Page 182, The actual robbers:** Noble, *The Walsh Street Killings*; Tame, *The Matriarch*; Read, *Chopper from the Inside*.

12 Into the New Century

Page 184, But the damage had been done: John Silvester, 'Cops, Robbers, drugs and money', *The Age*, 18 March 2003. **Page 185, His father George:** *R v Williams* [2008] VSCA 95. **Page 186, On 16 January 1998 he was killed:** John Silvester, 'Death of a Gangster', *The Sunday Age*, 18 January 1998. **Page 187, One remembers him:** Conversation with SL, 16 August 2006. **Page 187, It was purportedly placed:** *R v Lucas*, 2 VR 109 (1992); Anderson, *Shotgun City*; Silvester & Rule, *Leadbelly*. **Page 188, The list of people:** Silvester & Rule, *Leadbelly*. **Page 189, His killer was probably Dino Dibra:** Anderson, *Shotgun City*. **Page 190, However, ex-lawyer Andrew Fraser:** Fraser, *Snouts in the Trough*, p. 176. **Page 191, None of the Carlton Crew:** Adam Shand, 'Burial Ground', *Bulletin*, 6 April 2004. **Page 192, The killing had been slated:** *The Age*, 2 March 2005. **Page 192, He received a modest five-year minimum:** *R v Barbaro*, [2006] NSWCCA, 180. *R v McEachran* [2006] VSCA 290; *SMH*, 11, 25, 26 August 2004; *Observer*, 15 August 2004; *The Age*, 21 December 2005. **Page 192, With a career spanning three decades:** John Silvester et al., 'Modest Mobster who kept the Peace', *The Age*, 14 December 2003; Adam Shand, 'Mobsters Inc: How Melbourne became No.1 with a bullet', *Bulletin*, 18 February 2004. **Page 193, He was, said one Melbourne barrister:** Conversation with SL and JM, 22 February 2006. **Page 194, Indeed, the day before:** *The Sunday Age*, 14 December 2003. **Page 196, Quitter or not:** *Herald Sun*, 23 November 2004. **Page 197, On 9 February 2009:** Daniel Fogarty, 'Underworld killer jailed for life', *SMH*, 9 February 2009. **Page 198, Defteros, who adamantly denied:** *The Sunday Age*, 8 August 2004. **Page 198, He was remanded in custody:** *Geelong Advertiser*, 30 October 2004; *The Age*, 30 October 2004. For a series of highly entertaining accounts of the gang war, see the *Bulletin* articles by Adam Shand, including 6 & 15 April and 22 June 2004. **Page 199, Gatto was triumphantly acquitted:** Gatto with Noble, *I, Mick Gatto*; Silvester & Rule, *Underbelly*; *Leadbelly*; Wilkinson & Moor, *Mugshots*; *Melbourne Underworld News*, 17 May 2005. **Page 199, Around ten o'clock:** *Australian*, 8 February 2006. **Page 200, His son generously took:** *R v Holden* [2007] VSC 417; *Australian*, 7 December 2005; *The Age*, 24 May 2006. **Page 201, In June 2008 his appeals:** *R v Strawhorn* [2008] VSCA 101. **Page 201, In October 2003:** John Silvester, 'Bent Confessions of a Crooked Cop', *The Age*, 13 June 2003. **Page 202, Detective Senior Constable David Miechel:** *R v Miechel* [2006] VSC 359. **Page 202, In 2009 their appeals:** *R v Ferguson, R v Sadler, R v Cox* [2009]

230

VSCA 198. **Page 203, At the time he had been working:** John Silvester, 'End-of-year gangster wrap', *The Age*, 30 December 2006. **Page 203, As a result the Director:** Kate Hagan, 'Perjury Charges against Noel Ashby dropped', *The Age*, 9 February 2010. **Page 204, It appears that files:** Liam Houlihan, 'Lewis Moran police officer friend probed', *Herald Sun*, 7 November 2010. **Page 205, Ibrahim appeared to be:** *The Age*, 12 September 2003; 7 June, 12 July 2005; *Herald Sun*, 7 June, 12 July 2005; *Herald Sun*, 18 February 2006. **Page 206, 'There'll be the new New Boys':** Conversation with JM. **Page 206, 'The vacuum we've been:** *Melbourne Underworld News*, 17 May 2005. **Page 207, The judge's comments were condemned:** for a full account of this feud see Morton & Lobez, *Gangland Australia*. **Page 208, The Comancheros established Melbourne headquarters:** for more about Malkoun see Morton & Lobez, *Dangerous to Know*. **Page 208, He had also heard that one gang:** Cameron Houston, 'Bikie gangs battle for underworld', *The Age*, 18 April 2010; 'Bikie gang crackdown', abc.net.au/news, 17 August 2010; Nick McKenzie, 'Bikies, triads, officials linked in drug smuggling ring,' *4 Corners/The Age*, 30 August 2010; Cameron Houston & Maris Beck, 'Former boxer charged as bikie gangs recruit more muscle,' *The Age*, 12 September 2010; Geoff Wilkinson, 'Boom time for bikie gangs in Victoria', *Herald Sun*, 22 October 2010. **Page 209, Certainly, Desmond should never:** Read, *Chopper From the Inside*, p. 257; Sue Hewitt, 'The last Moran standing', *Herald Sun*, 15 April 2007. **Page 209, Read claimed that before:** Read, *Chopper From the Inside*, p. 259. **Page 212, Rather ambiguously:** Liam Houlihan, 'Carl Williams told of sex favours', *Herald Sun*, 16 May 2010. **Page 212, The some-time drug dealer:** *Ivanovic v The Queen* [2006] HCA Trans332. **Page 213, He also denied:** Mark Buttler 'I didn't kill Carl Williams, says former detective Paul Dale', *Herald Sun*, 16 February 2011. **Page 213, She later made what many:** Jon Kaila, 'Roberta Williams offers apology to rival Moran family', *Herald Sun*, 19 December 2010. **Page 213, Roberta Williams' fifth child:** Megan Norris, 'My baby is Carl's Gift', *New Idea*, 14 March 2011. **Page 214, The city's Asian Gang Squad:** Mark Buttler, 'Neighbours fear gang violence will spiral into gun battles as secret police report exposes fears of open warfare', *Herald Sun*, 20 May 2010. **Page 214, Weapons wielded by the gang:** Greg Roberts, 'Vic Police hunt armed gang after stabbing', *The Age*, 30 December 2010. **Page 214, It may not have reached:** In the Detroit war Harry Kalasho had two of his rivals Salem Munthir and Salem Gago killed by hitman Buck Lavell. The payment was $5000 each and a further $10 000 if their heads were deposited on the disputed turf of Detroit's Seven Mile. Lavell completed the contract but did not deposit the heads. **Page 215, Gangitano then tried:** Bezzina, *The Job*; Gatto, *I, Mick Gatto*; Keith Moor, 'Chaouk family members allegedly threatened to blow up police complex', *Herald Sun*, 17 September 2010. **Page 215, After that, threats were made:** Bezzina, *The Job*. Bezzina left Victoria Police after a reshuffle and became a manager of a branch of Tobin Brothers, the undertakers. **Page 215, 'I suddenly realised I was alone:** Norrie Ross, 'Accused killer Ahmed Hablas "shot Mohammed Haddara four times"', *Herald Sun*, 17 September 2010. **Page 216, 'His blood does not come cheap:** *R v Chaouk* [2000] VSCA 238; staff writers, 'Notorious Melbourne patriarch Macchour Chaouk, shot dead in Brooklyn', *Herald Sun*, 13 August

Notes

2010; Mark Buttler & Evonne Barry, 'A deadly rivalry', *Herald Sun*, 14 August 2010. **Page 216, This prompted a warning:** 'Bikie gang crackdown', abc.net.au/news, 17 August 2010. **Page 217, On 11 November he was sentenced:** Steve Lillebuen, 'Minute's silence, then jail', *Geelong Advertiser*, 12 November 2010. **Page 218, It was also immediately suggested:** Anthony Dowsley, 'Mokbel's life may be in danger', *Herald Sun*, 20 April 2011. **Page 220, Mokbel was also said:** Keith Moor, 'Businessman washed drug cash', Keith Moor, *Herald Sun*, 30 April 2007. **Page 220, Even with Mokbel's final conviction:** Anthony Dowsley, 'Concern for Tony Mokbel's safety over speculation of Crown deal', *Herald Sun*, 20 April 2011.

Selected Bibliography

Books

Allen, J, *Sex and Secrets: crimes involving Australian women since 1880*, Oxford University Press, Melbourne, 1990

Anderson, H, *Larrikin Crook: the rise and fall of Squizzy Taylor*, Jacaranda Press, Melbourne, 1971

Anderson, P, *Dirty Dozen: 12 true-crime stories that shocked Australia*, Hardie Grant Books, South Yarra, Vic., 2003

——*Shotgun City: Melbourne's gangland killings*, Hardie Grant Books, Prahran, Vic., 2004

Australian Dictionary of Biography, Melbourne University Publishing, Online Edition, Australian National University, Canberra, 2006

Barry, JV, *The Life and Death of John* Price: *a study in the exercise of naked power*, Melbourne University Press, Carlton, Vic., 1964

Beale, O, *A Compilation of Evidence from World Sources*, Angus & Robertson, Sydney, 1910

Berman, P & Childs, K, *Why Isn't She Dead?*, Gold Star Publications, Melbourne, 1972

Bezzina, C, *The Job: fighting crime from the inside*, Slattery Media Group, Victoria, 2010

Blaikie, G, *Remember Smith's Weekly*, Rigby, Sydney, 1966

Brennan, N, *John Wren: gambler, his life and times*, Hill of Content, Melbourne, 1971

Buggy, H, *The Real John Wren*, Widescope International Publishers, Melbourne, 1977

Caylock, G, *Charlie: as game as Ned Kelly*, Wild and Woolly, Glebe, NSW, 1998

Davison, G, Dunstan, D & McConville, C (eds), *The Outcasts of Melbourne*, Allen & Unwin, Sydney, 1985

Davison, G, McCarty, JW & McLeary, A (eds), *Australians, 1888*, Fairfax, Syme and Weldon Associates, Sydney, 1987

Selected Bibliography

Dower, A, *Deadline*, Hutchinson, Richmond, Vic., 1978

Fitzgerald, JD, *Studies in Australian Crime* (Second Series), Eagle Press, Sydney, 1924

Fitzroy Legal Service, *Police Shootings in Victoria 1987–1989*, Fitzroy Legal Service, Melbourne, 1992

Fraser, A, *Snouts in the Trough,* Hardie Grant Books, Prahran, Vic., 2010

Galbally, F, *Galbally for the Defence*, Penguin Books, Ringwood, Vic., 1994

Gatto, M with Noble, T, *I, Mick Gatto*, Victory Press, Carlton, Vic., 2009

Griffin, J, *John Wren: a life reconsidered*, Scribe Publications, Carlton North, Vic., 2004

Haldane, R, *The People's Force: a history of the Victoria Police*, Melbourne University Press, Carlton, Vic., 1986

Hansen, B, *The Awful Truth*, Brian Hansen Publications, Melbourne, 2004

Hickie, D, *Chow Hayes: gunman,* Angus & Robertson, Sydney, 1990

Illingworth, S, *Filthy Rat*, Fontaine Press, Fremantle, WA, 2007

Jackson, R, *In Your Face: the life and times of Billy 'The Texan' Longley*, ABC Books, Sydney, 2005

Kelly, V, *The Charge Is Murder,* Rigby, Adelaide, 1965

Lahey, J, *Damn You John Christie,* State Library of Victoria, Melbourne, 1993

Latch, B with Hitchings, B, *Mr X: police informer*, Dingo, Melbourne, 1975

Linnell S, *Don't Tell the Chief: the untold story of police, power and politics,* Wilkinson Publishing, Melbourne, 2010

Maltzahn, K, *Trafficked,* University of New South Wales Press, Sydney, 2008

McCalman, J, *Struggletown,* Melbourne University Press, Melbourne, 1984

Minchin, D, *The Money Movers*, Hutchinson, Melbourne, 1978

Morgan, K, *Gun Alley*, Simon & Schuster, Sydney, 2005

Morton, J & Lobez, S, *Gangland Australia*, Melbourne University Press, Carlton, Vic., 2008

——*Dangerous to Know*, Victory Press, Carlton, Vic., 2009

Morton, J & Robinson, R, *Shotgun and Standover*, Pan Macmillan, Sydney, 2010

Noble, T, *Walsh Street*, John Kerr, Richmond, Vic., 1991

Pearl, C, *Wild Men of Sydney*, WH Allen, London, 1958

Perkins, R et al (eds), *Sex Work and Sex Workers in Australia*,
       University of New South Wales Press, Sydney, 1994

Prior, T, *The Sinner's Club: confessions of a walk-up man*, Penguin
       Books, Ringwood, Vic., 1993

Read, MB, *Chopper From the Inside*, Floradale Productions, Smithfield,
       NSW, 1991

——*Chopper 2 Hits and Memories*, Floradale Productions, Smithfield,
       NSW, 1992

——*Chopper 3 How to Shoot Friends and Influence People*, Floradale
       Press, Smithfield, NSW, 2000

Robinson, LM, *Madame Brussels: this moral pandemonium*, Arcade
       Publications, Carlton, Vic., 2009

Silvester, J & A Rule, *Tough: 101 Australian gangsters*, Floradale Press
       and Sly Ink, Camberwell, Vic., 2002

——*Leadbelly: inside Australia's underworld wars*, Floradale Press and
       Sly Ink, Camberwell, Vic., 2004

Sullivan, M & Jeffries, S, *Legalising Prostitution Is Not the Answer:
       the example of Victoria, Australia*, Coalition Against Trafficking in
       Women, North Fitzroy, Melbourne, 2001

Tame, A, *The Matriarch*, Pan Macmillan, Sydney, 1996

Varley, H, *Henry Varley's Life-Story*, Alfred Holness, London, n.d.

Wainer, B, *It Isn't Nice*, Alpha Books, Sydney, 1972

Articles, reports and manuscripts

Attorney-General's Street Prostitution Advisory Group, Interim
       Report, Melbourne, September 2001

Barclay, I, Interactive Processes in Brothel Prostitution, Honours
       Thesis, Department of Political Science, University of Melbourne,
       2001

Beck, M, 'Inside Melbourne's sex trade', *Brisbane Times*, 12 March
       2009

'Blonde Underworld Queen dodged gaol', *Truth* (Melbourne), 4 April
       1941

'Bookie Robbery mobster finally runs out of lives', *The Age*,
       1 September 2010

Buggy, H, 'How "Squizzy" Taylor Died by the Gun', *The Argus*,
    3 December 1949

Buttler, M, 'Neighbours fear gang violence will spiral into gun battles
    as secret police report exposes fears of open warfare', *Herald Sun*,
    20 May 2010

Buttler, M & Barry, E, 'A deadly rivalry', *Herald Sun*, 14 August 2010

Buttler, M & Dowsley, A, 'Melbourne gangland figure dies', *Herald Sun*,
    12 October 2010

Chandler, J, 'See no evil, hear no evil … then there's "Granny Evil"',
    The Age, 7 February 2007

Chen, MY, 'Estimating the number of unlicensed brothels in
    Melbourne', *Australian and New Zealand Journal of Public Health*,
    vol. 34, issue 1, 2006

Christie, J, Private Papers, undated entry (probably 1897), State
    Library of Victoria

'Conman and Gunman', *Truth* (Sydney), 21 September 1924

Costigan, FX (Dir.), *Royal Commission on the Activities of the Federated
    Ship Painters and Dockers' Union*, Final Report, Canberra, 1984

Danilos, P, 'Saying Goodbye to a Colourful Criminal', *Herald Sun*,
    7 January 1995

'Death of a Thug', *Truth* (Melbourne), 6 August 1960

'Docklands' Dark Terror', *Truth* (Melbourne), 14 January 1928

Dowsley, A, 'Hatred drives gangland widow Wendy Peirce', *Herald
    Sun*, 8 January 2011

Duffy, M, 'Alive and kicking, a quiet achiever of the underworld', *SMH*,
    16 April 2010

'Five bullets—and death—for Razor Slasher Bruhn,' *Truth*
    (Melbourne), 2 July 1927

Flach, R, The Bearded Negro, unpublished manuscript, in possession
    of JM, 1963

Fogarty, D, 'Underworld killer jailed for life', *SMH*, 9 February 2009

Gill, R, *Herald,* 19 January 1972

'Gold Adulteration in Victoria', *Mercury*, 10 February 1898

Hadfield, S, 'Thai women caught in Melbourne sex slave scheme',
    Herald Sun, 23 April 2009

Hagan, K, 'Man found guilty in sex slave case', *The Age*, 18 October 2009

—— 'Perjury Charges against Noel Ashby dropped', *The Age*,
    9 February 2010

Hardiman, B, 'Police Accountability in Victoria', *Annual Report of the Ombudsman*, Government Printer, Melbourne, 2003

Hewitt, S, 'The last Moran standing', *Herald Sun*, 15 April 2007

Houlihan, L, 'Carl Williams told of sex favours', *Herald Sun*, 16 May 2010

—'Lewis Moran police officer friend probed', *Herald Sun*, 7 November 2010

'Is Buckley Dead or Alive?', *Truth* (Melbourne), 12 January 1924

Jeffreys, S, 'Prostitution Culture: Legalised brothel prostitution in Victoria, Australia', talk given at Swedish Ministry of Gender Equality Seminar on the Effect of Legalisation of Prostitution, Stockholm, 6 November 2002

Kaila, J, 'Roberta Williams offers apology to rival Moran family', *Herald Sun*, 19 December 2010

Khazar, M, 'Chopper's Whoppers', *Australian Penthouse*, December 1994

Lillebuen, S, 'Minute's silence, then jail', *Geelong Advertiser*, 12 November 2010

'Madame Brussels' Notorious Bawdy House: Her Junketing Jezebels', *Truth* (Melbourne), 10 March 1906

'Maloney Kids reverse routine', *Truth* (Melbourne), 15 July 1940

Maltzahn, K, 'So far, so good, but more can be done to end sex slavery', *The Age*, 18 June 2009

Marino, M, 'Sex in our city? Plenty apparently', *The Age*, 8 June 2003

McCarthy, J, 'The Commonwealth Block, Melbourne; Archaeological Investigation Report, Vol. 1, Historical and Archaeological Report', *Australian Construction Services*, prepared for the Department of Administrative Services and Telecom Australia, 1989

McConville, C, 'The location of Melbourne's prostitutes, 1870–1920', *Historical Studies*, vol. 19, no. 74, April 1980

McKenzie, N & Baker, R, 'Crime and Banishment', *SMH*, 23 February 2009

'Melbourne Pushes', *Ohinemuri Gazette* (NZ), 18 April 1910

Moor, K, 'Chaouk family members allegedly threatened to blow up police complex', Herald Sun, 17 September 2010

'Murder Mystery Still Unsolved', *Truth* (Melbourne), 18 January 1913

Murphy, P, 'Lured by wealth, sex slaves go home with little savings', *SMH*, 14 July 2003

Norton, J, 'Lechery and Lucre', *Truth* (Melbourne), 29 November 1906

'Notorious Melbourne patriarch Macchour Chaouk, shot dead in Brooklyn', *Herald Sun*, 13 August 2010

Pickering, S, Maher, J & Gerard, A, 'Working in Victoria Brothels', an independent report commissioned by Consumer Affairs Victoria, June 2009

'Police Treatment of Suspects', *The Argus*, 19 June 1936

Richards, D, 'Dockyard Vigilantes', *Australian Penthouse*, March 1980

—— 'Australia's Toughest Criminal Talks', *Bulletin*, 11 March 1980

—— 'How the Government Condones Waterfront Graft', *Bulletin*, 18 March 1980

—— 'Like Nelson, the Navy Turns a Blind Eye and Pays Up', *Bulletin*, 25 March 1980

—— 'Tax Rackets Lead to Death Threats', *Bulletin*, 2 April 1980

Roberts, G, 'Vic Police hunt armed gang after stabbing', *The Age*, 30 December 2010

Ross, N, 'Accused killer Ahmed Hablas "shot Mohammed Haddra four times"', *Herald Sun*, 17 September 2010

Rule, A, 'He's Mr Goldfingers', *The Sunday Age*, 12 March 2000

Ryan, M & Greenlees, D, 'Joey stays one jump ahead', *Sunday Press*, 5 September 1982

Shand, A, 'Mobsters Inc: How Melbourne became No.1 with a bullet', *Bulletin*, 18 February 2004

—— 'Burial Ground', *Bulletin*, 6 April 2004

—— 'Underworld twist on daughter of slain underworld hitman Victor Peirce', *Herald Sun*, 26 October 2010

Silvester, J, 'Cops, Robbers, drugs and money', *The Age*, 18 March 2003

—— 'Bent Confessions of a Crooked Cop', *The Age*, 13 June 2003

—— 'Coming Clean', *The Age*, 1 October 2005

—— 'End-of-year gangster wrap', *The Age*, 30 December 2006

Silvester, J et al., 'Modest Mobster who kept the Peace', *The Age*, 14 December 2003

'The Fitzroy Murder', *Advertiser* (Adelaide), 17 January 1913

'The Nelson Robbery', *Victorian Historical magazine*, vol. 73, no. 2, September 2002.

'The Push', *Timaru Herald*, 25 November 1899

'The Trotter Tragedy', *Truth* (Melbourne), 11 January 1913

Varley, H, *The War Between Heaven and Hell*, pamphlet, Melbourne, 1891

Walker, G, 'Temptress set free. But now she faces hell on the outside', *Sun*, 17 August 1989

Wilkinson, G, 'The Power of Peg', *Herald Sun*, 21 December 2002

Index

Note: page numbers in **bold** type refer to images.

Abbott, Ray, 67
Abdallah, Gary, 180
abortion, 8, 13, 174–5, 209
Abrahams, Evelyn, 154–5
Abrahams, John Charles, 70, 71–3
Adam, Fred 'Bluey', 85, 89, 90, 101, 110, 174, 175
Allard, Francis John, 89
Allard, Victor George, 135–6
Allen, Dennis 'Mr Death', **119**, 136, 156, 158–64
Allen, Peter, 158, 159, 160, 164–6
Allen, Sissy, 136
Allsop, Charles 'Prat-in', 32
Allsop, Rowena, 186–7
Anderson, James 'Paddles', 70, 71–3
Andrews, Norman, 49, 50
Andry, Earle Joseph, 75
Angilletta, Vincenzo, 111, 112
Anti-Mafia Commission, 112–13
Arena, Giuseppe 'Joe', 114
Arico, Rocco, 190
Armour, Geoffrey 'Nuts', 207, 209–10, 211
Ashby, Noel, 203, 204
Asling, Steven, 150–1
Aspel, Burt, 126
assault, 64–5, 70
Aydin, Ali, 204

Bailey, Robert George, 91
Baker, May, 42
Barbara, Antonio 'The Toad', 110
Barbaro, Giuseppe 'Joe', 192
Barbaro, Montana, 192
Barbaro, Pasquale, 117, 192, 198
Barci, Stephen, 150–1
Bariska, Tibor, 137–8
Barrett, George 'John Paul', 93
Barrett, William Sylvester, 69
Baum, Caroline 'Madame Brussels', 40–3, 44
Bayer, Hymie, 81
Bayliss, Francis, 129–30

Bayly, Albert, 75
Bazely, Arthur, 23, 25, 81
Bazin, Leon, 91, 94
Bazley, James Frederick 'Machine Gun', 126, 127, 129
Beatten, Mona, 74
Beaumont, James, 80
Beaumont, Jean, 47–8
Beckwith, Stan, 94
Belios, Jim, 189
Bennett, Ray 'Chuck', 129, 137, 141, 142–4, 144–6, 147, 149, 151, 152
Bennett, Robert David, 17
Benson, Abe, 5
Bent, Sir Thomas, 44
Benvenuto, Angelo, 114
Benvenuto, Francesco 'Frank', 114, 115, 189, 196
Benvenuto, Liborio, 113, 114
Berman, Peggy, 174–5
Berriman, Thomas, 27, 28
Biddlestone, Robert, 163
biker gangs *see* OMCG (outlaw motorcycle gangs)
Birch, Stanley 'Moocher', 77, 94, 96
Birch, Stanley Keith 'Big Moocher', 75
black market, 79–80
blackmail, 13, 33
Blamey, Thomas, 170–3
bodyguards, 114, 129, 137, 192
bombing, 10, 33, 36, 37, 116, 154, 162, 177–8
Bottazzi, Robert, 208
Bourke, Thomas, 2
Bradshaw, Norman 'The Chaffeur', 65–6, 82, 83, 84, 85–6, 87, 88, 90–1, 94, 100, 101, 102, 103, 104, 174
Brcic, Rosa, 52
Brearley, Lisa Maud, 155
Brennan, Thomas, 65
Brenner, Sarah, 45
Brewster, Bob, 83, 86, 87, 88
Brooks, Vickie, 164
Brooks, William, 170
Brophy, John O'Connell, 172–3
brothel wars, 176–7

Index

brothels, 33, 39–47, 51–4, 160, 161, 168, 171, 176, 207; see also prostitutes; prostitution
Brown, Alfred 'Darky', 127
Brown, Leslie Francis Eugene Xavier 'Lair', 74, 75, 76, 77, 90, 91
Brown, Lilian Vera Chrystobel, 61
Bruce, James, 23
Bruhn family, 55–61, 65–6
Bruhn, Billy, 60–1
Bruhn, Irene, 56, 57
Bruhn, Norman, 33, 35, 46, 55–7, 60, 196
Bruhn, Oscar, 60–1
Bruhn, Oscar Jnr, 60
Bruhn, Roy, 57–61
Bruhn, Stanley, 60
Buckley, Richard 'Grey Ghost', 15, 27–8, 31–2
Buggy, Hugh, 15
Buller-Murphy, Judge, 96
Bunning, Matthew, 202–3
Burgess, Murray, 132
burglary, 2, 4, 14, 15, 16, 24, 69
Bourke, Francis, 145
Burles, John, 69
Burles, Margaret, 69
Burles, Richard 'Shanghai', 69–70, 89
Burns, 'Mush', 33
Buttler, Mark, 212
Byrne, Rex, 37

Caine, Lewis, 197, 199
Cameron, Nellie, 46, 56
Cameron Royal Commission, 169–70
Carlton, Charlie, 81
Carpenter, Rob, 213
Carroll, Ian Revell 'Fingers', 129, 142, 151
Cartledge family, 64, 65, 69
Cartledge, Ada, 67–8
Cartledge, Adeline, 66
Cartledge, Blanche, 65, 67
Cartledge, David Lawrence 'Dopey', 64–5, 67
Cartledge, Gerald, 66
Cartledge, Henry, 64
Cartledge, Kenneth Roy, 65, 66, 67, 98
Cartledge, Leo, 66, 67, 68–9
Cartledge, Phyllis, 67
Cartwright, Walter, 8
Cassidy, Richard, 68
Cayeux, Jill Frances, 131
Caylock, Charlie, 32, 35–6
Chambers, Billy, 56
Chamings, Laurence Richard, 129, 130, 131

Chaouk, Macchour, **123**, 216–17
Chaouk, Matwali, 216, 217
Chaouk, Mohamed, 215
Chaouk, Mohamed Ali, 214–15
Chaouk, Omar, 215–16
Chaouk, Walid, 216
Charlton, Charlie, 81
Chartres-Abbott, Shane, 203–4
children, 7–8, 52–3, 68, 130, 191–2
Chokr, Ahmad,
Christie, John, 169
Christie, John, 2
Cingolani, Bruno, 155
Cirillo, Domenico, 112
Cirillo, Giovanni, 109
City Tattersall's Club, 9–10
Clarke, 'Nigger', 74
Clarke, Rayon, 65
Clayton, Margaret, 153
Clayton, Robert, 48–9, 50
Clinton, Leo, 64
Coates, James, 81, 83, 86–7
Coffey, John William, 61
Cole, Les, 211
Collingburn, Neil, 173–4
Collins, Sid, 157, 158, 185
Combine, The (brothel owners), 44–5
Combine, The (Painters and Dockers), 84–107
Combs, Raymond Theodore, 66
Condello, Mario, 197, 198, 199, 200
confidence tricksters, 2, 78, 89
Conlon, John, 14–15
Connell, Alfie, 132, 133
Connellan, Thomas, 126
Connolly, Gail, 104
consorting, 42, 46,, 67, 76, 77, 91, 94, 95, 125, 139
contract killings, 64, 86–7, 165, 184, 185, 191–2, 196, 197, 198, 204
Cooper, Constable, 20, 21
Corsetti, Danny, 127
Costello, Desmond Bernard 'Studd', 128, 129, 135
Costello, Peter, 46
Costigan, Francis Xavier, 139, 140
Cotter, Joseph 'Brownie', 23, 45
Counsel, Francis, 20
Cox, Russell 'Mad Dog', 150, 151–2, 182
Cox, Stephen, 202
Creed, Colin, 151
Croft, Peter, 76–7
Crotty, Robert, 126–7
Crowe, Cornelius, 10
Crutchy Push, 5

Cullen, Pat, 128
Cusack, John T, 112
Cutmore, 'Snowy', 6, 15, 18, 21, 33–5, 56
Cutmore, Bridget, 34, 35

Dale, Paul 'Killer', 202, 212–13
Daley, Matthew, 18–19, 20
Dalton, James, 41
Davis, Murray, 32
Day, Donny 'The Duck', 93
Day, Leslie Thomas, 93
De Sanctis, George, 82
Dean, John, 19
Deane, Helen Eva, 151
death sentence, 7, 9, 28–9, 31, 65, 69, 70, 109, 133
'debt bondage', 52
debt collectors, 144
Defteros, George, 186, 198
del Masi, Francesco, 112
Delaney, Francis, 36
Delouise, Vincenzo, 62
Demarte, Domenico, 108, 109, 111–12
Demsey, John Thomas, 60
Denning, Raymond, 152
Dew, Ernest 'Ikey', 96–7
Dias, Morris, 48–9
Dibra, Dino, 189, 189, 190, 196
Dix, Bobby, 127–8, 137
Dixon Report 1997, 51
dobbers see police informants
Dobbin, Joan, 85
Dodd, Dr Malcolm, 199
Donadio, Carl, 178
Donegan, Jimmy, 125, 126
Donoghue, Thomas, 2–3
Dorter, Thomas Leslie, 74
Douglas, George, 79
Dowdle, Percy, 30
Dower, Alan, 50, 90
Doyle, Jimmy, 99
Doyle, John, 139
Driscoll, Linus 'The Pom', 129, 137, 148
Drug Squad, 188, 219
drugs: amphetamines, 163, 183–4, 185, 187, 189; Asian syndicates, 126, 183; bikers, 115, 206; cannabis, 160; cocaine, 22, 30, 33, 47, 112–13, 115, 165, 219; dealing, 152, 158, 159, 160, 162; ecstasy, 115, 117; gangs, 214; heroin, 183; hotshots, 47, 150, 162, 166; Mafia, 112–13, 115; overdoses, 47; Romanian gangs, 183; and violence, 184
drugs war, 183–201, 208–11
Duffy, Frederick John, 109

Duggan, Jim, 48
Duncan, James, 1
Dunn, Dorothy, 108
Dunn QC, Phillip, 143, 147
Dunstan, Richard, 6

Edinburgh, Alfred, Duke of, 40, 168
Ellis, Edward, 86
Ellis, George, 30
Ellison, Johnny, 84–5
enforcers, 144, 158
ethnic communities: African gangs, 214; Asian gangs, 213–14; Chinese, 5, 45; Greek Club bombing, 36; Italian, 108–14; Lebanese, 215–18; Polynesian gang, 214; Yellow Clique, 214
Evans, Richard, 108
Eyre, Damian, 179

Fairlie Women's Prison, 63
false identities, 125
Fanesi, Joe, 76–7
Farrell, Anthony Leigh, 180–1
Farrugia, Michael, 209–10
Faure, Darlene, 62–3
Faure, Irene, 46, 57, 58, 62
Faure, Leslie Peter, 63
Faure, Leslie Thomas, 46, 57, 58, 62
Faure, Noel Ambrose, 62, 63, 196–7
Faure, Noel William, 57, 63–4
Faure, Norman Leslie, 62
Faure, Toni, 63, 64
Federated Ship Painters and Dockers' Union, 62, 84–107, 124–40, 196
Ferguson, Ian, 202
Field, Robert, 69
Finemore, Brian, 153
firearms trafficking, 104
Fitzroy Vendetta, 19–21
Flanigan, John, 1–2
Flannery, Chris 'Mr Rent-a-Kill', 145, 148, 161, 184
Fletcher, Archibald, 29–30
Flynn, Leonard, 92
Flynn, Leonard Patrick, 103
Flynn, William 'Porky', 6
Ford, Jack, 101, 174, 175
forgery, 25, 86
Foster, Leonard, 71, 72
Fox, Lindsay, 193
Francis, Charles, 26
Francis, Dr Shirley, 26
Fraser, Andrew, 190
Fraser, Sarah, 40
fraud, 2, 8

Index

Freeman, George, 139
Furina, Giuseppe, 113
Furlan, John, 116

Galbally, Frank, 92, 95, 102, 148
gambling, 103, 169; baccarat, 38, 81, 82,
    83, 86, 87, 90, 126; betting shops, 159;
    controlling, 81–2, 87–8; gaming, 25, 37,
    139; horseracing, 5, 9, 139, 141, 193;
    illegal, 37–8, 44, 100; totalisator, 9–10,
    43; two-up schools, 9, 18–19
Gangitano, Alphonse, 114, **122**, 184, 185,
    186–7, 188, 214
gangs: Bourke Street Rats, 4, 12;
    Bouverie Forty, 5–6; Bouverie Street,
    5; Brothers 4 Life, 213; Burke Street
    Rats, 4–5; Carlton Crew, 184, 185, 189,
    190, 191, 194, 197, 206; Central Crew,
    213; Chefs, 6; Devil's Raiders, 128;
    drug-dealing, 214; ethnic, 213–14;
    Fitzroy Checkers, 6; Fitzroy Forties, 5;
    Flying Angels, 6; Freeman Street, 5;
    Hawk Eyes, 6; Hoddle Street Lairies,
    3; Irishtown, 5; Kangaroo Gang, 141,
    193; Kings Park crew, 213; Little
    Campbells, 6; Magnetic Drill, 193;
    New Boys, 165, 184, 189, 190, 206; and
    nightclubs, 214; North Melbourne,
    6; Overcoat Boys, 157; resurgence,
    213–14, 218–19; Roses, 6; Stephen
    Street, 6; Sunshine Crew, 165, 184, 189,
    190, 206; Surrey Road, 156; Toecutters
    (Sydney), 129, 144, 156; Tracksuit
    Gang, 220; violence, 214; wars, 113–17;
    White Roses, 5; Williams Crew, 212;
    Woolpacks, 6; Young St Albans, 213;
    Young Spring Boys, 213
Garde-Wilson, Zarah, 197, 219
Gardiner, Edward, 45
Gardner, Sheryle Ann, 155
garrottings, 2–3, 39
Gatto, Dominic 'Mick', 186, 194, 195–6,
    198–9
Gaunson, David, 10
Genoa, Agnes, 57
Germanos, George, 190
'ghosting', 124, 138
Gilligan, John Francis, 25, 83, 86, 87, 88
Gillott, Sir Samuel, 43–4
ginger game, 13, 46, 49, 56, 65
Godfrey, Clarence, 29
gold, 1–2, 8, 91–2
Goldberg, Maurice, 74
Good, John, 40
Gordon, Terrence, 128–9

Gouroff, Victor, 161
Goussis, Evangelos, 197
Goyne, Lorraine, 177
Graham, Sidney James, 199–200
Grant, Peter, 137–8
Green, Frank, 57
Greenlees, Don, 94
Gregory, Peter, 181
Grey, Dolly, 13, 14–15, 19–20, 22, 46
Griffiths, Anne, 2
Griffiths, Thomas, 2
Grosvenor, William, 65
Gunther, Maud, 45

Hablas, Ahmed, 215–16
Haddara, Mohammed, 215–16
Haigh, Paul Steven, 154–5
Hall, John, 34
Hamer, John, 4
Hamilton, Emma, 9
Hamilton, Joey, 129
hangings, 17, 30–1, 50, 157
Hanlon, Hugh, 19
Hansen, Brian, 84
Harburton, Henry, 18
Harding, Gary, 132–4, 136, 137–8
Hardy, Frank, 11, 15
Hargreaves, Bernie, 94
Harkins, Violet, 98
Harries, William Patrick, 16
Harris, Blanche, 65, 67
Harrison, Beryl, 84–5, 89, 91, 100, 101
Harrison, Freddie 'The Frog', 25, 65–6,
    82, 83, 84–5, 86–7, 88–9, 91–2, 98–101,
    103, 139
Harrison, 'Dictionary' Harry, 81, 87
Harvey, Arthur, 2
Hatherley, Donald George, 155
Hatzakortzian, Paul, 203
Hayes, Chow, 50
Hayes, Robert, 98, 99
Hayes, Thomas 'Chopsey', 3
Hefti, Dominik, 178, 179, 182
Hegyalji, 'Mad' Charlie, 187–8
Helkett, Colonel Craigie, 168
Henderson, Christina, 71, 72
Hickey, Dominic, 52
Higgins, Paul William, 175–7
hitmen, 132, 137, 145, 147–8, 161, 195,
    218; *see also* contract killings
Ho Kam Ho, 54
Hodgson, Studholme George, 40, 41
Hodson, Nicola, 178
Hodson, Terence & Christine, 64, 178,
    202, 212–13, 218

Hoffa, Jimmy, 127
Holden, Graham, 200
Holland, Beryl, 84–5, 89, 91
Holland, Frank, 89
Holmes, Sylvia, 67–8
Honkys, Edward, 92
Hood, Sir Joseph, 13
Hoskings, Joan, 131–2
Houghton, Jedd, 180
housebreaking, 3, 12, 64, 66, 131
Howard, Alexander John, 25
Hughes, William 'Gunny', 4
Hull, Keith, 93

Ibrahim, Nicholas, 205
Italiano, Domenico 'The Pope', 110, 115–16
Ivanovic, Thomas 'Little Tommy', 212

Jackson, John, 15
Jackson, Mark 'Jacko', 157–8
Jacobson, Marty, 174–5
jailhouse lawyer, 164–5
James, John, 1
Jansen, Noella, 131–2
Jarvie, Mollie 'The Decoy Duck', 13, 22, 25
Jenkins, Percy 'Snowy', 37
Jensen, Graeme, 178–9, 180, 181, 182
Johnson, Matthew Charles, 212
Johnson, Raymond Andrew, 63
Jones, Gary, 162
Jones, John Mark, 106–7
Jones, Sir Ken, 208, 217
Judkins, George Alfred, 43
Judkins, William Henry, 43, 44

Kable, Barry 'The Bear', 130–1
Kable, Roy, 130
Kain, Jack, 47
Kaladjic, Thomaslav Dusko, 116
Kallipolitis, Paul, 190, 196
Kam Tin Ho, 54
Kane, Brian, 142, 144–5, 147, 148–50, 152
Kane, Judi, 144, 145, 146
Kane, Leslie, 63, 127, 135, 142, 144, 145,
    146–7, 186, 207
Kane, Raymond, 148
Kane, Suzanne, 207, 209, 211
Kaye QC, William, 174
Kelly, Irene Lorna, 21–2, 23
Kelly, Ned, 11, 168–9
Kelly, Osmond 'Hoppy', 128
Kelly, Ray, 73
Kelly, Siddy, 35
Kelly, Thomas, 35
Kemelfield, Simon, 38

Kenny, Anthony John, 163–4
Kent, William 'Old Bill', 49, 50
kidnapping, 47, 64, 128
Kim Syndicate, 81
King, 'No Toe', 33
King, Betty, 155, 200–201
King, John 'Scotty', 34
Kingdom, John Mervyn, 149
Kinneburgh, Graham 'The Munster',
    147, 184, 187, 192–4
Kinneburgh, Suzie, 194
Kirkham, Jack, 94
Kizon, John, 187
Knorr, Frances, 7–8
Koeppen, Willie, 153
Kolovrat, Nicholas, 130, 131
Korrington-Willis, Kenneth William 'Kid
    Stranger', 78–9

La Bastarda, 111
Lamb, Geoffrey, 175–7
Lander, Philip, 116
Lane, Hilda, 58
Lawson, Henry, 170
lawyers, 10, 15, 26, 52, 66, 72, 92, 93, 95,
    128, 129, 135, 137, 140, 143, 146, 147,
    148, 153, 172, 174, 175, 186, 193, 197,
    198
Laycock, Maurice, 4
Le Gallien, Richard Ross, 104
Lee, Jean, 48
Lee, Norman Leung, 142, 143–4, 145, 146,
    147, 150
Leigh, Kate, 89
Lelah, Fred, 52–3
'Lemon Tree', 124
Lenfield, Kim, 81
Lewis, Albert, 20
Lewis, Billy, 146
Lewis, Frederick, 20
Lewis, Joseph, 82
Lineham, Daniel, 171
Linnell, Stephen, 204
Lohse, Mark, 165
Longley, Billy 'The Texan', **120**, 126,
    127–8, 129, 132, 133, 134–5, 136–7, 138,
    139, 140, 142, 157
Longmore Commission, 169
'Lou the Lombard', 81, 90
Loughnan, John Patrick Joseph, 131–2,
    157
Loughnan, Richard, 24
Lowe, Justice, 77
Lowe, Nancy, 92
Lynch, Ruby, 45

Index

McAllister, Norman, 65
Macari, Peter, 143
McCabe, James, 203
McCormack, Cecil 'Scotchy', 72
McCubbin, Ambrose, 69
McCubbin, Benjamin, 69
Macdonald, Albert, 30
Macdonald, William, 22
McEachern, Malcolm, 42–3
McEachran, Mark and Cheryl, 192
McEvoy, Peter David, 180
McGinty, Patrick, 4
McGrath, David, 15
McGrindle, Robert Barklay, 45
McGuire, Danielle, 220
Macindoe, Hugh, 172
McIver, Alexander, 36
McIver, Norman, 36, 37
Mackay, Arthur, 58, 59
Mackay, Donald, 126
McKenzie, John, 77
McLaughlin, Frank, 34
McLeod, Norman, 149
McMahon, Brendon, 131
McNamara, Anthony, 150
McNamara, Anthony Paul, 142
MacRae, Alistair Farquhar 'Sandy', 113–14, 177
Madafferi, Antonio, 113, 116
Maddox, Lorna Carol, 82–3
Mafia (Honoured Society), 109–14
Maher, Judy, 69
Makin, John, 7
Malkoun, Amad 'Jay', 208
Mallia, Mark, 200
Maloney, Eva, 70
Maloney, Evelyn, 70
Maloney, James 'Red', 70, 71, 72
Maloney, Michael, 70
Maloney, Michael jnr, 70
Maloney, Tom, 70
Maloney, Violet, 70, 98
Manella, Giuseppe, 115
Manley, Jack, 89
Mann, Sir Frederick, 173
Mannella, Gerardo, 115, 188
Mannella, Vince, 115, 188
Mansfield, Karen, 114
manslaughter, 6, 74, 80–1
Mansour, Raymond, 188
Marafiote, Carmelo and Rosa, 113–14
Marafiote, Dominic, 113–14
market 'wars', 110–14, 189
Markham, 'Pretty' Dulcie, 71–2, 73, 75, 82, 88

Marks, Louise, 97
Marshall, Michael Ronald, 195, 198, 200, 218
Martin, Judge Bill, 157
Martini, Tony, 74
massage parlours, 51, 160, 161, 176
Masters, Florrie, 56
Matlock, Ada, 39
Matthews, Jack, 101
Matthews, Jack, 112, 174, 175
Mayer, Hymie, 38
Meagher, Doug, 140
Medici, Rocco, 113
Melbourne: brothels and prostitutes, 39–54; crime rate, 1–6; Fitzroy Vendetta, 19–21; infanticides, 7–8; Little Lon area, 39; market wars, 110–14, 189; wowsers, 42–4; see also gangs
Melbourne Wholesale Fruit & Vegetable Market, 113
Mendoza, Iris, 68
Mercante, Troy, 190
Mercuri, Santo, 178
Miechel, David, 202
Mikkelsen, Vinnie, 142, 145–6, 147, 149, 150
Milini, Rita, 39
Militano, Mark, 178
Miller, Maude, 42
Miller, Mavis Helen, 93
Miller, Robert, 56
Milne, Kenneth, 69
Minogue, Craig William, 154, 178
Minogue, Rodney, 178
Miscelli, Emanuelle, 67
Mitchell, William Henry, 167
Mladenich, Richard 'King Richard', 'Spade Brain', 190
Mokbel, Antonios 'Tony', 190–1, 218–20
Mokbel, Renate, 219, 220
Monaco, Antonio, 111
Monaghan, Robert, 66
Monaghan, Thomas, 21
money laundering, 114, 140, 143, 144, 152, 153, 202, 220
Moore, Allan 'Ginger', 3
Moore, John, 2
Moran, Desmond 'Tuppence', 208–9, 210, 211
Moran, Jason, **121**, 182, 184, 185–6, 187, 189, 191–2, 198, 200, 201, 209
Moran, Judy, **121**, 201, 209, 210–11
Moran, Lewis, 64, 182, 190, 196, 209, 211, 218, 220

Moran, Mark 'Handsome Harry', **121**, 184, 186, 189, 190, 191, 192, 200, 201, 209, 210
Moran, Molly Morva, 66, 67
Morgan, Alice, 45
Morgan, James, 1
Morris, Annie Marguerite, 97, 98
Morris, Arthur, 126
Morris, Cherie, 97
Morris, Horatio Raymond, 96, 97–8
Morris, Sam, 96
Morrison, John Lewis 'The Face', 130
Mullett, Paul, 204
Mulligan, John Michael, 25
Muratore, Alfonso, 114
Muratore, Vincenzo, 110–12
murder, 3, 4–5, 14, 15, 16, 21, 23, 28–9, 45–6, 47, 66, 67–8, 94, 96, 98, 109, 110, 126, 128, 138, 154; disposalists, 164
Murphy, Brian 'Skull', 136, 138, 140, 148, 173–4
Murray, Angus, 16–17, 26–7, 28–9, 32

Napier, Kenneth George, 104
National Crime Authority, 112, 140
Nelson, Alfred 'The Ferret', 127, 128, 135
Neville, Percy Charles 'Big', 'Tiny', 89–90
New Australians, 50–1, 96, 97, 108
Newman, George, 82, 87
Newman, George Henry, 86
newspapers and magazines: *The Age*, 11, 30, 136, 181, 216; *The Argus*, 7, 167; *Bulletin*, 138–9; *Canberra Times*, 61; *Herald*, 23, 24, 76, 77, 92, 101; *Herald Sun*, 154, 186, 187, 211–12; *Melbourne Underworld News*, 199, 206; *Smith's Weekly*, 37, 38; *Sydney Morning Herald*, 151; *Truth*, 28, 29, 30–1, 34, 35, 43, 44, 47, 48, 50, 57, 74–5, 80, 84, 95, 101, 109–10, 164, 174, 175; *Victoria Police Gazette*, 23, 26, 77, 85–6, 88, 103
Nguyen, Chyong, 214
Nicholls, Jack 'Puttynose', 125, 134, 137, 139–40
Nicholls, Percy, 70
Nicholson, Alexander, 170
Nixon, Christine, 199, 206
Norton, John, 43, 44
Nugan Hand Bank, 140
Nugent, Harold, 65–6, 74, 76, 77–8, 80, 84, 98–9, 100, 102
Nugent, Harold William Sydney, 73

O'Callaghan, Brian, 142, 149, 152
O'Callaghan, Thomas, 169
O'Connell, Raymond, 68
O'Connell, Timothy, 36
O'Connor, Biddy, 39
O'Connor, John, 7
O'Donnell, David 'Big', 9, 10
O'Reilly, Miles Patrick, 94
O'Sullivan, Timothy, 80–1
Office of Police Integrity, 203
Oliver, Pearl Lilian, 76–7
Olsen, John Thomas 'Jack', 23, 45–6
OMCG (outlaw motor cycle gangs): Bandidos OMCG, 201, 207, 208, 218; Black Uhlans, 115, 157, 158; Brothers, 207; Coffin Cheaters, 206–7; Comancheros, 206, 207, 208; Finks, 207, 208; God's Squad, 207; Hells Angels, 163, 206, 216; Nomads, 163; Rebels, 207; Resurrected, 206–7; Sons of Islam, 217
organised crime: Black Hand, 108; *La Bastarda*, 111; Mafia (Honoured Society), 109–14; *see also* drugs; gangs; OMCG
Osborn, Justice Robert, 203
outlaw motorcycle gangs *see* OMCG
Overcoat War, 138
Overland, Simon, 221
Ozerkam, Siam 'Sammy', 156–7

Paizes, Cristos 'Harry Carillo', 'The Old Greek', 82
Pallenberg, Henry, 43
Palmer, Darlene, 62–3
Palmer, John 'Piggy', 62–3, 138
Pasche, Greg, 160
Paton, Stephen Andrew, 219
Patrick, Dot, 55
Patten, Bill, 202
Payton, Stephen Andrew, 201–2
Pearce, Ronald, 6
Pearson, George, 94
Peddy, Edward, 3
Peddy, Edwin, 3
Peddy, John, 3–4
Peddy, William, 3
Peirce, Billy, 160
Peirce, Katie, 165, 166
Peirce, Lex, 160
Peirce, Victor, 114, 115, 164, 165, 180, 181, 188, 190
Peirce, Wendy, 115, 165, 166, 181
Pender, Ida 'Jazz Baby', 'Babe', 22, 23–4, 27, 29, 32, 33, 38, **118**

Pentridge, **123**; dockers in, 125, 138–9, 157; escapes, 7, 126, 131; Jika Jika fire, 157; prison snitches, 131, 137–8; warders, 92

Persson, Fred, 126

Pettingill family, 158–60, 166, 180

Pettingill, Jamie, 159, 160, 162–3, 166

Pettingill, Kath, 93, 136, 151, 156, 158, 160, 161, 162, 164, 165

Pettingill, Trevor, 162, 164, 166, 180

Pezzimenti, Domenico, 108–9

Phelan, Francis, 79

Phillips, Charles, 80

Pinakos, Jim, 187

Pitt, Michael, 38

Plumpton, Alfred, 41

Pohl, Jacob, 41

police, 1, 2; and abortion, 8, 174–5; attacks on, 3–4, 10, 14, 64, 73, 126; Beach Inquiry, 175; and brothels, 42, 44–5; brutality alleged, 89, 173–4; Cameron Royal Commission, 169–70; chief commissioners, 40, 167–73, 199, 221; corruption, 161, 167, 169, 171, 172, 174–6, 199, 201–4, 219; country police, 169; Drug Squad, 183, 184, 202–3, 219; imprisoned, 88–9, 104–5; moonlighting detectives, 141, 143; planting weapons, 96; preferment, 168; and Pushes, 3–4; recruitment, 167; Russell Street bombing, 154, 177–8; shot at, 3, 15, 20, 21, 62; strike, 170; Walsh Street murders, 179–81; and Wren, 9–10

police informants, 25, 33, 56–7, 87, 94, 95–6, 102, 103, 132, 136, 149, 158, 161, 163, 200

Pollitt, Roy 'Red Rat', 136, 161, 162

Powell, Mickey, 38

Power Without Glory, 11, 15, 170

Prendergast, Laurie, 145–6, 147, 148

Pretz, Edith May, 110

Price, John, 1–2

Pring, Ralph, 81

Prior, Tom, 92, 95, 137

prison: Ararat Prison, 140, 157; Barwon Prison, 211; deaths in, 155, 211–12; marriages in, 136; parole or early release, 154–5; solitary confinement, 27; Yatala Stockade Prison, 16; *see also* Pentridge

Project Pierglass, 53

prostitutes: children, 52–3; deported, 53; drugs, 163; escort agencies, 51; 'going rate', 44; mail-order brides, 158; 'mobile', 50–1; pimps, 47; recruited

with drugs, 53; Russian 'contract workers', 53; Thai 'contract workers', 52, 53; virgins, 41

prostitution, 98, 124, 169; annual spending on, 51–2; assignation houses, 40; call-girl networks, 42; Collins Street, 39; illegal, 51; legislation, 51; massage parlours, 51, 160, 161, 176; providers, 40; in residential areas, 40; in St Kilda, 48, 51, 91, 104; sex trafficking, 52–3; tabletop dancing, 51, 207

protection, 92, 176

providers, 40

punishments: floggings, 9, 17; hangings, 17, 30–1, 50, 157; hard labour, 2–3, 15, 16, 17, 77; lashing, 3, 27, 69; whipping, 6, 67, 131

Purdy, Charlie, 46

Purdy, Vera, 46–7, 57

Pushes (fighting gangs), 3–6

Queen Victoria Market, 108–9, 110, 111–14

Quendroux, Fernand, 37

Quinn, Barry Robert, 154

race fixing, 139, 185

Radev, Nikolai 'The Russian', 'The Bulgarian', 115, 191, 195, 196, 200, 205, 219

raffle-rigging, 115–16

rape, 9, 17, 69, 70, 158, 173

Rapke, Jeremy, 203, 204

Raymer, Charles, 104

Read, Mark Brandon 'Chopper', 107, **119**, 137, 138, 141, 154, 156–7, 165, 175, 185, 186, 209

receiving, 22, 59, 125, 129, 193

Reed, Peter Michael, 178

Regan, Gerald Francis 'Frank', 81, 82

Regan, John 'Nano the Magician', 144

Reid, Ernest Lionel, 59–60

Reilly, Dean Kenneth, 64

Richards, David, 138–9

Richter QC, Robert, 198–9

Riley, Murray, 139

Rischin, Miriam, 91, 103

robbery, 2, 3, 4, 6–7, 9, 14, 22, 33, 55, 58, 62, 63, 69, 88–9, 130–1; Ansett Air Freight terminal, 150; armed, 70, 73, 84, 85, 94, 146, 149, 151, 159, 178–9; armoured cars, 91, 94, 104–6, 125, 126, 127, 128, 129, 152–3; banks, 17, 27, 37, 59, 126, 141, 179; betting shops, 159;

demanding money with menaces, 67, 102, 103; gold, 1, 167; Great Bookie Robbery, 129, 141–4, 150–1, 152; Great Train Robbery (UK), 141, 143, 144; jewellery, 18, 22, 25, 32, 33, 47, 89, 153, 193; safebreaking, 23, 192; Town Hall robbery, 15
Robertson, Peter, 163, 164
Robinson, Horace Clive, 47
Robinson, Leanne, 44
Roccisano, Ilario & Domenico, 109
Rogerson, Roger, 157–8, 161
Rollison, WA, 15
Romeo, Antonio, 109
Rosenes, Malcolm, 201, 219
Russell, Trevor, 150
Russell Street bombing, 154, 177–8
Ryan, Eugene, 75
Ryan, Jason, 164, 180–1
Ryan, Margaret Ellen 'Mona', 57–8, 59, 60, 61
Ryan, Mike, 94

Sadler, Glenn, 202
Sales, Robert, 166
Schultz-Trinus, Ethel, 97, 98
'Scotch Maud', 39
Scriva, Michele, 108, 109, 112
sex trafficking, 52–3
Shannon, Pat, 47, 59–60, 125–6, 129, 130, 131–3, 134, 136, 137, 139, 157
Shannon, Pearl, 47
Shaw, Stanley, 67, 68
Sheargold, William, 96–7
Sheehan, Terrance Clyde, 102
'shoddy drop', 22
Shortell, Constable, 3
Silvester, John, 191, 206
Simpson, Lindsay, 136, 161–2
Skelton, Lance, 86
Skirrett, Arthur, 19
Slater, Henry 'Long Harry', 18, 19, 20–1, 23, 35
Slater, James Robert, 176–7
sly-grog, 16–17, 19, 97, 103, 124, 167, 169
Smart, Herbert, 68
Smith, Dennis William 'Fatty', 'Greedy', 142, 143, 150, 152
Smith, Harold 'Dodger', 6
Smith, James 'The Jockey', 141
Smith, Dr John, 207
Smith, Mark Anthony, 191–2
Smith, Norman, 35
Smith, Percy William 'Midnight Rover', 74–5

Smith, Wayne, 155
Snowball Gang, 104
Socko, Stanislaus, 97–8
Sofra, Giuseppe, 113
Sparks, John Henry, 7
Sproule, Doug, 126, 128, 137
Standish, Captain Frederick, 40, 168
standover men, 13, 25, 33, 46, 50, 63, 64, 68, 74, 82, 84, 92, 96, 98, 102–103, 108, 124, 130, 138, 142, 144, 156, 160, 174, 189, 195, 200, 205, 209, 215; Sydney, 89–90, 93, 104
Stanhope, Wayne, 161, 164
Stanley, Lady, 25
Stevens, Lorna, 63
Stewart, Fiona, 216
Stirling, Louis 'The Count', 22
Stokes, Henry, 15, 18, 20–1, 24–5, 36–7, 38, 87, 191, 35, 81, 85, 86
Strawhorn, Wayne, 201, 202
Stretton, LEB, 172
Stuart-Jones, Dr Reginald, 47
Sulley, Brian, 130
Sullivan, Michael, 70
'supper joints', 44–5
Sydney; bent cop Rogerson, 157–8, 161; Double Bay Mob, 73; OMCG clash, 206; prison breaks, 149, 151; Pushes, 6; Snowball Gang, 104; standover men, 89–90, 93, 104, 144; Surry Hills murder, 21; Toecutters, 129, 144, 156
Syme, Geoffrey, 3

Tame, Adrian, 164, 165
Tattslotto robbery, 153
Taylor, Constable Angela, 154, 178
Taylor, Gloria, 22
Taylor, Joseph Leslie 'Squizzy', 11, 12–36, 38, **117**
Taylor, Kevin, 132–4, 137, 138, 157
Taylor, Stanley, 178
Taylor, Thomas, 11, 28, 32, 36
Templeton, David, 197
theft, 2, 18, 22, 67, 69; pickpockets, 5, 12, 13, 46; from Qantas, 143; shoplifting, 12, 46, 193; thieves' ponce, 92; from Victorian Railways, 34–5
Theodore, William, 8
Thomas, Peggy, 69
Thompson, Edward, 7
Thompson, Harold 'Bush', 14
Thompson, June, 135
Thompson, Willy, 195
Thorson, William, 20
three-card merchants, 2

Index

Tiffen, Lawrence, 73
Tobin, Detective Ray, 102
Tong Yang, 165–6
Torney, Lee Patrick, 199–200
Toveski, Steve, 217
Towerson, Henry 'Long Harry', 2–3
Tracey, Mabel, 171
Travers, Roy, 34, 35
Trotter, Arthur, 14, 15
Trunley, Abe, 81
Truscott, Frank, 63
Tsakmakis, Alex, 153–4
Turner, Joey, 127
Turner, John 'Beeper', 106
Turner, Joseph Patrick 'Joey', 50, 84, 92–3, 94–6, 97, 102, 104–5, 106
Turner, Lilian, 97
Twentyman, Les, 214
Twist, Jack Eric, 84, 88–9, 91–2, 95, 98–9, 100, 101, 102, 103, 106, 137
Tynan, Steven, 179
unions: Builders Labourers Federation, 24; Federated Ship Painters and Dockers, 62, 84–107, 124–40, 196

Varley, Henry, 41
Varney, James, 47
Vaughan, Madge, 36–7
Veniamin, Andrew 'Benji', 115, 165, 184, 189, 190, 191, 195–6, 197, 198–9
Vernon, Robert, 95
Versace, Giuseppe 'Fat Joe', 108–9, 111
Victoria Club, 141, 142–3, 150
Victorian Railways payroll theft, 24–5
Vodopic, Joseph, 64

Waghorn, Frankie, 107
Wagnegg, Helga, 162, 164
Wainer, Dr Bertram, 174, 175
Walker, Bruce, 153
Walker, John, 137
Walker, Levi, 169
Walkerden, Leslie Ernest 'Scotland Yard', 75, 82, 86
Walkerden, Gladys, 82
Walkley, John, 4
Wallace, George 'The Midnight Raper', 25
Walsh, Gavan, 88
Walsh, Sandra, 149–50
Walsh Street murders, 179–81
Ward, Alexander, 15
wartime (WWII), 71–83

waterfront; Federated Ship Painters and Dockers, 62, 84–107, 124–40, 196; wartime, 80
Watson, Ella 'Decoy Duck', 25
Wei Tang, 53
West, Iain, 178
West, Phyllis, 70, 71, 72, 73
White Australia Policy, 108
Whitford, Harold, 93–4
Whiting, Ted, 19, 20
Whitton, Evan, 175
Williams, Alan, 136, 161, 161–2
Williams, Betty, 201
Williams, Carl, 122, 184, 185, 189, 190, 191, 196, 198–9, 200–201, 211–12, 213
Williams, Dhakota, 201, 212
Williams, George, 185, 198, 204, 212
Williams, Giuseppe, 213
Williams, Roberta, 201, 213
Williams, Thomas, 1
Williamson, John, 16
Wilson, Annie, 42
Wilson, Douglas and Isobel, 126
Wilson, Herbert, 33, 34, 35
Winch, Fred, 169
Wingy, 144–5
witness protection, 164, 181
women: hanged, 7, 48, 49, 50; see also prostitutes
Wood, Hayley, 115
Woon, Leslie, 141–2
Wootton, Charles Edward 'Inky', 74, 100
Wootton, Charles Joseph, 74, 100, 101, 107, 127, 129, 139
Workman, Gregory John, 185, 186
Worseldine, Ernest, 6
wowsers, 42–4
Wren, Arthur, 9
Wren, John, 8–11, 31, 43
Wright, Alfred Charles 'Lou', 80–1
Wright, Bella, 39
Wright, Charley, 39
Wright, Lou 'The Godfather', 99–100, 124–5, 137
Wrout, Herbert, 64, 196, 210

Ymer, Ishmael, 66
Young, Jay, 166

Zayat, Sam, 205
Zemour, Raymond, 198
Zervas, Peter, 206